THE DIARIES OF FRANZ KAFKA
1914–1923

THE DIARIES OF
FRANZ KAFKA
1914-1923

EDITED BY Max Brod

SCHOCKEN BOOKS · NEW YORK

TRANSLATED BY MARTIN GREENBERG, WITH
THE CO-OPERATION OF HANNAH ARENDT

First SCHOCKEN PAPERBACK edition 1965

10 9 8 7   86

CONTENTS *

* Only longer compositions, or those of a finished nature, are listed here.

THE DIARIES OF FRANZ KAFKA
1914–1923

January 2. A lot of time well spent with Dr. Weiss.

January 4. We had scooped out a hollow in the sand, where we felt quite comfortable. At night we rolled up together inside the hollow, Father covered it over with the trunks of trees, scattering underbrush on top, and we were as well protected as we could be from storms and wild beasts. "Father," we would often call out in fright when it had already grown dark under the tree trunks and Father had still not appeared. But then we would see his feet through a crack, he would slide in beside us, would give each of us a little pat, for it calmed us to feel his hand, and then we would all fall asleep as it were together. In addition to our parents we were five boys and three girls; the hollow was too small for us, but we should have felt afraid if we had not been so close to one another at night.

January 5. Afternoon. Goethe's father was senile when he died. At the time of his father's last illness Goethe was working on *Iphigenie*.

"Take that woman home, she's drunk," some court official said to Goethe about Christiane.

August, a drunkard like his mother, vulgarly ran around with common women. Ottilie, whom he did not love but was made to marry by his father for social reasons.

Wolf, the diplomat and writer.

Walter, the musician, couldn't pass his examinations. Withdrew into the Gartenhaus for months; when the Czarina wanted to see him: "Tell the Czarina that I am not a wild animal." "My constitution is more lead than iron."

Wolf's petty, ineffectual literary efforts.

The old people in the garret rooms. Eighty-year-old Ottilie, fifty-year-old Wolf, and their old acquaintances.

Only in such extremes does one become aware of how every person is lost in himself beyond hope of rescue, and one's sole consolation in this is to observe other people and the law governing them and everything. How, outwardly, Wolf can be guided, moved here or there, cheered up, encouraged, induced to work systematically—and how, inwardly, he is held fast and immovable.

Why don't the Tchuktchis simply leave their awful country; considering their present life and wants they would be better off anywhere else. But they cannot; all things possible do happen, only what happens is possible.

A wine cellar had been set up in the small town of F. by a wine dealer from the larger city near by. He had rented a small vaulted cellar in a house on the Ringplatz, painted oriental decorations on the walls and had put in old plush furniture almost past its usefulness.

January 6. Dilthey: *Das Erlebnis und die Dichtung:* Love for humanity, the highest respect for all the forms it has taken; stands back quietly in the best post from which he can observe. On Luther's early writings: "the mighty shades, attracted by murder and blood, that step from an invisible world into the visible one."—Pascal.

Letter for A. to his mother-in-law. Liesl kissed the teacher.

January 8. Fantl recited *Tête d'or:*[1] "He hurls the enemy about like a barrel."

Uncertainty, aridity, peace—all things will resolve themselves into these and pass away.

What have I in common with Jews? I have hardly anything in common with myself and should stand very quietly in a corner, content that I can breathe.

Description of inexplicable emotions. A.: Since that happened, the sight of women has been painful to me; it is neither sexual excitement nor pure sorrow, it is simply pain. That's the way it was too before I felt sure of Liesl.

January 12. Yesterday: Ottilie's love affairs, the young Englishmen.—Tolstoy's engagement; I have a clear impression of a young, sensitive and violent person, restraining himself, full of forebodings. Well dressed, dark and dark blue.

The girl in the coffeehouse. Her tight skirt, her white, loose, fur-trimmed silk blouse, bare throat, close-fitting gray hat. Her full, laughing, eternally pulsating face; friendly eyes, though a little affected. My face flushes whenever I think of F.

Clear night on the way home; distinctly aware of what in me is mere dull apathy, so far removed from a great clarity expanding without hindrance.

Nikolai, *Literaturbriefe.*

There are possibilities for me, certainly; but under what stone do they lie?

Carried forward on the horse——

Youth's meaninglessness. Fear of youth, fear of meaninglessness, of the meaningless rise of an inhuman life.

Tellheim: "He has—what only the creations of true poets possess—that spontaneous flexibility of the inner life which, as circumstances alter, continually surprises us by revealing entirely new facets of itself." [2]

January 19. Anxiety alternating with self-assurance at the office. Otherwise more confident. Great antipathy to "Metamorphosis." Unreadable ending. Imperfect almost to its very marrow. It would have turned out much better if I had not been interrupted at the time by the business trip.

January 23. B., the chief auditor, tells the story of a friend of his, a half-pay colonel who likes to sleep beside an open window: "During the night it is very pleasant; but in the morning, when I have to shovel the snow off the ottoman near the window and then start shaving, it is unpleasant."

Memoirs of Countess Thürheim: Her mother: "Her gentle nature made her especially fond of Racine. I have often heard her praying God that He might grant him eternal peace."

There is no doubt that at the great dinners given in his

honor at Vienna by the Russian ambassador Count Rasu-
movsky, he (Suvorov) ate like a glutton the food served
upon the table without pausing for a soul. When he was
full he would get up and leave the guests to themselves.

To judge by an engraving, a frail, determined, pedantic
old man.

"It wasn't your fate," my mother's lame consolation.
The bad part of it is, that at the moment it is almost all
the consolation that I need. There is my weak point and
will remain my weak point; otherwise the regular, hardly
varying, semiactive life I have led these last days (worked
at the office on a description of our bureau's activities; A.'s
worries about his bride; Ottla's Zionism; the girls' enjoyment of the Salten-Schildkraut lecture; reading the memoirs of Thürheim; letters to Weiss and Löwy; proofread-
ing "Metamorphosis") has really pulled me together and
instilled some resolution and hope in me.

January 24. Napoleonic era: the festivities came hard
upon each other, everyone was in a hurry "to taste to the
full the joys of the brief interlude of peace." "On the
other hand, the women exercised an influence as if in
passing, they had really no time to lose. In those days love
expressed itself in an intensified enthusiasm and a greater
abandonment." "In our time there is no longer any excuse
for passing an empty hour."

Incapable of writing a few lines to Miss Bl., two letters
already remain unanswered, today the third came. I grasp
nothing correctly and at the same time feel quite hale,
though hollow. Recently, when I got out of the elevator
at my usual hour, it occurred to me that my life, whose

days more and more repeat themselves down to the smallest detail, resembles that punishment in which each pupil must according to his offense write down the same meaningless (in repetition, at least) sentence ten times, a hundred times or even oftener; except that in my case the punishment is given me with only this limitation: "as many times as you can stand it."

A. cannot calm himself. In spite of the confidence he has in me and in spite of the fact that he wants my advice, I always learn the worst details only incidentally in the course of the conversation, whereupon I have always to suppress my sudden astonishment as much as I can—not without a feeling that my indifference in face of the dreadful news either must strike him as coldness, or on the contrary must greatly console him. And in fact so I mean it. I learn the story of the kiss in the following stages, some of them weeks apart: A teacher kissed her; she was in his room; he kissed her several times; she went to his room regularly because she was doing some needlework for A.'s mother and the teacher had a good lamp; she let herself be kissed without resistance; he had already made her a declaration of his love; she still goes for walks with him in spite of everything, wanted to give him a Christmas present; once she wrote, Something unpleasant has happened to me but nothing came of it.

A. questioned her in the following way: How did it happen? I want to know all the details. Did he only kiss you? How often? Where? Didn't he lie on you? Did he touch you? Did he want to take off your clothes?

Answer: I was sitting on the sofa with my sewing, he on the other side of the table. Then he came over, sat down beside me and kissed me; I moved away from him toward the arm of the sofa and was pressed down with my head against the arm. Except for the kiss, nothing happened.

During the questioning she once said: "What are you thinking of? I *am* a virgin."

Now that I think of it, my letter to Dr. Weiss was written in such a way that it could all be shown to F. Suppose he did that today and for that reason put off his answer?

January 26. Unable to read Thürheim, though she has been my delight these past few days. Letter to Miss Bl. now sent on its way. How it has hold of me and presses against my brow. Father and Mother playing cards at the same table.

The parents and their grown children, a son and a daughter, were seated at table Sunday noon. The mother had just stood up and was dipping the ladle into the round-bellied tureen to serve the soup, when suddenly the whole table lifted up, the tablecloth fluttered, the hands lying on the table slid off, the soup with its tumbling bacon balls spilled into the father's lap.

The way I almost insulted my mother just now because she had lent Elli [3] *Die böse Unschuld*, which I had myself intended to offer her only yesterday. "Leave me my books! I have nothing else." Speeches of this kind in a real rage.

The death of Thürheim's father: "The doctors who came in soon thereafter found his pulse very weak and gave the invalid only a few more hours to live. My God, it was my father they were speaking of! A few hours only, and then dead."

January 28. Lecture on the miracles of Lourdes. Free-thinking doctor; bares his strong and energetic teeth, takes great delight in rolling his words. "It is time that German thoroughness and probity stand up to Latin charlatanism." Newsboys of the *Messager de Lourdes: "Superbe guérison de ce soir!" "Guérison affirmée!"*—Discussion: "I am a simple postal official, nothing more." "Hôtel de l'univers." —Infinite sadness as I left, thinking of F. Am gradually calmed by my reflections.

Sent letter and Weiss' *Galeere* to Bl.

Quite some time ago A.'s sister was told by a fortune-teller that her eldest brother was engaged and that his fiancée was deceiving him. At that time he rejected all such stories in a rage. I: "Why only at that time? It is as false today as it was then. She hasn't deceived you, has she?" He: "It's true that she hasn't, isn't it?"

February 2. A.: A girl friend's lewd letter to his fiancée. "If we were to take everything as seriously as when we were under the domination of the confessional sermons." "Why were you so backward in Prague, better to have one's fling on a small scale than a large." I interpret the letter according to my own opinion, in favor of his fiancée, with several good arguments occurring to me.

Yesterday A. was in Schluckenau. Sat in the room with her all day holding the bundle of letters (his only baggage) in his hand and didn't stop questioning her. Learned nothing new; an hour before leaving he asked her: "Was the light out during the kissing?" and learned the news, which makes him inconsolable, that the second time W. kissed her he switched off the light. W. sat sketching on one side of the table, L. sat on the other (in W.'s room, at 11 P.M.) and read *Asmus Semper* aloud. Then W. got up, went to the chest to get something (a compass, L. thinks, A. thinks a contraceptive), then suddenly switched off the light, overwhelmed her with kisses; she sank down on the sofa, he held her arms, her shoulders, and kept saying, "Kiss me!"

L. on another occasion: "W. is very clumsy." Another time: "I didn't kiss him." Another time: "I felt as if I were lying in your arms."

A. "I must find out the truth, mustn't I?" (he is thinking of having her examined by a doctor). "Only suppose I learn on the wedding night that she has been lying. Perhaps she's so calm only because he used a contraceptive."

Lourdes: Attack on faith in miracles, also attack on the church. With equal justification he could argue against the churches, processions, confessions, the unhygienic practices everywhere, since it can't be proved that prayer does any good. Karlsbad is a greater swindle than Lourdes; Lourdes has the advantage that people go there out of deepest conviction. What about the crackpot notions people have concerning operations, serum therapy, vaccination, medicines?

On the other hand: The huge hospitals for the pilgrimaging invalids; the filthy piscinas; the brancards waiting for the special trains; the medical commission; the great incandescent crosses on the mountains; the Pope receives three millions a year. The priest with the monstrance passes by, a woman screams from her stretcher, "I am cured!" Her tuberculosis of the bone continues unchanged.

The door opened a crack. A revolver appeared and an outstretched arm.

Thürheim II 35, 28, 37: nothing sweeter than love, nothing pleasanter than flirtation; 45, 48: Jews.

February 10. Eleven o'clock, after a walk. Fresher than usual. Why?

1. Max said I was calm.
2. Felix is going to be married (was angry with him).
3. I remain alone, unless F. will still have me after all.
4. Mrs. X.'s invitation; I think how I shall introduce myself to her.

By chance I walked in the direction opposite to my usual one, that is, Kettensteg, Hradčany, Karlsbrücke. Ordinarily I nearly collapse on this road; today, coming from the opposite direction, I felt somewhat lifted up.

February 11. Hastily read through Dilthey's *Goethe;* tumultuous impression, carries one along, why couldn't one set oneself afire and be destroyed in the flames? Or obey, even if one hears no command? Or sit on a chair in the middle of one's empty room and look at the floor? Or shout "Forward!" in a mountain defile and hear answering shouts and see people emerge from all the bypaths in the cliffs.

February 13. Yesterday at Mrs. X.'s. Calm and energetic, an energy that is perfect, triumphant, penetrating, that finds its way into everything with eyes, hands and feet. Her frankness, a frank gaze. I keep remembering the ugly, huge, ceremonious Renaissance hats with ostrich feathers that she used to wear; she repelled me so long as I didn't know her personally. How her muff, when she hurries toward the point of her story, is pressed against her body and yet twitches. Her children, A. and B.

Reminds one a good deal of W. in her looks, in her self-forgetfulness in the story, in her complete absorption, in her small, lively body, even in her hard, hollow voice, in her talk of fine clothes and hats at the same time that she herself wears nothing of the sort.

View from the window of the river. At many points in the conversation, in spite of the fact that she never allows it to flag, my complete failure, vacant gaze, incomprehension of what she is saying; I mechanically drop the silliest remarks at the same time that I am forced to see how closely she attends to them; I stupidly pet her little child.

Dreams: In Berlin, through the streets to her house, calm and happy in the knowledge that, though I haven't arrived at her house yet, a slight possibility of doing so exists; I shall certainly arrive there. I see the streets, on a white house a sign, something like "The Splendors of the North" (saw it in the paper yesterday); in my dream "Berlin W" has been added to it. Ask the way of an affable, red-nosed old policeman who in this instance is stuffed into a sort of butler's livery. Am given excessively detailed directions, he even points out the railing of a small park in the distance which I must keep hold of for safety's sake when I go past. Then advice about the trolley, the subway, etc. I can't follow him any longer and ask in a fright, knowing full well that I am underestimating the distance: "That's about half an hour away?" But the old man answers, "I can make it in six minutes." What joy! Some man, a shadow, a companion, is always at my side, I don't know who it is. Really have no time to turn around, to turn sideways.

Live in Berlin in some pension or other apparently filled with young Polish Jews; very small rooms. I spill a bottle of water. One of them is tapping incessantly on a small typewriter, barely turns his head when he is asked for something. Impossible to lay hands on a map of Berlin. In the hand of one of them I continually notice a book that looks like a map. But it always proves to be something entirely different, a list of the Berlin schools, tax statistics, or something of the sort. I don't want to believe it, but, smiling, they prove it to me beyond any doubt.

February 14. There will certainly be no one to blame if I should kill myself, even if the immediate cause should for instance appear to be F.'s behavior. Once, half asleep, I pictured the scene that would ensue if, in anticipation of the end, the letter of farewell in my pocket, I should come to her house, should be rejected as a suitor, lay the letter on the table, go to the balcony, break away from all those who run up to hold me back, and, forcing one hand after another to let go its grip, jump over the ledge. The letter, however, would say that I was jumping because of F., but that even if my proposal had been accepted nothing essential would have been changed for me. My place is down below, I can find no other solution, F. simply happens to be the one through whom my fate is made manifest; I can't live without her and must jump, yet—and this F. suspects—I couldn't live with her either. Why not use tonight for the purpose, I can already see before me the people talking at the parents' gathering this evening, talking of life and the conditions that have to be created for it—but I cling to abstractions, I live completely entangled in life, I won't do it, I am cold, am sad that a shirt collar is pinching my neck, am damned, gasp for breath in the mist.

February 15. How long this Saturday and Sunday seem in retrospect. Yesterday afternoon I had my hair cut, then wrote the letter to Bl., then was over at Max's new place for a moment, then the parents' gathering, sat next to L.W., then Baum (met Kr. in the trolley), then on the way home Max's complaints about my silence, then my longing for suicide, then my sister returned from the parents' gathering unable to report the least thing. In bed until ten, sleepless, sorrow after sorrow. No letter, not here, not in the office, mailed a letter to Bl. at the Franz-Josef station, saw G. in the afternoon, walked along the Moldau, read aloud at his house; his queer mother who ate sandwiches and played solitaire; walked around alone for two hours; decided to leave Berlin Friday, met Khol,[4] at home with my brothers-in-law and sisters, then the discussion of his engagement at Weltsch's (J.K.'s putting out the candles), then at home attempted by my silence to elicit aid and sympathy from my mother; now my sister tells me about her meeting, the clock strikes a quarter to twelve.

At Weltsch's, in order to comfort his mother who was upset, I said: "I too am losing Felix by this marriage. A friend who is married is none." Felix said nothing, naturally couldn't say anything, but he didn't even want to.

The notebook begins with F., who on May 2, 1913, made me feel uncertain; this same beginning can serve as conclusion too, if in place of "uncertain" I use a worse word.[5]

February 16. Wasted day. My only joy was the hope that last night has given me of sleeping better.

I was going home in my usual fashion in the evening after work, when, as though I had been watched for, they excitedly waved to me from all three windows of the Genzmer house to come up.

February 22. In spite of my drowsy head, whose upper left side is near aching with restlessness, perhaps I am still able quietly to build up some greater whole wherein I might forget everything and be conscious only of the good in one.

Director at his table. Servant brings in a card.
DIRECTOR: Witte again, this is a nuisance, the man is a nuisance.

February 23. I am on my way. Letter from Musil.[6] Pleases me and depresses me, for I have nothing.

A young man on a beautiful horse rides out of the gate of a villa.

March 8. A prince can wed the Sleeping Beauty, or someone even harder to win to, but the Sleeping Beauty can be no prince.

It happened that when Grandmother died only the nurse was with her. She said that just before Grandmother died she lifted herself up a little from the pillow so that she seemed to be looking for someone, and then peacefully lay back again and died.

There is no doubt that I am hemmed in all around, though by something that has certainly not yet fixed itself in my flesh, that I occasionally feel slackening, and that could be burst asunder. There are two remedies, marriage or Berlin; the second is surer, the first more immediately attractive.

I dived down and soon everything felt fine. A small shoal floated by in an upward-mounting chain and disappeared in the green. Bells borne back and forth by the drifting of the tide—wrong.

March 9. Rense walked a few steps down the dim passageway, opened the little papered door of the dining room and said to the noisy company, almost without regarding them: "Please be a little more quiet. I have a guest. Have some consideration."

As he was returning to his room and heard the noise continuing unabated, he halted a moment, was on the verge of going back again, but thought better of it and returned to his room.

A boy of eighteen was standing at the window, looking down into the yard. "It is quieter now," he said when Rense entered, and lifted his long nose and deep-set eyes to him.

"It isn't quieter at all," said Rense, taking a swallow from the bottle of beer standing on the table. "It's impossible ever to have any quiet here. You'll have to get used to that, boy."

I am too tired, I must try to rest and sleep, otherwise I am lost in every respect. What an effort to keep alive! Erecting a monument does not require the expenditure of so much strength.

The general argument: I am completely lost in F.

Rense, a student, sat studying in his small back room.

The maid came in and announced that a young man wished to speak to him. "What is his name?" Rense asked. The maid did not know.

I shall never forget F. in this place, therefore shan't marry. Is that definite?

Yes, that much I can judge of: I am almost thirty-one years old, have known F. for almost two years, must therefore have some perspective by now. Besides, my way of life here is such that I can't forget, even if F. didn't have such significance for me. The uniformity, regularity, comfort and dependence of my way of life keep me unresistingly fixed wherever I happen to be. Moreover, I have a more than ordinary inclination toward a comfortable and dependent life, and so even strengthen everything that is pernicious to me. Finally, I am getting older, any change becomes more and more difficult. But in all this I foresee a great misfortune for myself, one without end and without hope; I should be dragging through the years up the ladder of my job, growing ever sadder and more alone as long as I could endure it at all.

But you wanted that sort of life for yourself, didn't you?

An official's life could benefit me if I were married. It would in every way be a support to me against society, against my wife, against writing, without demanding too many sacrifices, and without on the other hand degenerating into indolence and dependence, for as a married man I should not have to fear that. But I cannot live out such a life as a bachelor.

But you could have married, couldn't you?

I couldn't marry then; everything in me revolted against it, much as I always loved F. It was chiefly concern over my literary work that prevented me, for I thought marriage would jeopardize it. I may have been right, but in any case it is destroyed by my present bachelor's life. I have written nothing for a year, nor shall I be able to write anything in the future; in my head there is and remains the one single thought, and I am devoured by it. I wasn't able to consider it all at the time. Moreover, as a result of my dependence, which is at least encouraged by this way of life, I approach everything hesitantly and complete nothing at the first stroke. That was what happened here too.

Why do you give up all hope eventually of having F.?

I have already tried every kind of self-humiliation. In the Tiergarten I once said: "Say 'yes'; even if you consider your feeling for me insufficient to warrant marriage, my love for you is great enough to make up the insufficiency, and strong enough in general to take everything on itself." In the course of a long correspondence I had alarmed F. by my peculiarities, and these now seemed to make her uneasy. I said: "I love you enough to rid myself of anything that might trouble you. I will become another person." Now, when everything must be cleared up, I can confess that even at the time when our relationship was at its most affectionate, I often had forebodings, and fears, founded on trifling occurrences, that F. did not love me very much, not with all the force of the love she was capable of. F. has now realized this too, though not without my assistance. I am almost afraid that after my last two visits F. even feels a certain disgust for me, despite the fact that outwardly we are friendly, call each other "Du," walk arm in arm together. The last thing I remember of her is the quite hostile grimace she made in the entrance hall of her house when I was not satisfied to kiss her glove but pulled it open and kissed her hand. Added to this there is the fact that, despite her promise to be punctual in the future in her correspond-

ence, she hasn't answered two of my letters, merely tele-
graphed to promise letters but hasn't kept her promise; indeed, she hasn't even so much as answered my mother.
There can be no doubt of the hopelessness in all this.

One should really never say that. Didn't your previous
behavior likewise seem hopeless from F.'s point of view?

That was something else. I always freely confessed my
love for her, even during what appeared to be our final
farewell in the summer; I was never so cruelly silent; I had
reasons for my behavior which, if they could not be ap-
proved, could yet be discussed. F.'s only reason is the complete insufficiency of her love. Nevertheless, it is true that I
could wait. But I cannot wait in double hopelessness: I cannot see F. more and more slipping from my grasp, and
myself more and more unable to escape. It would be the
greatest gamble I could take with myself, although—or because—it would best suit all the overpowering evil forces
within me. "You never know what will happen" is no argument against the intolerableness of an existing state of
affairs.

Then what do you want to do?

Leave Prague. Counter the greatest personal injury that
has ever befallen me with the strongest antidote at my dis-
posal.

Leave your job?

In light of the above, my job is only a part of the general
intolerableness. I should be losing only what is intolerable
in any case. The security, the lifelong provision, the good
salary, the fact that it doesn't demand all my strength—
after all, so long as I am a bachelor all these things mean
nothing to me and are transformed into torments.

Then what do you want to do?

I could answer all such questions at once by saying: I have nothing to lose; every day, each tiniest success, is a gift; whatever I do is all to the good. But I can also give a more precise answer: as an Austrian lawyer, which, speaking seriously, I of course am not, I have no prospects; the best thing I might achieve for myself in this direction I already possess in my present post, and it is of no use to me. Moreover, in the quite impossible event I should want to make some money out of my legal training, there are only two cities that could be considered: Prague, which I must leave, and Vienna, which I hate and where I should inevitably grow unhappy because I should go there with the deepest conviction of that inevitability. I therefore have to leave Austria and—since I have no talent for languages and would do poorly at physical labor or at a business job—go to Germany, at least at first, and in Germany to Berlin, where the chances of earning a living are best. Also, there, in journalism, I can make best and directest use of my ability to write, and so find a means of livelihood at least partially suited to me. Whether in addition I shall be capable of inspired work, that I cannot say at present with any degree of certainty. But I think I know definitely that from the independence and freedom I should have in Berlin (however miserable I otherwise would be) I should derive the only feeling of happiness I am still able to experience.

But you are spoiled.

No, I need a room and a vegetarian diet, almost nothing more.

Aren't you going there because of F.?

No, I choose Berlin only for the above reasons, although I love it and perhaps I love it because of F. and because of the aura of thoughts that surrounds F.; but that I can't help.

It is also probable that I shall meet F. in Berlin. If our being together will help me to get F. out of my blood, so much the better, it is an additional advantage Berlin has.

Are you healthy?

No—heart, sleep, digestion.

A small furnished room. Dawn. Disorder. The student is in bed asleep, his face to the wall. There is a knock at the door. Silence. A louder knock. The student sits up in fright, looks at the door.

STUDENT: Come in.

MAID (*a frail girl*): Good morning.

STUDENT: What do you want? It's still night.

MAID: Excuse me, but a gentleman is asking for you.

STUDENT: For me? (*Hesitates.*) Nonsense! Where is he?

MAID: He is waiting in the kitchen.

STUDENT: What does he look like?

MAID (*smiling*): Well, he's still a boy, he's not very handsome; I think he's a Yid.

STUDENT: And that wants to see me in the middle of the
night? But I don't need your opinion of my guests, do
you hear? Send him in. Be quick about it. (*The student
fills the small pipe lying on the chair beside his bed and
smokes it.*)

KLEIPE *stands at the door and looks at the student, who
calmly smokes on with his eyes turned toward the ceiling. Short, erect, a large, long, somewhat crooked,
pointed nose, dark complexion, deep-set eyes, long
arms.*

STUDENT: How much longer? Come over here to the bed
and say what you want. Who are you? What do you
want? Quick! Quick!

KLEIPE (*walks very slowly toward the bed and at the same*

time attempts to gesture something in explanation. He stretches his neck and raises and lowers his eyebrows to assist his speech): What I mean to say is, I am from Wulfenshausen too.

STUDENT: Really? That's nice, that's very nice. Then why didn't you stay there?

KLEIPE: Only think! It is the home town of both of us, a beautiful place, but still a miserable hole.

It was Sunday afternoon, they lay in bed in one another's arms. It was winter, the room was unheated, they lay beneath a heavy feather quilt.

March 15. The students wanted to carry Dostoevsky's chains behind his coffin. He died in the workers' quarter, on the fifth floor of a tenement house.

Once, during the winter, at about five o'clock in the morning, the half-clothed maid announced a visitor to the student. "What's that? What did you say?" the student, still half asleep, was asking, when a young man entered, carrying a lighted candle that he had borrowed from the maid. He raised the candle in one hand the better to see the student and lowered his hat in his other hand almost to the floor, so long was his arm.

Only this everlasting waiting, eternal helplessness.

March 17. Sat in the room with my parents, leafed through magazines for two hours, on and off simply stared before me; in general simply waited for ten o'clock to arrive and for me to be able to go to bed.

March 27. On the whole passed in much the same way.

Hass hurried to get aboard the ship, ran across the gang-plank, climbed up on deck, sat down in a corner, pressed his hands to his face and from then on no longer concerned himself with anyone. The ship's bell sounded, people were running along, far off, as though at the other end of the ship someone were singing with full voice.

They were just about to pull in the gangplank when a small black carriage came along, the coachman shouted from the distance, he had to exert all his strength to hold back the rearing horse; a young man sprang out of the carriage, kissed an old, white-bearded gentleman bending forward under the roof of the carriage, and with a small valise in his hand ran aboard the ship, which at once pushed off from the shore.

It was about three o'clock in the morning, but in the summer, and already half light. Herr von Irmenhof's five horses—Famos, Grasaffe, Tournemento, Rosina and Bra-bant—rose up in the stable. Because of the sultry night the stable door had been left ajar; the two grooms slept on their backs in the straw, flies hovered up and down above their open mouths, there was nothing to hinder them. Grasaffe stood up so that he straddled the two men under him, and, watching their faces, was ready to strike down at them with his hoofs at their slightest sign of awakening. Meanwhile the four others sprang out of the stable in two easy leaps, one behind the other; Grasaffe followed them.

Through the glass door Anna saw the lodger's room was dark; she went in and turned on the electric light to make the bed ready for the night. But the student was sitting half reclined upon the sofa, smiling at her. She excused herself and turned to leave. But the student asked her to stay and to pay no attention to him. She did stay, in fact, and did her work, casting an occasional sidelong glance at the student.

April 5. If only it were possible to go to Berlin, to become independent, to live from one day to the next, even to go hungry, but to let all one's strength pour forth instead of husbanding it here, or rather—instead of one's turning aside into nothingness! If only F. wanted it, would help me!

April 8. Yesterday incapable of writing even one word. Today no better. Who will save me? And the turmoil in me, deep down, scarcely visible; I am like a living lattice-work, a lattice that is solidly planted and would like to tumble down.

Today in the coffeehouse with Werfel. How he looked from the distance, seated at the coffeehouse table. Stooped, half reclining even in the wooden chair, the beautiful profile of his face pressed against his chest, his face almost wheezing in its fulness (not really fat); entirely indifferent to the surroundings, impudent and without flaw. His dangling glasses by contrast make it easier to trace the delicate outlines of his face.

May 6. My parents seem to have found a beautiful apartment for F. and me; I ran around for nothing one entire beautiful afternoon. I wonder whether they will lay me in my grave too, after a life made happy by their solicitude.

A nobleman, Herr von Griesenau by name, had a coachman, Joseph, whom no other employer would have put up with. He lived in a ground-floor room near the gatekeeper's lodge, for he was too fat and short of breath to climb stairs. All he had to do was drive a coach, but even for this he was employed only on special occasions, to honor a visitor perhaps; otherwise, for days on end, for weeks on end, he lay on a couch near the window, with remarkable rapidity blinking his small eyes deep-sunken in fat as he looked out of the window at the trees which——

Joseph the coachman lay on his couch, sat up only in order to take a slice of bread and butter and herring from a little table, then sank back again and stared vacantly around as he chewed. He laboriously sucked in the air through his large round nostrils; sometimes, in order to breathe in enough air, he had to stop chewing and open his mouth; his large belly trembled without stop under the many folds of his thin, dark blue suit.

The window was open, an acacia tree and an empty square were visible through it. It was a low ground-floor window. Joseph saw everything from his couch and everybody on the outside could see him. It was annoying, but he hadn't been able to climb stairs for the last six months at least, ever since he had got so fat, and thus was obliged to live on a lower story. When he had first been given this room near the gatekeeper's lodge, he had pressed and kissed the hands of his employer, Herr von Griesenau, with tears in his eyes, but now he knew its disadvantages: the eternal observation he was subjected to, the proximity of the unpleasant gatekeeper, all the commotion at the entrance gate and on the square, the great distance from the rest of the servants and the consequent estrangement and neglect that he suffered—he was now thoroughly acquainted with all these disadvantages and in fact intended to petition the Master to permit him to move back to his old room. What

after all were all these newly hired fellows standing uselessly around for, especially since the Master's engagement? Let them simply carry him up and down the stairs,
rare and deserving man that he was.

An engagement was being celebrated. The banquet was
at an end, the company got up from the table; all the
windows were open, it was a warm and beautiful evening
in June. The fiancée stood in a circle of friends and acquaintances, the others were gathered in small groups;
now and then there was an outburst of laughter. The man
to whom she was engaged stood apart, leaning in the doorway to the balcony and looking out.

After some time the mother of the fiancée noticed him,
went over to him and said: "Why are you standing here
all alone? Aren't you joining Olga? Have you quarreled?"

"No," he answered, "we haven't quarreled."

"Very well," the mother said, "then join your fiancée!
Your behavior is beginning to attract attention."

The horror in the merely schematic.

The landlady of the rooming house, a decrepit widow
dressed in black and wearing a straight skirt, stood in the
middle room of her empty house. It was still perfectly
quiet, the bell did not stir. The street, too, was quiet; the
woman had purposely chosen so quiet a street because she
wanted good roomers, and those who insist on quiet are
the best.

May 27. Mother and sister in Berlin. I shall be alone with
my father in the evening. I think he is afraid to come up.
Should I play cards [Karten] with him? (I find the letter

K offensive, almost disgusting, and yet I use it; it must be
very characteristic of me.) How Father acted when I
touched F.

The first appearance of the white horse was on an au-
tumn afternoon, in a large but not very busy street in the
city of A. It passed through the entranceway of a house
in whose yard a trucking company had extensive store-
rooms; thus it would often happen that teams of horses,
now and then a single horse as well, had to be led out
through the entranceway, and for this reason the white
horse attracted little attention. It was not, however, one
of the horses belonging to the trucking company. A workman tightening the cords around a bale of goods in front
of the gate noticed the horse, looked up from his work
and then into the yard to see whether the teamster was
following after. No one came. The horse had hardly
stepped into the road when it reared up mightily, struck
several sparks from the pavement, for a moment was on
the point of falling, but at once regained its balance, and
then trotted neither rapidly nor slowly up the street, which
was almost deserted at this twilight hour. The workman
cursed what he thought had been the carelessness of the
teamsters, shouted several names into the yard; some men
came out in response, but when they immediately perceived that the horse was not one of theirs, simply stopped
short together in the entranceway, somewhat astonished.
A short interval elapsed before some of them thought what
to do; they ran after the horse for a distance, but, failing
to catch sight of it again, soon returned.
In the meantime the horse had already reached the
outermost streets of the suburbs without being halted. It
accommodated itself to the life of the streets better than

horses running alone usually do. Its slow pace could frighten no one, it never strayed out of the roadway or from its own side of the street; when it was obliged to stop for a vehicle coming out of a cross street, it stopped; had the most careful driver been leading it by the halter it could not have behaved more perfectly. Still, of course, it was a conspicuous sight; here and there someone stopped and looked after it with a smile, a teamster in a passing beer wagon jokingly struck down at the horse with his whip; it was frightened, of course, and reared, but did not quicken its pace.

It was just this incident, however, that a policeman saw; he went over to the horse, who at the very last moment had tried to turn off in another direction, took hold of the reins (despite its light frame it wore the harness of a dray horse) and said, though in a very friendly way: "Whoa! Now where do you think you are running off to?" He held on to it for some time in the middle of the road, thinking that the animal's owner would soon be along after the runaway.

It has meaning but is weak; its blood flows thin, too far from the heart. There are still some pretty scenes in my head but I will stop regardless. Yesterday the white horse appeared to me for the first time before I fell asleep; I have an impression of its first stepping out of my head, which was turned to the wall, jumping across me and down from the bed and then disappearing. The last is unfortunately not refuted by the fact of my having begun the story.

If I am not very much mistaken, I am coming closer. It is as though the spiritual battle were taking place in a clearing somewhere in the woods. I make my way into the woods, find nothing, and out of weakness immediately hasten out again; often as I leave the woods I hear, or think I hear, the clashing weapons of that battle. Perhaps the eyes of the warriors are seeking me through the darkness of the woods, but I know so little of them, and that little is deceptive.

A heavy downpour. Stand and face the rain, let its iron rays pierce you; drift with the water that wants to sweep you away but yet stand fast, and upright in this way abide the sudden and endless shining of the sun.

The landlady dropped her skirts and hurried through the rooms. A cold, haughty woman. Her projecting lower jaw frightened roomers away. They ran down the steps, and when she looked after them through the window they covered their faces as they ran. Once a gentleman came for a room, a solid, thickset young man who constantly kept his hands in his coat pockets. It was a habit, perhaps, but it was also possible that he wanted to conceal the trembling of his hands.

"Young man," said the woman, and her lower jaw jutted forward, "you want to live here?"

"Yes," the young man said, tossing his head upward.

"You will like it here," the woman said, leading him to a chair on which she sat him down. In doing this she noticed a stain on his trousers, kneeled down beside him and began to scrape at the stain with her fingernails.

"You're a dirty fellow," she said.

"It's an old stain."

"Then you are an old dirty fellow."

"Take your hand away," he said suddenly, and actually

pushed her away. "What horrible hands you have." He caught her hand and turned it over. "All black on top, whitish below, but still black enough and"—he ran his fingers inside her wide sleeve—"there is even some hair on your arm."

"You're tickling me," she said.

"Because I like you. I don't understand how they can say that you are ugly. Because they did say it. But now I see that it isn't true at all."

And he stood up and walked up and down the room. She remained on her knees and looked at her hand.

For some reason this made him furious; he sprang to her side and caught her hand again.

"You're quite a woman," he then said, and clapped her long thin cheek. "It would really add to my comfort to live here. But it would have to be cheap. And you would not be allowed to take in other roomers. And you would have to be faithful to me. I am really much younger than you and can after all insist on faithfulness. And you would have to cook well. I am used to good food and never intend to disaccustom myself."

Dance on, you pigs; what concern is it of mine?

But it has more reality than anything I have written this past year. Perhaps after all it is a matter of loosening the joint. I shall once more be able to write.

Every evening for the past week my neighbor in the adjoining room has come to wrestle with me. He was a stranger to me, even now I haven't yet spoken to him. We merely shout a few exclamations at one another, you can't call that "speaking." With a "well then" the struggle is begun; "scoundrel!" one of us sometimes groans under the grip of the other; "there" accompanies a surprise thrust; "stop!" means the end, yet the struggle always goes on a little while longer. As a rule, even when he is already at the door he leaps back again and gives me a push that sends me to the ground. From his room he then calls good night to me through the wall. If I wanted to give up this acquaintance once and for all I should have to give up my room, for bolting the door is of no avail. Once I had the door bolted because I wanted to read, but my neighbor hacked the door in two with an ax, and, since he can part with something only with the greatest difficulty once he has taken hold of it, I was even in danger of the ax.

I know how to accommodate myself to circumstances. Since he always comes to me at a certain hour, I take up some easy work beforehand which I can interrupt at once, should it be necessary. I straighten out a chest, for example, or copy something, or read some unimportant book. I have to arrange matters in this way—no sooner has he appeared in the door than I must drop everything, slam the chest to at once, drop the penholder, throw the book away, for it is only fighting that he wants, nothing else. If I feel particularly strong I tease him a little by first attempting to elude him. I crawl under the table, throw chairs under his feet, wink at him from the distance, though it is of course in bad taste to joke in this very one-sided way with a stranger. But usually our bodies close in battle at once. Apparently he is a student, studies all day and wants some hasty exercise in the evening before he goes to bed. Well, in me he has a good opponent; accidents aside, I perhaps am the stronger and more skilful of the two. He, however, has more endurance.

May 28. Day after tomorrow I leave for Berlin. In spite

of insomnia, headaches and worries, perhaps in a better
state than ever before.

Once he brought a girl along. While I say hello to her,
not watching him, he springs upon me and jerks me into
the air. "I protest," I cried, and raised my hand.

"Keep quiet," he whispered in my ear. I saw that he was
determined to win at all costs, even by resorting to unfair
holds, so that he might shine before the girl.

"He said 'Keep quiet' to me," I cried, turning my head to
the girl.

"Wretch!" the man gasped in a low voice, exerting all
his strength against me. In spite of everything he was able
to drag me to the sofa, put me down on it, knelt on my
back, paused to regain his breath, and said: "Well, there
he lies."

"Just let him try it again," I intended to say, but after
the very first word he pressed my face so hard into the
upholstery that I was forced to be silent.

"Well then," said the girl, who had sat down at my table
and was reading a half-finished letter lying there, "shouldn't
we leave now? He has just begun to write a letter."

"He won't go on with it if we leave. Come over here,
will you? Touch him, here on his thigh, for instance; he's
trembling just like a sick animal."

"I say leave him alone and come along." Very reluctantly
the man crawled off me. I could have thrashed him soundly
then, for I was rested while all his muscles had been tensed
in the effort to hold me down. He was the one who had
been trembling and had thought that it was I. He was still
trembling even now. But I let him alone because the girl
was present.

"You will probably have drawn your own conclusions

as to this battle," I said to the girl, walked by him with a bow and sat down at the table to go on with the letter. "And who is trembling?" I asked, before beginning to write, and held the penholder rigid in the air in proof that it was not I. I was already in the midst of my writing when I called out a short adieu to them in the distance, but kicked out my foot a little to indicate, at least to myself, the farewell that they both probably deserved.

May 29. Tomorrow to Berlin. Is it a nervous or a real, trustworthy security that I feel? How is that possible? Is it true that if one once acquires a confidence in one's ability to write, nothing can miscarry, nothing is wholly lost, while at the same time only seldom will something rise up to a more than ordinary height? Is this because of my approaching marriage to F.? Strange condition, though not entirely unknown to me when I think back.

Stood a long time before the gate with Pick. Thought only of how I might quickly make my escape, for my supper of strawberries was ready for me upstairs. Everything that I shall now note down about him is simply a piece of shabbiness on my part, for I won't let him see any of it, or am content that he won't see it. But I am really an accessory to his behavior so long as I go about in his company, and therefore what I say of him applies as well to me, even if one discounts the pretended subtlety that lies in such a remark.

I make plans. I stare rigidly ahead lest my eyes lose the imaginary peepholes of the imaginary kaleidoscope into which I am looking. I mix noble and selfish intentions in confusion; the color of the noble ones is washed away, in recompense passing off onto the merely selfish ones. I invite heaven and earth to take part in my schemes, at the same time I am careful not to forget the insignificant little people one can draw out of every side street and who for the time being are more useful to my schemes. It is of course only the beginning, always only the beginning. But as I stand here in my misery, already the huge wagon of my schemes comes driving up behind me, I feel underfoot the first small step up, naked girls, like those on the carnival floats of happier countries, lead me backward up the steps; I float because the girls float, and raise my hand to command silence. Rosebushes stand at my side, incense burns, laurel wreaths are let down, flowers are strewn before and over me; two trumpeters, as if hewn out of stone, blow fanfares, throngs of little people come running up, in ranks behind leaders; the bright, empty, open squares become dark, tempestuous and crowded: I feel myself at the farthest verge of human endeavor, and, high up where I am, with suddenly acquired skill spontaneously execute a trick I had admired in a contortionist years ago—I bend slowly backward (at that very moment the heavens strain to open to disclose a vision to me, but then stop), draw my head and trunk through my legs and gradually stand erect again. Was this the ultimate given to mankind? It would seem so, for already I see the small horned devils leaping out of all the gates of the land, which lies broad and deep beneath me, overrunning the countryside; everything gives way in the center under their feet, their little tails expunge everything, fifty devils' tails are already scouring my face; the ground begins to yield, first one of my feet sinks in and then the other; the screams of the girls pursue me into the depths into which I plummet, down a shaft precisely the width of my body but infinitely deep. This infinity tempts one to no extraordinary accomplishments, anything that I should do would be insignificant; I fall insensibly and that is best.

Dostoevsky's letter to his brother on life in prison.

June 6. Back from Berlin. Was tied hand and foot like a criminal. Had they sat me down in a corner bound in real chains, placed policemen in front of me and let me look on simply like that, it could not have been worse. And that was my engagement; everybody made an effort to bring me to life, and when they couldn't, to put up with me as I was. F. least of all, of course, with complete justification, for she suffered the most. What was merely a passing occurrence to the others, to her was a threat.

We couldn't bear it at home even a moment. We knew that they would look for us. But despite its being evening we ran away. Hills encircled our city; we clambered up them. We set all the trees to shaking as we swung down the slope from one to the other.

The posture of the clerks in the store shortly before closing time in the evening: hands in trouser pockets, a trifle stooped, looking from the vaulted interior past the open door onto the square. Their tired movements behind the counters. Weakly tie up a package, distractedly dust a few boxes, pile up used wrapping paper.

An acquaintance comes and speaks to me. He makes the following statement: Some say this, but I say exactly the opposite. He cites the reasons for his opinion. I wonder. My hands lie in my trouser pockets as if they had been dropped there, and yet as relaxed as if I had only to turn my pockets inside out and they would quickly drop out again.

I had closed the store, employees and customers departed carrying their hats in hand. It was a June evening, eight o'clock already but still light. I had no desire to take a walk, I never feel an inclination to go walking; but neither did I want to go home. When my last apprentice had turned the corner I sat down on the ground in front of the closed store.

An acquaintance and his young wife came by and saw me sitting on the ground. "Why, look who is sitting here," he said. They stopped, and the man shook me a little, despite the fact that I had been calmly regarding him from the very first.

"My God, why are you sitting here like this?" his young wife asked.

"I am going to give up my store," I said. "It isn't going too badly, and I can meet all my obligations, even if only just about. But I can't stand the worries, I can't control the clerks, I can't talk to the customers. From tomorrow on I won't even open the store. I've thought it all over carefully." I saw how the man sought to calm his wife by taking her hand between both of his.

"Fine," he said, "you want to give up your store; you aren't the first to do it. We too"—he looked across at his wife—"as soon as we have enough to take care of ourselves (may it be soon), won't hesitate to give up our store any more than you have done. Business is as little a pleasure to us as it is to you, believe me. But why do you sit on the ground?"

"Where shall I go?" I said. Of course, I knew why they were questioning me. It was sympathy and astonishment as well as embarrassment that they felt, but I was in no position whatsoever to help them too.

"Don't you want to join us?" I was recently asked by an acquaintance when he ran across me alone after midnight in a coffeehouse that was already almost deserted. "No, I don't," I said.

It was already past midnight. I sat in my room writing a letter on which a lot depended for me, for with the letter I hoped to secure an excellent post abroad. I sought to remind the acquaintance to whom I was writing—by chance, after a ten-year interval, I had been put in touch with him again by a common friend—of past times, and at the same time make him understand that all my circumstances pressed me to leave the country and that in the absence of good and far-reaching connections of my own, I was placing my greatest hopes in him.

It was getting on toward nine o'clock in the evening before Bruder, a city official, came home from his office. It was already quite dark. His wife was waiting for him in front of the gate, clutching her little girl to her. "How is it going?" she asked.

"Very badly," said Bruder. "Come into the house and I'll tell you everything." The moment they set foot in the house, Bruder locked the front door. "Where is the maid?" he asked.

"In the kitchen," his wife replied.

"Good; come!"

The table lamp was lit in the large, low living room, they all sat down and Bruder said: "Well, this is how things stand. Our men are in full retreat. As I understand it

from unimpeachable reports that have been received at
City Hall, the fighting at Rumdorf has gone entirely against
us. Moreover, the greater part of the troops have already
withdrawn from the city. They are still keeping it secret
so as not to add enormously to the panic in the city; I
don't consider that altogether wise, it would be better to
tell the truth frankly. However, my duty demands that
I be silent. But of course there is no one to prevent me
from telling you the truth. Besides, everybody suspects
the real situation, you can see that everywhere. Everybody is shutting up his house, hiding whatever can be
hidden." [7]

It was about ten o'clock in the evening before Bruder, a
city official, came home from his office; nevertheless he
at once knocked on the door that separated his room from
Rumford's, the furniture dealer, from whom he rented
the room. Though he could hear only an indistinct response, he went in. Rumford was seated at the table with
a newspaper; his fat was troubling him this hot July
evening, he had thrown his coat and vest on the sofa;
his shirt——

Several city officials were standing by the stone ledge
of a window in City Hall, looking down into the square.
The last of the rear guard was waiting below for the command to retreat. They were young, tall, red-cheeked fellows who held their quivering horses tightly reined. Two
officers rode slowly back and forth in front of them. They
were apparently waiting for a report. They sent out nu-
merous riders who disappeared at a gallop up a steeply
ascending side street opening off the square. None had
yet returned.

The city official Bruder, still a young man but wearing a full beard, had joined the group at the window. Since he enjoyed higher rank and was held in particular esteem because of his abilities, they all bowed courteously and made way for him at the window ledge. "This must be the end," he said, looking down on the square. "It is only too apparent."

"Then it is your opinion, Councillor," said an arrogant young man who in spite of Bruder's approach had not stirred from his place and now stood close to him in such a way that it was impossible for them to look at each other; "then it is your opinion that the battle has been lost?"

"Certainly. There can be no doubt of it. Speaking in confidence, our leadership is bad. We must pay for all sorts of old sins. This of course is not the time to talk of it, everybody must look out for himself now. We are indeed face to face with final collapse. Our visitors may be here by this evening. It may be that they won't even wait until evening but will arrive here in half an hour."

I step out of the house for a short stroll. The weather is beautiful but the street is startlingly empty, except for a municipal employee in the distance who is holding a hose and playing a huge arc of water along the street. "Unheard of," I say, and test the tension of the arc. "An insignificant municipal employee," I say, and again look at the man in the distance.

At the corner of the next intersection two men are fighting; they collide, fly far apart, guardedly approach one another and are at once locked together in struggle again. "Stop fighting, gentlemen," I say.

The student Kosel was studying at his table. He was so deeply engrossed in his work that he failed to notice it getting dark; in spite of the brightness of the May day, dusk began to descend at about four o'clock in the afternoon in this ill-situated back room. He read with pursed lips, his eyes, without his being aware of it, bent close to the book. Occasionally he paused in his reading, wrote short excerpts from what he had read into a little notebook, and then, closing his eyes, whispered from memory what he had written down. Across from his window, not five yards away, was a kitchen and in it a girl ironing clothes who would often look across at Karl.

Suddenly Kosel put his pencil down and listened. Someone was pacing back and forth in the room above, apparently barefooted, making one round after another. At every step there was a loud splashing noise, of the kind one makes when one steps into water. Kosel shook his head. These walks which he had had to endure for perhaps a week now, ever since a new roomer had moved in, meant the end, not only of his studying for today, but of his studying altogether, unless he did something in his own defense.

There are certain relationships which I can feel distinctly but which I am unable to perceive. It would be sufficient to plunge down a little deeper; but just at this point the upward pressure is so strong that I should think myself at the very bottom if I did not feel the currents moving below me. In any event, I look upward to the surface whence the thousand-times-refracted brilliance of the light falls upon me. I float up and splash around on the surface, in spite of the fact that I loathe everything up there and——

"Herr Direktor, a new actor has arrived," the servant was heard distinctly to announce, for the door to the anteroom was wide open. "I merely wish to *become* an actor," said Karl in an undertone, and in this way corrected the servant's announcement. "Where is he?" the director asked, craning his neck.

The old bachelor with the altered cut to his beard.

The woman dressed in white in the center of the Kinsky Palace courtyard. Distinct shadow under the high arch of her bosom in spite of the distance. Stiffly seated.

June 11.
TEMPTATION IN THE VILLAGE [8]

One summer, toward evening, I arrived in a village where I had never been before. It struck me how broad and open were the paths. Everywhere one saw tall old trees in front of the farmhouses. It had been raining, the air was fresh, everything pleased me. I tried to indicate this by the manner in which I greeted the people standing in front of the gates; their replies were friendly even if somewhat aloof. I thought it would be nice to spend the night here if I could find an inn.

I was just walking past the high, ivy-covered wall of a farm when a small door opened in the wall, three faces peered out, vanished, and the door closed again. "Strange," I said aloud, turning to one side as if I had someone with me. And, as if to embarrass me, there in fact stood a tall man next to me with neither hat nor coat, wearing a black knitted vest and smoking a pipe. I quickly recovered myself and said, as though I had already known that he was there: "The door! Did you see the way that little door opened?"

"Yes," the man said, "but what's strange in that? It was the tenant farmer's children. They heard your footsteps and looked out to see who was walking by here so late in the evening."

"The explanation is a simple one, of course," I said with a smile. "It's easy for things to seem queer to a stranger. Thank you." And I went on.

But the man followed me. I wasn't really surprised by that, the man could be going the same way; yet there was no reason for us to walk one behind the other and not side by side. I turned and said, "Is this the right way to the inn?"

The man stopped and said, "We don't have an inn, or rather we have one but it can't be lived in. It belongs to the community and, years ago now, after no one had applied for the management of it, it was turned over to an old cripple whom the community already had to provide for. With his wife he now manages the inn, but in such a way that you can hardly pass by the door, the smell coming out of it is so strong. The floor of the parlor is slippery with dirt. A wretched way of doing things, a disgrace to the village, a disgrace to the community."

I wanted to contradict the man; his appearance provoked me to it, this thin face with yellowish, leathery, bony cheeks and black wrinkles spreading over all of it at every movement of his jaws. "Well," I said, expressing no further surprise at this state of affairs, and then went on: "I'll stop there anyway, since I have made up my mind to spend the night here."

"Very well," the man quickly said, "but this is the path you must take to reach the inn," and he pointed in the direction I had come from. "Walk to the next corner and then turn right. You'll see the inn sign at once. That's it."

I thanked him for the information and now walked past him again while he regarded me very closely. I had no way of guarding against the possibility that he had given me wrong directions, but was determined not to be put out of countenance either by his forcing me to march past him now, or by the fact that he had with such remarkable abruptness abandoned his attempts to warn me against the inn. Somebody else could direct me to the inn as well, and if it were dirty, why then for once I would simply sleep in dirt, if only to satisfy my stubbornness. Moreover, I did not have much of a choice; it was already dark, the roads were muddy from the rain and it was a long way to the next village.

By now the man was behind me and I intended not to trouble myself with him any further when I heard a woman's voice speak to him. I turned. Out of the darkness under a group of plane trees stepped a tall, erect woman. Her skirts shone a yellowish-brown color, over her head and shoulders was a black coarse-knit shawl. "Come home now, won't you?" she said to the man; "why aren't you coming?"

"I'm coming," he said; "only wait a little while. I want to see what that man is going to do. He's a stranger. He's hanging around here for no reason at all. Look at him."

He spoke of me as if I were deaf or did not understand his language. Now to be sure it did not much matter to me what he said, but it would naturally be unpleasant for me were he to spread false reports about me in the village, no matter of what kind. For this reason I said to the woman: "I'm looking for the inn, that's all. Your husband has no right to speak of me that way and perhaps give you a wrong impression of me."

But the woman hardly looked at me and went over to her husband (I had been correct in thinking him her husband; there was such a direct, self-evident relationship between the two), and put her hand on his shoulder: "If there is anything you want, speak to my husband, not to me."

"But I don't want anything," I said, irritated by the manner in which I was being treated; "I mind my business, you mind yours. That's all I ask." The woman tossed her head; that much I was able to make out in the dark, but not the expression in her eyes. Apparently she wanted to say something in reply, but her husband said, "Keep still!" and she was silent.

Our encounter now seemed definitely at an end; I turned, about to go on, when someone called out, "Sir!" It was probably addressed to me. For a moment I could not tell where the voice came from, but then I saw a young man sitting above me on the farmyard wall, his legs dangling down and knees bumping together, who insolently said to me: "I have just heard that you want to spend the night in the village. You won't find livable quarters anywhere except here on this farm."

"On this farm?" I asked, and involuntarily—I was furious about it later—cast a questioning glance at the man and wife, who still stood there pressed against each other watching me.

"That's right," he said, with the same arrogance in his reply that there was in all his behavior.

"Are there beds to be had here?" I asked again, to make sure and to force the man back into his role of landlord.

"Yes," he said, already averting his glance from me a

little, "beds for the night are furnished here, not to everyone, but only to those to whom they are offered."

"I accept," I said, "but will naturally pay for the bed, just as I would at the inn."

"Please," said the man, who had already been looking over my head for a long time, "we shall not take advantage of you."

He sat above like a master, I stood down below like a petty servant; I had a great desire to stir him up a little by throwing a stone up at him. Instead I said, "Then please open the door for me."

"It's not locked," he said.

"It's not locked," I grumbled in reply, almost without knowing it, opened the door and walked in. I happened to look up at the top of the wall immediately afterward; the man was no longer there, in spite of its height he had apparently jumped down from the wall and was perhaps discussing something with the man and wife. Let them discuss it, what could happen to me, a young man with barely three gulden in cash and the rest of whose property consisted of not much more than a clean shirt in his rucksack and a revolver in his trouser pocket. Besides, the people did not look at all as if they would rob anyone. But what else could they want of me?

It was the usual sort of neglected garden found on large farms, though the solid stone wall would have led one to expect more. In the tall grass, at regular intervals, stood cherry trees with fallen blossoms. In the distance one could see the farmhouse, a one-story rambling structure. It was already growing quite dark; I was a late guest; if the man on the wall had lied to me in any way, I might find myself in an unpleasant situation. On my way to the house I met no one, but when a few steps away from the house I saw, in the room into which the open door gave, two tall old people side by side, a man and wife, their faces toward the door, eating some sort of porridge out of a bowl. I could not make anything out very clearly in the darkness but now and then something on the man's coat sparkled like gold, it was probably his buttons or perhaps his watch chain.

I greeted them and then said, not crossing the threshold for the moment: "I happened to be looking in the village for a place to spend the night when a young man sitting on your garden wall told me it was possible to rent a room for the night here on the farm." The two old people had put their spoons into the porridge, leaned back on their bench, and looked at me in silence. There was none too great hospitality in their demeanor. I therefore added, "I hope the information given me was correct and that I haven't needlessly disturbed you." I said this very loudly, for they might perhaps have been hard of hearing.

"Come nearer," said the man after a little pause.

I obeyed him only because he was so old, otherwise I should naturally have had to insist that he give a direct answer to my direct question. At any rate, as I entered I said, "If putting me up causes you even the slightest difficulty, feel free to tell me so; I don't absolutely insist on it. I can go to the inn, it wouldn't matter to me at all."

"He talks so much," the woman said in a low voice.

It could only have been intended as an insult, thus it was with insults that they met my courtesy; yet she was an old woman, I could not say anything in my defense. And my very defenselessness was perhaps the reason why this remark to which I dared not retort had so much greater

an effect on me than it deserved. I felt there was some justification for a reproach of some sort, not because I had
talked too much, for as a matter of fact I had said only
what was absolutely necessary, but because of other reasons that touched my existence very closely. I said nothing
further, insisted on no reply, saw a bench in a dark corner
near by, walked over and sat down.

The old couple resumed their eating, a girl came in from
the next room and placed a lighted candle on the table.
Now one saw even less than before, everything merged
in the darkness, only the tiny flame flickered above the
slightly bowed heads of the two old people. Several children came running in from the garden, one fell headlong
and cried, the others stopped running and now stood dispersed about the room; the old man said, "Go to sleep,
children."

They gathered in a group at once, the one who had been
crying was only sobbing now, one boy near me plucked at
my coat as if he meant that I was to come along; since I
wanted to go to sleep too, I got up and, adult though I
was, went silently from the room in the midst of the children as they loudly chorused good night. The friendly
little boy took me by the hand and made it easier for me
to find my way in the dark. Very soon we came to a ladder, climbed up it and were in the attic. Through a small
open skylight in the roof one could just then see the thin
crescent of the moon; it was delightful to step under the
skylight—my head almost reached up to it—and to breathe
the mild yet cool air. Straw was piled on the floor against
one wall; there was enough room for me to sleep too. The
children—there were two boys and three girls—kept laughing while they undressed; I had thrown myself down in
my clothes on the straw, I was among strangers, after all,

and they were under no obligation to take me in. For a little while, propped up on my elbows, I watched the half-naked children playing in a corner. But then I felt so tired that I put my head on my rucksack, stretched out my arms, let my eyes travel along the roof beams awhile longer and fell asleep. In my first sleep I thought I could still hear one boy shout, "Watch out, he's coming!" whereupon the noise of the hurried tripping of the children running to their beds penetrated my already receding consciousness.

I had surely slept only a very short time, for when I awoke the moonlight still fell almost unchanged through the window on the same part of the floor. I did not know why I had awakened—my sleep had been dreamless and deep. Then near me, at about the height of my ear, I saw a very small bushy dog, one of those repulsive little lap dogs with disproportionately large heads encircled by curly hair, whose eyes and muzzle are loosely set into their heads like ornaments made out of some kind of lifeless horny substance. What was a city dog like this doing in the village! What was it that made it roam the house at night? Why did it stand next to my ear? I hissed at it to make it go away; perhaps it was the children's pet and had simply strayed to my side. It was frightened by my hissing but did not run away, only turned around, then stood there on its crooked little legs and I could see its stunted (especially by contrast with its large head) little body.

Since it continued to stand there quietly, I tried to go back to sleep, but could not; over and over again in the space immediately before my closed eyes I could see the dog rocking back and forth with its protruding eyes. It was unbearable, I could not stand the animal near me; I rose and picked it up in my arms to carry it outside. But though it had been apathetic until then, it now began to defend itself and tried to seize me with its claws. Thus I was forced to hold its little paws fast too—an easy matter, of course; I was able to hold all four in one hand. "So, my pet," I said to the excited little head with its trembling curls, and went into the dark with it, looking for the door.

Only now did it strike me how silent the little dog was, it neither barked nor squeaked, though I could feel its blood pounding wildly through all its arteries. After a few steps— the dog had claimed all my attention and made me careless—greatly to my annoyance, I stumbled over one of the sleeping children. It was now very dark in the attic, only a little light still came through the skylight. The child sighed, I stood still for a moment, dared not move even my toe away lest any change waken the child still more. It was too late; suddenly, all around me, I saw the children rising up in their white shifts as though by agreement, as though on command. It was not my fault; I had made only one child wake up, though it had not really been an awakening at all, only a slight disturbance that a child should have easily slept through. But now they were awake. "What do you want, children?" I asked. "Go back to sleep."

"You're carrying something," one of the boys said, and all five children searched my person.

"Yes," I said; I had nothing to hide, if the children wanted to take the dog out, so much the better. "I'm taking this dog outside. It was keeping me from sleeping. Do you know whose it is?"

"Mrs. Cruster's," at least that's what I thought I made of their confused, indistinct drowsy shouts which were intended not for me but only for each other.

"Who is Mrs. Cruster?" I asked, but got no further answer from the excited children. One of them took the dog, which had now become entirely still, from my arm and hurried away with it; the rest followed.

I did not want to remain here alone, also my sleepiness had left me by now; for a moment I hesitated, it seemed to me that I was meddling too much in the affairs of this house where no one had shown any great confidence in me; but finally I ran after the children. I heard the pattering of their feet a short distance ahead of me, but often stumbled in the pitch darkness on the unfamiliar way and once even bumped my head painfully against the wall. We came into the room in which I had first met the old people; it was empty, through the door that was still standing open one could see the moonlit garden.

"Go outside," I said to myself, "the night is warm and bright, you can continue your journey or even spend the night in the open. After all, it is so ridiculous to run about after the children here." But I ran nevertheless; I still had a hat, stick and rucksack up in the attic. But how the children ran! With their shifts flying they leaped through the moonlit room in two bounds, as I distinctly saw. It occurred to me that I was giving adequate thanks for the lack of hospitality shown me in this house by frightening the children, causing a race through the house and myself making a great din instead of sleeping (the sound of the children's bare feet could hardly be heard above the tread of my heavy boots)—and I had not the faintest notion of what would come of all this.

Suddenly a bright light appeared. In front of us, in a room with several windows opened wide, a delicate-looking woman sat at a table writing by the light of a tall, splendid table lamp. "Children!" she called out in astonishment; she hadn't seen me yet, I stayed back in the shadow outside the door. The children put the dog on the table; they obviously loved the woman very much, kept trying to look into her eyes, one girl seized her hand and caressed it; she made no objection, was scarcely aware of it. The dog stood before her on the sheet of letter paper on which she had just been writing and stretched out its quivering little tongue toward her, the tongue could be plainly seen a short distance in front of the lampshade. The children now begged to be allowed to remain and tried to wheedle the woman's consent. The woman was undecided, got up, stretched her arms and pointed to the single bed and the hard floor. The children refused to give it any importance and lay down on the floor wherever they happened to be, to try it; for a while everything was quiet. Her hands folded in her lap, the woman looked down with a smile at the children. Now and then one raised its head, but when it saw the others still lying down, lay back again.

One evening I returned home to my room from the office somewhat later than usual—an acquaintance had detained me below at the house entrance for a long time—opened the door (my thoughts were still engrossed by our conversation, which had consisted chiefly of gossip about people's social standing), hung my overcoat on the hook and was about to cross over to the washstand when I heard a strange, spasmodic breathing. I looked up and, on top of the stove that stood deep in the gloom of a corner, saw something alive. Yellowish glittering eyes stared at me; large round woman's breasts rested on the shelf of the stove, on either side beneath the unrecognizable face; the creature seemed to consist entirely of a mass of soft white flesh; a thick yellowish tail hung down beside the stove, its tip ceaselessly passing back and forth over the cracks of the tiles.

The first thing I did was to cross over with long strides and sunken head—nonsense! nonsense! I kept repeating like a prayer—to the door that led to my landlady's rooms. Only later I realized that I had entered without knocking. Miss Hefter——

It was about midnight. Five men held me, behind them a sixth had his hand raised to grab me. "Let go," I cried, and whirled in a circle, making them all fall back. I felt some sort of law at work, had known that this last effort of mine would be successful, saw all the men reeling back with raised arms, realized that in a moment they would all throw themselves on me together, turned toward the house entrance—I was standing only a short distance from it—lifted the latch (it sprang open of itself, as it were, with extraordinary rapidity), and escaped up the dark stairs. On the top floor stood my old mother in the open door-way of our apartment, a candle in her hand. "Look out! look out!" I cried while still on the floor below, "they are coming after me!"

"Who? Who?" my mother asked. "Who could be coming after you, son?" my mother asked.

"Six men," I said breathlessly.

"Do you know them?" my mother asked.

"No, strangers," I said.

"What do they look like?"

"I barely caught a glimpse of them. One has a black full beard, one a large ring on his finger, one has a red belt, one has his trousers torn at the knee, one has only one eye open, and the last bares his teeth."

"Don't think about it any more," my mother said. "Go to your room, go to sleep, I've made the bed."

My mother! This old woman already proof against the

assaults of life, with a crafty wrinkle round her mouth, mouth that unwittingly repeated eighty-year-old follies.

"Sleep now?" I cried——

June 12. Kubin. Yellowish face, sparse hair lying flat on his skull, from time to time a heightened sparkle in his eyes.

W., half blind, detached retina; has to be careful not to fall or be pushed, for the lens might fall out and then it would be all over with. Has to hold the book close to his eyes when he reads and try to catch the letters through the corners of his eyes. Was in India with Melchior Lechter, fell ill with dysentery; eats everything, every piece of fruit he finds lying in the dust of the street.

P. sawed a silver chastity belt off a skeleton; pushed aside the workers who had dug it up somewhere in Rumania, re-assured them by saying that he saw in the belt a valuable trifle which he wanted as a souvenir, sawed it open and pulled it off. If he finds a valuable Bible or picture or page that he wants in a village church, he tears what he wants out of the book, off the wall, from the altar, puts a two-heller piece down as compensation and his conscience is clear.—Loves fat women. Every woman he has had has been photographed. The bundle of photographs that he shows every visitor. Sits at one end of the sofa, his visitor, at a considerable distance from him, at the other. P. hardly looks across and yet always knows which picture is on top and supplies the necessary explanations: This was an old widow; these were the two Hungarian maids; etc.—Of Kubin: "Yes, Master Kubin, you are indeed on the way up; in ten or twenty years, if this keeps on, you may come to occupy a position like that of Bayros." [9]

Dostoevsky's letter to a woman painter.

The life of society moves in a circle. Only those burdened with a common affliction understand each other. Thanks to their affliction they constitute a circle and provide each other mutual support. They glide along the inner borders of their circle, make way for or jostle one another gently in the crowd. Each encourages the other in the hope that it will react upon himself, or—and then it is done passionately—in the immediate enjoyment of this reaction. Each has only that experience which his affliction grants him; nevertheless one hears such comrades exchanging immensely varying experiences. "This is how you are," one says to the other; "instead of complaining, thank God that this is how you are, for if this were not how you are, you would have this or that misfortune, this or that shame." How does this man know that? After all, he belongs—his statement betrays it—to the same circle as does the one to whom he spoke; he stands in the same need of comfort. In the same circle, however, one knows only the same things. There exists not the shadow of a thought to give the comforter an advantage over the comforted. Thus their conversations consist only of a coming-together of their imaginations, outpourings of wishes from one upon the other. One will look down at the ground and the other up at a bird; it is in such differences that their intercourse is realized. Sometimes they will unite in faith and, their heads together, look up into the unending reaches of the sky. Recognition of their situation shows itself, however, only when they bow down their heads in common and the common hammer descends upon them.

June 14. How I calmly walk along while my head twitches and a branch feebly rustles overhead, causing me the worst discomfort. I have in me the same calm, the same assurance as other people, but somehow or other inverted.

June 19. The excitements of the last few days. The calm that is transferred from Dr. W. to me. The worries he takes upon himself for me. How they moved back into me early this morning when I awoke about four after a deep sleep. Pištekovo divadlo.[10] Löwenstein. Now the crude, exciting novel by Soyka. Anxiety. Convinced that I need F.

How the two of us, Ottla and I, explode in rage against every kind of human relationship.

The parents' grave, in which the son (Pollak, a graduate of a commercial school) is also buried.[11]

June 25. I paced up and down my room from early morning until twilight. The window was open, it was a warm day. The noises of the narrow street beat in uninterruptedly. By now I knew every trifle in the room from having looked at it in the course of my pacing up and down. My eyes had traveled over every wall. I had pursued the pattern of the rug to its last convolution, noted every mark of age it bore. My fingers had spanned the table across the middle many times. I had already bared my teeth repeatedly at the picture of the landlady's dead husband.
Toward evening I walked over to the window and sat down on the low sill. Then, for the first time not moving restlessly about, I happened calmly to glance into the interior of the room and at the ceiling. And finally, finally, unless I were mistaken, this room which I had so violently upset began to stir. The tremor began at the edges of the thinly plastered white ceiling. Little pieces of plaster broke off and with a distinct thud fell here and there, as if at random, to the floor. I held out my hand and some plaster fell into it too; in my excitement I threw it over my head into the

street without troubling to turn around. The cracks in the ceiling made no pattern yet, but it was already possible somehow to imagine one. But I put these games aside when a bluish violet began to mix with the white; it spread straight out from the center of the ceiling, which itself remained white, even radiantly white, where the shabby electric lamp was stuck. Wave after wave of the color—or was it a light?—spread out toward the now darkening edges. One no longer paid any attention to the plaster that was falling away as if under the pressure of a skilfully applied tool. Yellow and golden-yellow colors now penetrated the violet from the side. But the ceiling did not really take on these different hues; the colors merely made it somewhat transparent; things striving to break through seemed to be hovering above it, already one could almost see the outlines of a movement there, an arm was thrust out, a silver sword swung to and fro. It was meant for me, there was no doubt of that; a vision intended for my liberation was being prepared.

I sprang up on the table to make everything ready, tore out the electric light together with its brass fixture and hurled it to the floor, then jumped down and pushed the table from the middle of the room to the wall. That which was striving to appear could drop down unhindered on the carpet and announce to me whatever it had to announce. I had barely finished when the ceiling did in fact break open. In the dim light, still at a great height, I had judged it badly, an angel in bluish-violet robes girt with gold cords sank slowly down on great white silken-shining wings, the sword in its raised arm thrust out horizontally. "An angel, then!" I thought; "it has been flying toward me all the day and in my disbelief I did not know it. Now it will speak to me." I lowered my eyes. When I raised them again the angel was still there, it is true, hanging rather far off under the ceiling (which had closed again), but it was no living angel, only a painted wooden figurehead off the prow of some ship, one of the kind that hangs from the ceiling in sailors' taverns, nothing more.

The hilt of the sword was made in such a way as to hold candles and catch the dripping tallow. I had pulled the electric light down; I didn't want to remain in the dark, there was still one candle left, so I got up on a chair, stuck the candle into the hilt of the sword, lit it and then sat late into the night under the angel's faint flame.

June 30. Hellerau to Leipzig with Pick. I behaved terribly. Couldn't ask a question, answer one, or move; was barely able to look him in the eye. The Navy League agitator, the fat, sausage-eating Thomas couple in whose house we lived, Prescher, who took us there; Mrs. Thomas, Hegner, Fantl and Mrs. Adler, the woman and the child, Anneliese, Mrs. K., Miss P., Mrs. Fantl's sister, K., Mendelssohn (the brother's child; Alpinum, cockchafer larvae, pine-needle bath); tavern in the forest called Natura, Wolff, Haas; reading *Narciss* aloud in the Adler garden, sightseeing in the Dalcroze house, evening in the tavern in the forest, Bugra—terror after terror.

Failures: didn't find the Natura, ran up and down Struvestrasse; wrong trolley to Hellerau; no room in the tavern in the forest; forgot that I was supposed to get a telephone call from E.[12] there, hence went back; Fantl had left; Dalcroze in Geneva; next morning got to the tavern in the forest too late (F. had telephoned for nothing); decided to go not to Berlin but Leipzig; pointless trip; by mistake, a local train; Wolff was just going to Berlin; Lasker-Schüler appropriated Werfel; pointless visit to the exhibition;

finally, to cap it all, quite pointlessly dunned Pick for an old debt in the Arco.

July 1. Too tired.

July 5. To have to bear and to be the cause of such suffering!

July 23. The tribunal in the hotel. Trip in the cab. F.'s face. She patted her hair with her hand, wiped her nose, yawned. Suddenly she gathered herself together and said very studied, hostile things she had long been saving up. The trip back with Miss Bl.[13] The room in the hotel; heat reflected from the wall across the street. Afternoon sun, in addition. Energetic waiter, almost an Eastern Jew in his manner. The courtyard noisy as a boiler factory. Bad smells. Bedbug. Crushing it a difficult decision. Chambermaid astonished: There are no bedbugs anywhere; once only did a guest find one in the corridor.

At her parents'. Her mother's occasional tears. I recited my lesson. Her father understood the thing from every side. Made a special trip from Malmö to meet me, traveled all night; sat there in his shirt sleeves. They agreed that I was right, there was nothing, or not much, that could be said against me. Devilish in my innocence. Miss Bl.'s apparent guilt.

Evening alone on a bench on Unter den Linden. Stomach-ache. Sad-looking ticket-seller. Stood in front of people, shuffled the tickets in his hands and you could only get rid of him by buying one. Did his job properly in spite of all his apparent clumsiness—on a full-time job of this kind you can't keep jumping around; he must also try to remember people's faces. When I see people of this kind I always think: How did he get into this job, how much does he make, where will he be tomorrow, what awaits him in his old age, where does he live, in what corner does he stretch out his arms before going to sleep, could I do his job, how should I feel about it? All this together with my stomach-ache. Suffered through a horrible night. And yet almost no recollection of it.

In the Restaurant Belvedere on the Strahlau Brücke with E. She still hopes it will end well, or acts as if she does. Drank wine. Tears in her eyes. Ships leave for Grünau, for Schwertau. A lot of people. Music. E. consoled me, though I wasn't sad; that is, my sadness has to do only with myself, but as such it is inconsolable. Gave me *The Gothic Rooms*. Talked a lot (I knew nothing). Especially about how she got her way in her job against a venomous white-haired old woman who worked in the same place. She would like to leave Berlin, to have her own business. She loves quiet. When she was in Sebnitz she often slept all day on Sunday. Can be gay too.

Why did her parents and aunt wave after me? Why did F. sit in the hotel and not stir in spite of the fact that everything was already settled? Why did she telegraph me: "Expecting you, but must leave on business Tuesday"? Was I expected to do something? Nothing could have been more natural. From nothing (interrupted by Dr. Weiss, who walks over to the window)——

July 27. The next day didn't visit her parents again. Merely sent a messenger with a letter of farewell. Letter dishonest and coquettish. "Don't think badly of me." Speech from the gallows.

Went twice to the swimming pool on the Strahlauer Ufer. Lots of Jews. Bluish faces, strong bodies, wild running. Evening in the garden of the Askanischer Hof. Ate rice à la Trautmannsdorf and a peach. A man drinking wine watched my attempts to cut the unripe little peach with my knife. I couldn't. Stricken with shame under the old man's eyes, I let the peach go completely and ten times leafed through *Die Fliegenden Blätter*. I waited to see if he wouldn't at last turn away. Finally I collected all my strength and in defiance of him bit into the completely juiceless and expensive peach. A tall man in the booth near me occupied with nothing but the roast he was painstakingly selecting and the wine in the ice bucket. Finally he lit a long cigar; I watched him over my *Fliegende Blätter*.

Left from the Lehrter railroad station.[14] Swede in shirt sleeves. Strong-looking girl with all the silver bracelets. Changing trains in Buchen during the night. Lübeck. Hotel Schützenhaus dreadful. Cluttered walls, dirty clothes under the sheet, neglected building; a bus boy was the only servant. Afraid of the room, I went into the garden and sat down over a bottle of mineral water. Opposite me a hunchback drinking beer and a thin, anemic young man who was smoking. Slept nevertheless, but was awakened early in the morning by the sun shining through the large window straight into my face. The window looked out on the railroad tracks; incessant noise of the trains. Relief and happiness after moving to the Hotel Kaiserhof on the Trave.

Trip to Travemünde. Mixed bathing. View of the beach. Afternoon on the sand. My bare feet struck people as indecent. Near me a man who was apparently an American. Instead of eating lunch walked past all the pensions and restaurants. Sat among the trees in front of the Kurhaus and listened to the dinner music.

In Lübeck a walk on the Wall. Sad, forlorn-looking man on a bench. Bustle on the Sportplatz. Quiet square, people on stairs and stones in front of every door. Morning from the window. Unloading timber from a sailboat. Dr. Weiss at the railroad station. Unfailing resemblance to Löwy. Unable to make up my mind on Gleschendorf. Meal in the Hansa dairy. "The Blushing Virgin." Shopping for dinner. Telephone conversation with Gleschendorf. Trip to Marienlyst. Ferry. Mysterious disappearance of a young man wearing a raincoat and hat and his mysterious reappearance in the carriage on the trip from Vaggerloese to Marienlyst.

July 28. Despairing first impression of the barrenness, the miserable house, the bad food with neither fruit nor vegetables, the quarrels between W. and H. Decided to leave the next day. Gave notice. Stayed nevertheless. A reading from *Überfall;* I was unable to listen, to enjoy it with them, to judge. W.'s improvised speeches. Beyond me. The man writing in the middle of the garden; fat face, black eyes, pomaded long hair brushed straight back. Rigid stare, looked right and left out of the corners of his eyes. *The children, uninterested, sat around his table like flies.—I am more and more unable to think, to observe, to determine the truth of things, to remember, to speak, to share an experience; I am turning to stone, this is the truth.* I am more and more unable even in the office. If I can't take refuge in some work, I am lost. Is my knowledge of this as clear as the thing itself? I shun people not because I want to live quietly, but rather because I want to die quietly. I think of the walk we, E. and I, took from the trolley to the Lehrter railroad station. Neither of us spoke, I thought nothing but that each step taken was that much of a gain for me. And E. is nice to me, believes in me for some incomprehensible reason, in spite of having seen me before the tribunal; now and then I even feel the effect of this faith in me, without, however, fully believing in the feeling.

The first time in many months that I felt any life stir in me in the presence of other people was in the compartment on the return trip from Berlin, opposite the Swiss woman. She reminded me of G.W. Once she even exclaimed: Children! She had headaches, her blood gave her so much trouble. Ugly, neglected little body; bad, cheap dress from a Paris department store. Freckles on her face. But small feet; a body completely under control because of its diminutive size, and despite its clumsiness, round, firm cheeks, sparkling, inextinguishable eyes.

The Jewish couple who lived next to me. Young people, shy and unassuming; her large hooked nose and slender body; he had a slight squint, was pale, short and stout; at night he coughed a little. They often walked one behind the other. Sight of the tumbled bed in their room.

Danish couple. The man often very proper in a dinner jacket, the woman tanned, a weak yet coarse-featured face. Were silent a good deal; sometimes sat side by side, their heads inclined toward one another as on a cameo.

The impudent, good-looking youngster. Always smoking cigarettes. Looked at H. impudently, challengingly, admiringly, scornfully and contemptuously, all in one glance. Sometimes he paid her no attention at all. Silently demanded a cigarette from her. Soon thereafter, from the distance, offered her one. Wore torn trousers. If anyone is going to spank him, it will have to be done this summer; by next summer he will be doing the spanking. Strokes the arms of almost all the chambermaids; not humbly, however, not with embarrassment but rather like some lieutenant whose still childish face permitted him liberties that

would later be denied him. How he makes as if to chop off
the head of a doll with his knife at the dinner table.

Lancers. Four couples. By lamp light and to phonograph
music in the main hall. After each figure a dancer hurried
to the phonograph and put on a new record. A decorous,
graceful and earnestly executed dance, especially on the
part of the men. Cheerful, red-cheeked fellow, a man of the
world, whose inflated stiff shirt made his broad, high chest
seem even higher; the pale nonchalant fellow with a superior air, joking with everyone; beginning of a paunch; loud,
ill-fitting clothes; many languages; read *Die Zukunft;* the
gigantic father of the goitrous, wheezing family; you were
able to recognize them by their labored breathing and infantile bellies; he and his wife (with whom he danced very
gallantly) demonstratively sat at the children's table, where
indeed his offspring were most heavily represented.

The proper, neat, trustworthy gentleman with a face
looking almost sulky in its utter solemnity; modesty and
manliness. Played the piano. The gigantic German with
dueling scars on his square face whose puffed lips came together so placidly when he spoke. His wife, a hard and
friendly Nordic face, accentuated, beautiful walk, accentuated freedom of her swaying hips. Woman from Lübeck
with shining eyes. Three children, including Georg who,
thoughtless as a butterfly, alighted beside complete strangers. Then in childish talkativeness asked some meaningless
question. For example, we were sitting and correcting the
"Kampf." [15] Suddenly he appeared and in a matter-of-fact,
trustful and loud voice asked where the other children had
run off to.

The stiff old gentleman who was a demonstration of
what the noble Nordic longheads look like in old age.

Decayed and unrecognizable; yet beautiful young long-heads were also running around there.

July 29. The two friends, one of them blond, resembling Richard Strauss, smiling, reserved, clever; the other dark, correctly dressed, mild-mannered yet firm, too dainty, lisped; both of them gourmets, kept drinking wine, coffee, beer, brandy, smoked incessantly, one poured for the other; their room across from mine full of French books; wrote a great deal in the stuffy writing room when the weather was mild.

Joseph K., the son of a rich merchant, one evening after a violent quarrel with his father—his father had reproached him for his dissipated life and demanded that he put an immediate stop to it—went, with no definite purpose but only because he was tired and completely at a loss, to the house of the corporation of merchants which stood all by itself near the harbor. The doorkeeper made a deep bow, Joseph looked casually at him without a word of greeting. "These silent underlings do everything one supposes them to be doing," he thought. "If I imagine that he is looking at me insolently, then he really is." And he once more turned to the doorkeeper, again without a word of greeting; the latter turned toward the street and looked up at the overcast sky.

I was in great perplexity. Only a moment ago I had known what to do. With his arm held out before him the boss had pushed me to the door of the store. Behind the two counters stood my fellow clerks, supposedly my friends, their gray faces lowered in the darkness to conceal their expressions.

"Get out!" the boss shouted. "Thief! Get out! Get out, I say!"

"It's not true," I shouted for the hundredth time; "I didn't steal! It's a mistake or a slander! Don't you touch me! I'll sue you! There are still courts here! I won't go! For five years I slaved for you like a son and now you treat me like a thief. I didn't steal; for God's sake, listen to me, I didn't steal."

"Not another word," said the boss, "you're fired!"

We were already at the glass door, an apprentice darted out in front of us and quickly opened it; the din coming in from what was indeed an out-of-the-way street brought me back to reality; I halted in the doorway, arms akimbo, and, as calmly as I could despite my breathlessness, merely said, "I want my hat."

"You'll get it," the boss said, walked back a few steps, took the hat from Grassmann, one of the clerks, who had jumped over the counter, tried to throw it to me but missed his aim, and anyway threw it too hard, so that the hat flew past me into the street.

"You can keep the hat now," I said, and went out into the street. And now I was in a quandary. I had stolen, had slipped a five-gulden bill out of the till to take Sophie to the theater that evening. But she didn't even want to go to the theater; payday was three days off, at that time I should have had my own money; besides, I had committed the theft stupidly, in broad daylight, near the glass window of the office in which the boss sat looking at me. "Thief!" he shouted, and sprang out of the office. "I didn't steal," was the first thing I said, but the five-gulden bill was in my hand and the till open.

Made my jottings on the trip in another notebook. Began

things that went wrong. But I will not give up in spite of insomnia, headaches, a general incapacity. I've summoned up my last resources to this end. I made the remark that "I don't avoid people in order to live quietly, but rather in order to be able to die quietly." But now I will defend myself. For a month, during the absence of my boss, I'll have the time.

July 30. Tired of working in other people's stores, I had opened up a little stationery store of my own. Since my means were limited and I had to pay cash for almost everything——

I sought advice, I wasn't stubborn. It was not stubbornness when I silently laughed with contorted face and feverishly shining cheeks at someone who had unwittingly proffered me advice. It was suspense, a readiness on my part to be instructed, an unhealthy lack of stubbornness.

The director of the Progress Insurance Company was always greatly dissatisfied with his employees. Now every director is dissatisfied with his employees; the difference between employees and directors is too vast to be bridged by means of mere commands on the part of the director and mere obedience on the part of the employees. Only mutual hatred can bridge the gap and give the whole enterprise its perfection.

Bauz, the director of the Progress Insurance Company, looked doubtfully at the man standing in front of his desk applying for a job as attendant with the company. Now and then he also glanced at the man's papers lying before him on the desk.

"You're tall enough," he said, "I can see that; but what can you do? Our attendants must be able to do more than lick stamps; in fact, that's the one thing they don't have to be able to do, because we have machines to do that kind of thing. Our attendants are part officials, they have responsible work to do; do you feel you are qualified for that? Your head is shaped peculiarly. Your forehead recedes so. Remarkable. Now, what was your last position? What? You haven't worked for a year? Why was that? You had pneumonia? Really? Well, that isn't much of a recommendation, is it? Naturally, we can employ only people who are in good health. Before you are taken on you will have to be examined by the doctor. You are quite well now? Really? Of course, that could be. Speak up a little! Your whispering makes me nervous. I see here that you're also married, have four children. And you haven't worked for a year! Really, man! Your wife takes in washing? I see. Well, all right. As long as you're already here, have the doctor examine you now; the attendant will show you the way. But that doesn't mean that you will be hired, even if the doctor's opinion is favorable. By no means. In any event, you'll receive our decision in writing. To be frank, I may as well tell you at once: I'm not at all impressed with you. We need an entirely different kind of attendant. But have yourself examined in any case. And now go, go. Trembling like that won't do you any good. I have no authority to hand out favors. You're willing to do any kind of work? Certainly. Everyone is. That's no special distinction. It merely indicates the low opinion you have of yourself. And now I'm telling you for the last time: Go along and don't take up any more of my time. This is really enough."

Bauz had to strike the desk with his hand before the man

let himself be led out of the director's office by the attendant.

I mounted my horse and settled myself firmly in the saddle. The maid came running to me from the gate and announced that my wife still wanted to speak to me on an urgent matter; would I wait just a moment, she hadn't quite finished dressing yet. I nodded and sat quietly on my horse, who now and then gently raised his forelegs and reared a little. We lived on the outskirts of the village; before me, in the sun, the highway mounted a slope whose opposite side a small wagon had just ascended, which now came driving down into the village at a rapid pace. The driver brandished his whip, a woman in a provincial yellow dress sat in the dark and dusty interior of the wagon.

I was not at all surprised that the wagon stopped in front of my house.

July 31. I have no time.[16] General mobilization. K. and P. have been called up. Now I receive the reward for living alone. But it is hardly a reward; living alone ends only with punishment. Still, as a consequence, I am little affected by all the misery and am firmer in my resolve than ever. I shall have to spend my afternoons in the factory; I won't live at home, for Elli and the two children are moving in with us. But I will write in spite of everything, absolutely; it is my struggle for self-preservation.

August 1. Went to the train to see K. off. Relatives everywhere in the office. Would like to go to Valli's.

August 2. Germany has declared war on Russia.—Swimming in the afternoon.

August 3. Alone in my sister's apartment. It is lower down than my room, it is also on a side street, hence the neighbors' loud talking below, in front of their doors. Whistling too. Otherwise complete solitude. No longed-for wife to open the door. In one month I was to have been married. The saying hurts: You've made your bed, now lie in it. You find yourself painfully pushed against the wall, apprehensively lower your eyes to see whose hand it is that pushes you, and, with a new pain in which the old is forgotten, recognize your own contorted hand holding you with a strength it never had for good work. You raise your head, again feel the first pain, again lower your gaze; this up-and-down motion of your head goes on without pause.

August 4. When I rented the place for myself I probably signed something for the landlord by which I bound myself to a two- or even six-year lease. Now he is basing his demand on this agreement. My stupidity, or rather, my general and utter helplessness. Drop quietly into the river. Dropping probably seems so desirable to me because it reminds me of "being pushed."

August 5. The business almost settled, by the expenditure of the last of my strength. Was there twice with Malek as witness, at Felix's to draft the lease, at the lawyers' (6 kr.), and all of it unnecessary; I could and should have done it all myself.

August 6. The artillery that marched across the Graben. Flowers, shouts of hurrah! and *nazdar!* [17] The rigidly silent, astonished, attentive black face with black eyes.

I am more broken down than recovered. An empty vessel, still intact yet already in the dust among the broken fragments; or already in fragments yet still ranged among those that are intact. Full of lies, hate and envy. Full of incompetence, stupidity, thickheadedness. Full of laziness, weakness and helplessness. Thirty-one years old. I saw the two agriculturists in Ottla's picture. Young, fresh people possessed of some knowledge and strong enough to put it to use among people who in the nature of things resist their efforts somewhat. One of them leading beautiful horses; the other lies in the grass, the tip of his tongue playing between his lips in his otherwise unmoving and absolutely trustworthy face.

I discover in myself nothing but pettiness, indecision, envy and hatred against those who are fighting and whom I passionately wish everything evil.

What will be my fate as a writer is very simple. My talent for portraying my dreamlike inner life has thrust all other matters into the background; my life has dwindled dreadfully, nor will it cease to dwindle. Nothing else will ever satisfy me. But the strength I can muster for that portrayal is not to be counted upon: perhaps it has already vanished forever, perhaps it will come back to me again, although the circumstances of my life don't favor its return. Thus I waver, continually fly to the summit of the mountain, but then fall back in a moment. Others waver too, but in lower regions, with greater strength; if they are in danger of falling, they are caught up by the kinsman who walks beside them for that very purpose. But I waver on the heights; it is not death, alas, but the eternal torments of dying.

Patriotic parade. Speech by the mayor. Disappears, then reappears, and a shout in German: "Long live our beloved monarch, hurrah!" I stand there with my malignant look. These parades are one of the most disgusting accompaniments of the war. Originated by Jewish businessmen who are German one day, Czech the next; admit this to themselves, it is true, but were never permitted to shout it out as loudly as they do now. Naturally they carry many others along with them. It was well organized. It is supposed to be repeated every evening, twice tomorrow and Sunday.

August 7. Even if you have not the slightest sensitivity to individual differences, you still treat everyone in his own way. L. of Binz, in order to attract attention, poked his stick at me and frightened me.

Yesterday and today wrote four pages, trivialities difficult to surpass.

Strindberg is tremendous. This rage, these pages won by fist-fighting.

Chorus from the tavern across the way. I just went to the window. Sleep seems impossible. The song is coming through the open door of the tavern. A girl's voice is leading them. They are singing simple love songs. I hope a policeman comes along. There he comes. He stops in front of the door for a moment and listens. Then calls out: "Landlord!" The girl's voice: "Vojtíšku." [18] A man in trousers and shirt jumps forward out of a corner. "Close the door! You're making too much noise." "Oh sorry, sorry," says the landlord, and with delicate and obliging gestures, as if he were dealing with a lady, first closes the door behind him, then opens it to slip out, and closes it again. The policeman (whose behavior, especially his anger, is incomprehensible, for the singing can't disturb

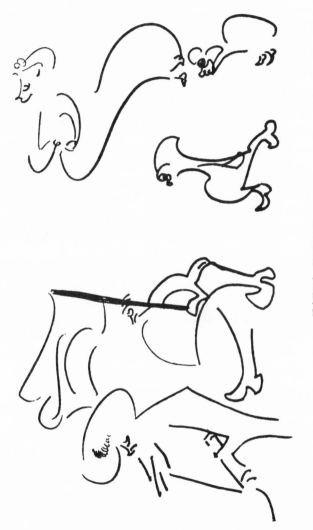

KAFKA SKETCH

him but must rather sweeten his monotonous round)
marches off; the singers have lost all desire to sing.

August 11. I imagine that I have remained in Paris, walk
through it arm in arm with my uncle, pressed close to his
side.

August 12. Didn't sleep at all. Lay three hours in the
afternoon on the sofa, sleepless and apathetic; the same at
night. But it mustn't thwart me.

August 15. I have been writing these past few days, may
it continue. Today I am not so completely protected by
and enclosed in my work as I was two years ago,[19] nevertheless have the feeling that my monotonous, empty, mad
bachelor's life has some justification. I can once more carry
on a conversation with myself, and don't stare so into complete emptiness. Only in this way is there any possibility of
improvement for me.

[MEMOIRS OF THE KALDA RAILROAD]

During one period of my life—it is many years ago now—
I had a post with a small railroad in the interior of Russia. I
have never been so forsaken as I was there. For various reasons that do not matter now, I had been looking for just
such a place at the time; the more solitude ringing in my
ears the better I liked it, and I don't mean now to make any
complaint. At first I had only missed a little activity. The
little railroad may originally have been built with some
commercial purpose in view, but the capital had been insufficient, construction came to a halt, and instead of ter-
minating at Kalda, the nearest village of any size, a five

days' journey from us by wagon, the railroad came to an end at a small settlement right in the wilderness, still a full day's journey from Kalda.

Now even if the railroad had extended to Kalda it would perforce have remained an unprofitable venture for an indefinite period, for the whole notion of it was wrong; the country needed roads, not railroads, nor could the railroad manage at all in its present state; the two trains running daily carried freight a light wagon could have hauled, and its only passengers were a few farm hands during the summer. But still they did not want to shut down the railroad altogether, for they went on hoping that if it were kept in operation they could attract the necessary capital for furthering the construction work. Even this hope was, in my opinion, not so much hope as despair and laziness. They kept the railroad in operation so long as there were still supplies and coal available, the wages of their few workers they paid irregularly and not in full, as though they were gifts of charity; as for the rest, they waited for the whole thing to collapse.

It was by this railroad, then, that I was employed, living in a wooden shed left standing from the time of the railroad's construction, and now serving at the same time as a station. There was only one room, in which a bunk had been set up for me—and a desk for any writing I might have to do. Above it was installed the telegraphic apparatus. In the spring, when I arrived, one train would pass the station very early in the day—later this was changed—and it sometimes happened that a passenger would alight at the station while I was still asleep. In that case, of course—the nights there were very cool until midsummer—he did not remain outside in the open but knocked, I would unbolt the door and then we would often pass hours in chatting. I lay on my bunk, my guest squatted on the floor or, following my instructions, brewed tea which we then drank together sociably. All these village people were distinguished by a great sociability. Moreover, I perceived that I was not particularly suited to stand a condition of utter solitude, admit as I had to that my self-imposed solitude had already, after a short time, begun to dissipate my past sorrows. I have in general found that it is extremely difficult for a misfortune to dominate a solitary person for any length of time. Solitude is powerful beyond everything else, and drives one back to people. Naturally, you then attempt to find new ways, ways seemingly less painful but in reality simply not yet known.

I became more attached to the people there than I should have thought possible. It was naturally not a regular contact with them that I had. All the five villages with which I had to do were several hours distant from the station as well as from each other. I dared not venture too far from the station, lest I lose my job. And under no circumstances did I want that, at least not in the beginning. For this reason I could not go to the villages themselves, and had to depend on the passengers or on people not deterred by the long journey that had to be made to visit me. During the very first month such people dropped in; but no matter how friendly they were, it was easy to see that they came only on the chance of transacting some business with me, nor did they make any attempt to conceal their purpose. They brought butter, meat, corn, all sorts of things; at first, so long as I had any money, I habitually bought everything almost sight unseen, so welcome were these people to me, some of them especially. Later, though, I limited my purchases, among other reasons because I thought I noticed a certain contempt on their part for the manner in which I bought things. Besides, the train also brought me food, food, however, that was very bad and even more expensive than that which the peasants brought.

Originally I had intended to plant a small vegetable garden, to buy a cow, and in this way make myself as self-sufficient as I could. I had even brought along gardening tools and seed; there was a great deal of uncultivated ground around my hut stretching away on one level without the slightest rise as far as the eye could see. But I was too weak to conquer the soil. A stubborn soil that was frozen solid until spring and that even resisted the sharp edge of my new ax. Whatever seed one sowed in it was lost. I had attacks of despair during this labor. I lay in my bunk for days, not coming out even when the trains arrived. I would simply put my head through the window, which was right above my bunk, and report that I was sick. Then the train crew, which consisted of three men, came in to get warm, though they found very little warmth —whenever possible I avoided using the old iron stove that so easily blew up. I preferred to lie there wrapped in an old warm coat and covered by the various skins I had bought from the peasants over a period of time. "You're often sick," they said to me. "You're a sickly person. You won't leave this place alive." They did not say this to depress me, but rather strove straightforwardly to speak the truth whenever possible. Their eyes usually goggled peculiarly at such times.

Once a month, but always on a different day of the month, an inspector came to examine my record book, to collect the money I had taken in and—but not always—to pay me my salary. I was always warned of his arrival a day in advance by the people who had dropped him at the last station. They considered this warning the greatest favor they could do me in spite of the fact that I naturally always had everything in good order. Nor was the slightest effort needed for this. And the inspector too always came into the station with an air as if to say, this time I shall unquestionably uncover the evidence of your mismanagement. He always opened the door of the hut with a push of his knee, giving me a look at the same time. Hardly had he opened my book when he found a mistake. It took me a long time to prove to him, by recomputing it before his eyes, that the mistake had been made not by me but by him. He was always dissatisfied with the amount I had taken in, then clapped his hand on the book and gave me a sharp look again. "We'll have to shut down the railroad," he would say each time. "It will come to that," I usually replied.

After the inspection had been concluded, our relationship would change. I always had brandy ready and, whenever possible, some sort of delicacy. We drank to each other; he sang in a tolerable voice, but always the same two songs. One was sad and began: "Where are you going, O child in the forest?" The other was gay and began like this: "Merry comrades, I am yours!"— It depended on the mood I was able to put him in, how large an instalment I got on my salary. But it was only at the beginning of these entertainments that I watched him with any purpose in mind; later we were quite at one, cursed the company shamelessly, he whispered secret promises into my ear about the career he would help me to achieve, and finally we fell together on the bunk in an embrace that often lasted ten hours unbroken. The next morning he went on his way, again my superior. I stood beside the train and saluted; often as not he turned to me while getting aboard and said, "Well, my little friend, we'll meet again in a month. You know what you have at stake." I can still see the bloated face he turned to me with an effort, every feature in his face stood prominently forth, cheeks, nose, lips.

This was the one great diversion during the month when I let myself go; if inadvertently some brandy had been left over, I guzzled it down immediately after the inspector left. I could generally hear the parting whistle of the train while it gurgled into me. The thirst that followed a night of this sort was terrible; it was as if another person were within me, sticking his head and throat out of my mouth and screaming for something to drink. The inspector was provided for, he always carried a large supply of liquor on his train; but I had to depend on whatever was left over.

But then the whole month thereafter I did not drink, did not smoke either; I did my work and wanted nothing more. There was, as I have said, not very much to do, but what there was I did thoroughly. It was my duty every day, for instance, to clean and inspect the track a kilometer on either side of the station. But I did not limit myself to what was required and often went much farther, so far that I was barely able to make out the station. In clear weather the station could be seen at a distance of perhaps five kilometers, for the country was quite flat. And then, if I had gone so far off that the hut in the distance only glimmered before my eyes, I sometimes saw—it was an optical illusion—many black dots moving toward the hut. There were whole companies, whole troops. But sometimes someone really came; then, swinging my ax, I ran all the long way back.

I finished my work toward evening and finally could retreat into my hut. Generally no visitors came at this hour, for the journey back to the villages was not entirely safe at night. All sorts of shiftless fellows drifted about in the neighborhood; they were not natives, however, and others would take their place from time to time, but then the original ones would come back again. I got to see most of them, they were attracted by the lonely station; they were not really dangerous, but you had to deal firmly with them.

They were the only ones who disturbed me during the long twilight hours. Otherwise I lay on my bunk, gave no thought to the past, no thought to the railroad, the next train did not come through till between ten and eleven at night; in short, I gave no thought to anything. Now and then I read an old newspaper thrown to me from the train; it contained the gossip of Kalda, which would have interested me but which I could not understand from disconnected issues. Moreover, in every issue there was an instalment of a novel called "The Commander's Revenge." I once dreamed of this commander, who always wore a dagger at his side, on one particular occasion even held it between his teeth. Besides, I could not read much, for it got dark early and kerosene or a tallow candle was prohibitively expensive. Every month the railroad gave me only half a liter of kerosene, which I used up long before the end of the month merely in keeping the signal light lit half an hour for the train every evening. But this light wasn't at all necessary, and later on, at least on moonlit nights, I would neglect to light it. I correctly foresaw that with the passing of summer I should stand in great need of kerosene. I therefore dug a hole in one corner of the hut, put an old tarred beer keg in it, and every month poured in the kerosene I had saved. It was covered with straw and could attract no attention. The more the hut stank of kerosene, the happier I was; the smell got so strong because the old and rotten staves of the keg had soaked up the kerosene. Later, as a precaution, I buried the keg outside the hut; for once the inspector had boasted to me of a box of wax matches, and when I had asked to see them, threw them one after the other blazing into the air. Both of us, and especially the kerosene, were in real danger; I saved everything by throttling him until he dropped all the matches.

In my leisure hours I often considered how I might prepare for winter. If I was freezing even now, during the warm part of the year—and they said it was warmer than it had been for many years—it would fare very badly with me during the winter. That I was hoarding kerosene was only a whim, if I had been acting sensibly, I should have had to lay up many things for the winter; there was little doubt that the company would not be especially solicitous of my welfare; but I was too heedless, or rather, I was not heedless but I cared too little about myself to want to make much of an effort. Now, during the warm season, things were going tolerably, I left it at that and did nothing further.

One of the attractions that had drawn me to this station had been the prospect of hunting. I had been told that the country was extraordinarily rich in game, and I had already put down a deposit on a gun I wanted sent to me when I had saved up a little money. Now it turned out that there was no trace of game animals here, only wolves and bears were reported, though during the first few months I had failed to see any; otherwise there were only unusually large rats which I had immediately caught sight of running in packs across the steppe as if driven by the wind. But the game I had been looking forward to was not to be found. The people hadn't misinformed me; a region rich in game did exist, but it was a three days' journey away— I had not considered that directions for reaching a place in this country, with its hundreds of kilometers of uninhabited areas, must necessarily be uncertain. In any event, for the time being I had no need of the gun and could use the money for other purposes; still, I had to provide myself with a gun for the winter and I regularly laid money aside for that purpose. As for the rats that sometimes attacked my provisions, my long knife sufficed to deal with them.

During the first days, when I was still eagerly taking in everything, I spitted one of these rats on the point of my knife and held it before me at eye level against the wall. You can see small animals clearly only if you hold them before you at eye level; if you stoop down to them on the ground and look at them there, you acquire a false, imperfect notion of them. The most striking feature of these rats was their claws—large, somewhat hollow, and yet pointed at the ends, they were well suited to dig with. Hanging against the wall in front of me in its final agony, it rigidly stretched out its claws in what seemed to be an unnatural way; they were like small hands reaching out to you.

In general these animals bothered me little, only sometimes woke me up at night when they hurried by the hut in a patter of running feet on the hard ground. If I then sat up and perhaps lit a small wax candle, I could see a rat's claws sticking in from the outside and working feverishly at some hole it was digging under the boards. This work was all in vain, for to dig a hole big enough for itself it would have had to work days on end, and yet it fled with the first brightening of the day; despite this it labored on like a workman who knew what he was doing. And it did good work; the particles it threw up as it dug were imperceptible indeed, on the other hand its claw was probably never used without result. At night I often watched this at length, until the calm and regularity of it put me to sleep. Then I would no longer have the energy to put out the little candle, and for a short while it would shine down for the rat at its work.

Once, on a warm night, when I had again heard these claws at work, I cautiously went outside without lighting a candle in order to see the animal itself. Its head, with its sharp snout, was bowed very low, pushed down almost between its forelegs in the effort to crowd as close as possible to the wood and dig its claws as deep as possible under it. You might have thought there was someone inside the hut holding it by the claws and trying bodily to pull the animal in, so taut was every muscle. And yet everything was ended with one kick, by which I killed the beast. Once fully awake, I could not tolerate any attack on my only possession, the hut.

To safeguard the hut against these rats I stopped all the holes with straw and tow and every morning examined the floor all around. I also intended to cover the hard-packed earthen floor of the hut with planks; such a flooring would also be useful for the winter. A peasant from the next village, Jekoz by name, long ago had promised to bring me some well-seasoned planks for this purpose, and I had often entertained him hospitably in return for this promise, nor did he stay very long away from me but came every fortnight, occasionally bringing shipments to send by the railroad; but he never brought the planks. He had all sorts of excuses for this, usually that he himself was too old to carry such a load, and his son, who would be the one to bring the planks, was just then hard at work in the fields. Now according to his own account, which seemed correct enough, Jekoz was considerably more than seventy years old; but he was a tall man and still very strong. Besides, his excuses varied, and on another occasion he spoke of the difficulties of obtaining planks as long as those I needed. I did not press him, had no urgent need for the planks, it was Jekoz himself who had given me the idea of a plank flooring in the first place; perhaps a flooring would do no good at all; in short, I was able to listen calmly to the old man's lies. My customary greeting was: "The planks, Jekoz!" At once the apologies began in a half-stammer, I was called inspector or captain or even just telegrapher, which had a particular meaning for him; he promised me not only to bring the planks very shortly, but also, with the help of his son and several neighbors, to tear down my whole hut and build me a solid house in its stead. I listened until I grew tired, then pushed him out. While yet in the doorway, in apology he raised his supposedly feeble arms, with which he could in reality have throttled a grown man to death. I knew why he did not bring the planks; he supposed that when the winter was closer at hand I should have a more pressing need for them and would pay a better price; besides, as long as the boards were not delivered he himself would be more important to me. Now he was of course not stupid and knew that I was aware of what was in the back of his mind, but in the fact that I did not exploit this knowledge he saw his advantage, and this he preserved.

But all the preparations I had been making to secure the hut against the animals and protect myself against the winter had to be interrupted when (the first three months of my service were coming to an end) I became seriously ill. For years I had been spared any illness, even the slightest indisposition, but now I became indisputably sick. It began with a heavy cough. About two hours upcountry from the station there was a little brook, where I used to go to fetch my supply of water in a barrel on a wheelbarrow. I often bathed there too, and this cough was the result. The fits of coughing were so severe that I had to double up when I coughed, I imagined I should not be able to survive the coughing unless I doubled up and so gathered together all my strength. I thought my coughing would terrify the train crew, but they knew all about it, called it the wolf's cough. After that I began to hear the howl in the cough. I sat on the little bench in front of the hut and greeted the train with a howl, with a howl I accompanied it on its way when it departed. At night, instead of lying down, I knelt on the bunk and pressed my face into the skins at least to spare myself hearing my howls. I waited tensely until the bursting of some vital blood vessel should put an end to everything. But nothing of the kind happened and the coughing even abated after a few days. There is a tea that cures it, and one of the locomotive engineers promised to bring me some, but explained that it must be drunk only on the eighth day after the coughing began, otherwise it was of no use. On the eighth day he did in fact bring it, and I remember how not only the train crew but the passengers as well, two young peasants, came into my hut, for it was accounted lucky to hear the first cough after the drinking of the tea. I drank, coughed the first mouthful into the faces of my guests, but then immediately felt a real relief, though indeed the coughing had already been easier during the last two days. But a fever remained and did not go down.

This fever tired me a great deal, I lost all my resistance; sometimes, quite unexpectedly, sweat would break out on my forehead, my whole body would tremble, and regardless of where I was I had to lie down and wait until I came to my senses again. I clearly perceived that I was not getting better, but worse, and that it was essential that

I go to Kalda and stay there a few days until my condition improved.

August 21. Began with such hope and was then repulsed by all three stories; today more so than ever. It may be true that the Russian story ought to be worked on only after *The Trial*. In this ridiculous hope, which apparently has only some mechanical notion behind it of how things work, I start *The Trial* again.—The effort wasn't entirely without result.

August 29. The end of one chapter a failure; another chapter, which began beautifully, I shall hardly—or rather certainly not—be able to continue as beautifully, while at the time, during the night, I should certainly have succeeded with it. But I must not forsake myself, I am entirely alone.

August 30. Cold and empty. I feel only too strongly the limits of my abilities, narrow limits, doubtless, unless I am completely inspired. And I believe that even in the grip of inspiration I am swept along only within these narrow limits, which, however, I then no longer feel because I am being swept along. Nevertheless, within these limits there is room to live, and for this reason I shall probably exploit them to a despicable degree.

A quarter to two at night. Across the street a child is crying. Suddenly a man in the same room, as near to me as if he were just outside the window, speaks. "I'd rather jump out of the window than listen to any more of that." He nervously growls something else, his wife, silent except for her shushing, tries to put the child to sleep again.

September 1. In complete helplessness barely wrote two pages. I fell back a great deal today, though I slept well. Yet if I wish to transcend the initial pangs of writing (as well as the inhibiting effect of my way of life) and rise up into the freedom that perhaps awaits me, I know that I must not yield. My old apathy hasn't completely deserted me yet, as I can see, and my coldness of heart perhaps never. That I recoil from no ignominy can as well indicate hopelessness as give hope.

September 13. Again barely two pages. At first I thought my sorrow over the Austrian defeats and my anxiety for the future (anxiety that appears ridiculous to me at bottom, and base too) would prevent me from doing any writing. But that wasn't it, it was only an apathy that forever comes back and forever has to be put down again. There is time enough for sorrow when I am not writing. The thoughts provoked in me by the war resemble my old worries over F. in the tormenting way in which they devour me from every direction. I can't endure worry, and perhaps have been created expressly in order to die of it. When I shall have grown weak enough—it won't take very long—the most trifling worry will perhaps suffice to rout me. In this prospect I can also see a possibility of postponing the disaster as long as possible. It is true that, with the greatest effort on the part of a nature then comparatively unweakened, there was little I was able to do against my worries over F.; but I had had the great support of my writing only in the first days of that period; henceforth I will never allow it to be taken from me.

October 7. I have taken a week's vacation to push the novel on. Until today—it is Wednesday night, my vacation

ends Monday—it has been a failure. I have written little
and feebly. Even last week I was on the decline, but could
not foresee that it would prove so bad. Are these three
days enough to warrant the conclusion that I am unworthy
of living without the office?

October 15. Two weeks of good work; full insight into
my situation occasionally. Today, Thursday (Monday
my vacation is over, I have taken an additional week), a
letter from Miss Bl. I don't know what to do about it, I
know it is certain that I shall live on alone (if I live at
all—which is *not* certain), I also don't know whether I love
F. (I remember the aversion I felt at the sight of her dancing with her severe eyes lowered, or when she ran her
hand over her nose and hair in the Askanischer Hof
shortly before she left, and the numberless moments of
complete estrangement); but in spite of everything the
enormous temptation returns again, I played with the letter all through the evening; I don't work though I could
(even if I've had excruciating headaches this whole past
week). I'm noting down from memory the letter I wrote
to Miss Bl.:

"What a strange coincidence, Grete, that it was just today I received your letter. I will not say with what it
coincided, that concerns only me and the things that were
troubling me tonight as I went to bed, about three. (Suicide; letter full of instructions to Max.)

"Your letter was a great surprise to me. Not because
you wrote to me. Why shouldn't you write to me? Though
you do say that I hate you; but it isn't true. Were the
whole world to hate you, I still shouldn't, and not only
because I have no right to do so. You sat as a judge over
me in the Askanischer Hof—it was awful for you, for

me, for everyone—but it only *seemed* so; in reality all the time I was sitting in your place and sit there to this day.

"You are completely mistaken about F. I don't say this to worm details from you. I can think of no detail—and my imagination has so often gone back and forth across this ground that I can trust it—I say I can think of no detail that could persuade me you are not mistaken. What you suggest is completely impossible; it makes me unhappy to think that F. should perhaps be deceiving herself for some undiscoverable reason. But that is also impossible.

"I have always believed your interest to be honest and free from any personal consideration. Nor was your last letter an easy one to write. I warmly thank you for it."

What did this accomplish? The letter sounds unyielding, but only because I was ashamed, because I considered it irresponsible, because I was afraid to be yielding; by no means because I did not want to yield. That was the only thing I did want. It would be best for all of us if she would not answer, but she will answer and I shall wait for her answer.

. . . [20] I have now lived calmly for two months without any real contact with F. (except through the correspondence with E.), have dreamed of F. as though of someone who was dead and could never live again, and now, when I am offered a chance to come near her, she is at once the center of everything again. She is probably also interfering with my work. How very much a stranger she has sometimes seemed to me these latter days when I would think of her, of all the people I had ever met the most remote; though at the same time I told myself that this was simply because F. had been closer to me than any other person, or at least had been thrust so close to me by other people.

Leafed through the diary a little. Got a kind of inkling of the way a life like this is constituted.

October 21. For four days almost no work at all, only an hour or so all the time and only a few lines, but slept better; as a result almost got rid of my headaches. No reply from Bl.; tomorrow is the last possible day.

October 25. My work almost completely at a standstill. What I write seems to lack independence, seems only the pale reflection of earlier work. Reply from Bl. arrived; I am completely undecided as to how to answer it. Thoughts so base that I cannot even write them down. Yesterday's sadness. . . .

November 1. Yesterday, after a long time, made a great deal of progress; today again virtually nothing; the two weeks since my vacation have been almost a complete loss.—Part of the day—it's Sunday—has been beautiful. In Chotek Park read Dostoevsky's pamphlet in his own defense. The guard at the castle and the corps headquarters. The fountain in the Thun palace.—Much self-satisfaction all day. And now I completely balk at any work. Yet it isn't balking; I see the task and the way to it, I simply have to push past small obstacles but cannot do it.—Toying with thoughts of F.

November 3. In the afternoon a letter to E., looked through a story by Pick, "Der blinde Gast," and made some corrections, read a little Strindberg, then didn't sleep, home at half-past eight, back at ten in fear of headaches which had already begun; and because I had slept very little during the night, did not work any more, partly too because I was afraid to spoil a fair passage I had written yesterday. Since August, the fourth day on which I have written nothing. The letters are the cause of it; I'll try to write none at all or only very short ones. How embarrassed I now am, and how it agitates me. Yesterday evening my excessive happiness after having read several lines by Jammes, whom otherwise I don't care for, but whose French (it is a description of a visit to a poet who was a friend of his) had so strong an effect on me.

November 4. P. back.[21] Shouting, excited past all bounds. Story about the mole burrowing under him in the trenches which he looked upon as a warning from heaven to leave that spot. He had just got away when a bullet struck a soldier crawling after him at the moment he was over the mole.—His captain. They distinctly saw him taken prisoner. But the next day found him naked in the woods, pierced through by bayonets. He probably had had money on him, they wanted to search him and rob him of it, but he—"the way officers are"—wouldn't voluntarily submit to being touched.—P. almost wept with rage and excitement when he met his boss (whom in the past he had admired ridiculously, out of all measure) on the train, elegantly dressed, perfumed, his opera glass dangling from his neck, on his way to the theater. (A month later he himself did the same with a ticket given him by this boss. He went to see *Der ungetreue Eckehart*, a comedy.) [22] Slept one night in the castle of Princess Sapieha; one night, while his unit was in reserve, right in front of the Austrian batteries; one night in a peasant cottage, where two women were sleeping in each of the two beds standing right and left against each wall, a girl behind the stove, and eight soldiers on the floor.—Punishment given soldiers. Stand bound to a tree until they turn blue.

November 12. Parents who expect gratitude from their children (there are even some who insist on it) are like usurers who gladly risk their capital if only they receive interest.

November 24. Yesterday on Tuchmachergasse, where they distribute old clothing to the refugees from Galicia. Max, his mother, Mr. Chaim Nagel. The intelligence, the patience, the friendliness, the industry, the affability, the wit, the dependability of Mr. Nagel. People who, within their sphere, do their work so thoroughly that you believe they could succeed in anything on earth—yet it is part of their perfection too that they don't reach out for anything beyond their sphere.

The clever, lively, proud and unassuming Mrs. Kannegiesser from Tarnow, who wanted only two blankets, but nice ones, and who nevertheless, in spite of Max's influence, got only old, dirty ones, while the new blankets were put aside for the better people in another room, together with all the best things. Then, they didn't want to give her good ones because she needed them for only two days until her linen arrived from Vienna; they aren't permitted to take back used articles because of the danger of cholera.

Mrs. Lustig, with a lot of children of every size and her fresh, self-assured, sprightly little sister. She spent so much time looking for a dress for a little girl that Mrs.

Brod shouted at her: "Now you take this or you won't get anything." But then Mrs. Lustig answered in an even louder shout, ending with a wide, violent sweep of her arm: "The *mitzveh* [good deed] is worth more than all these *shmattes* (rags)."

November 25. Utter despair, impossible to pull myself together; only when I have become satisfied with my sufferings can I stop.

November 30. I can't write any more. I've come up against the last boundary, before which I shall in all likelihood again sit down for years, and then in all likelihood begin another story all over again that will again remain unfinished. This fate pursues me. And I have become cold again, and insensible; nothing is left but a senile love for unbroken calm. And like some kind of beast at the farthest pole from man, I shift my neck from side to side again and for the time being should like to try again to have F. back. I'll really try it, if the nausea I feel for myself doesn't prevent me.

December 2. Afternoon at Werfel's with Max and Pick. Read "In the Penal Colony" aloud; am not entirely dissatisfied, except for its glaring and ineradicable faults. Werfel read some poems and two acts of *Esther, Kaiserin von Persien*. The acts carry one away. But I am easily carried away. The criticisms and comparisons put forward by Max, who was not entirely satisfied with the piece, disturb me, and I am no longer so sure of my impression of the play as a whole as I was while listening to it, when it overwhelmed me. I remember the Yiddish actors. W.'s handsome sisters. The elder one leaned against the chair, often looked at the mirror out of the corner of her eye, and then—as if she were not already devoured by my eyes—gently pointed a finger to a brooch pinned to her blouse. It was a low-cut dark blue blouse, her throat was covered with a tulle scarf. Repeated account of something that happened at the theater: some officers kept saying to each other in a loud voice during *Kabale und Liebe:* "Speckbacher is cutting a figure," by which they meant an officer leaning against the side of a box.

The day's conclusion, even before meeting Werfel: Go on working regardless of everything; a pity I can't work today, for I am tired and have a headache, already had preliminary twinges in the office this morning. I'll go on working regardless of everything, it must be possible in spite of the office or the lack of sleep.

Dreamed tonight. With Kaiser Wilhelm. In the castle. The beautiful view. A room similar to that in the Tabaks-kollegium.[23] Meeting with Matilde Serav. Unfortunately forgot everything.

From *Esther:* God's masterpieces fart at one another in the bath.

December 5. A letter from E. on the situation in her family. My relation to her family has a consistent meaning only if I conceive of myself as its ruin. This is the only natural explanation there is to make plausible everything that is astonishing in the relation. It is also the only connection I have at the moment with her family; otherwise I am completely divorced from it emotionally, although not more effectually, perhaps, than I am from the whole world. (A picture of my existence apropos of this would portray a useless stake covered with snow and frost, fixed loosely and slantwise into the ground in a deeply plowed field on the edge of a great plain on a dark winter's night.) Only ruin has effect. I have made F. unhappy, weakened the resistance of all those who need her so much now, contributed to the death of her father, come between F. and E., and in the end made E. unhappy too, an unhappiness that gives every indication of growing worse. I am in the harness and it is my fate to pull the load. The last letter to her that I tortured out of myself she considers calm; it "breathes so much calmness," as she puts it. It is of course not impossible that she puts it this way out of delicacy, out of forbearance, out of concern for me. I am indeed sufficiently punished in general, even my position in my own family is punishment enough; I have also suffered so much that I shall never recover from it (my sleep, my memory, my ability to think, my resistance to the tiniest worries have been weakened past all cure—strangely enough, the consequences of a long period of imprisonment are about the same); for the moment, however, my relationship to them causes me little suffering, at least less than F. or E. There is of course something tormenting in the fact that I am now supposed to take a Christmas trip with E., while F. will remain in Berlin.

December 8. Yesterday for the first time in ever so long an indisputable ability to do good work. And yet wrote only the first page of the "mother" chapter,[24] for I had barely slept at all two nights, in the morning already had had indications of a headache, and had been too anxious about the next day. Again I realized that everything writ-

ten down bit by bit rather than all at once in the course
of the larger part (or even the whole) of one night is
inferior, and that the circumstances of my life condemn
me to this inferiority.

December 9. Together with E. K. of Chicago. He is
almost touching. Description of his placid life. From eight
to half-past five in the mail-order house. Checking the
shipments in the textile department. Fifteen dollars a
week. Two weeks' vacation, one week with pay; after
five years both weeks with pay. For a while, when there
wasn't much to do in the textile department, he helped out
in the bicycle department. Three hundred bicycles are
sold a day. A wholesale business with ten thousand employees. They get all their customers by sending out
catalogues. The Americans like to change their jobs, they
don't particularly like to work in summer; but he doesn't
like to change, doesn't see the point of it, you lose time
and money by it. So far he has had two jobs, each for
five years, and when he returns—he has an indefinite leave—
he will go back to the same job, they can always use him,
but can always do without him too. Evenings he generally stays at home, plays cards with friends; sometimes,
for diversion, an hour at the movies, in summer a walk,
Sunday a boatride on the lake. He is wary of marriage,
even though he is already thirty-four years old, since
American women often marry only in order to get divorced, a simple matter for them, but very expensive for
the man.

December 13. Instead of working—I have written only
one page (exegesis of the "Legend" [25])—looked through
the finished chapters and found parts of them good. Al-

ways conscious that every feeling of satisfaction and happiness that I have, such, for example, as the "Legend" in particular inspires in me, must be paid for, and must be paid for moreover at some future time, in order to deny me all possibility of recovery in the present.

Recently at Felix's. On the way home told Max that I shall lie very contentedly on my deathbed, provided the pain isn't too great. I forgot—and later purposely omitted—to add that the best things I have written have their basis in this capacity of mine to meet death with contentment. All these fine and very convincing passages always deal with the fact that someone is dying, that it is hard for him to do, that it seems unjust to him, or at least harsh, and the reader is moved by this, or at least he should be. But for me, who believe that I shall be able to lie contentedly on my deathbed, such scenes are secretly a game; indeed, in the death enacted I rejoice in my own death, hence calculatingly exploit the attention that the reader concentrates on death, have a much clearer understanding of it than he, of whom I suppose that he will loudly lament on his deathbed, and for these reasons my lament is as perfect as can be, nor does it suddenly break off, as is likely to be the case with a real lament, but dies beautifully and purely away. It is the same thing as my perpetual lamenting to my mother over pains that were not nearly so great as my laments would lead one to believe. With my mother, of course, I did not need to make so great a display of art as with the reader.

December 14. My work goes forward at a miserable crawl, in what is perhaps its most important part, where a good night would stand me in such stead.

At Baum's in the afternoon. He was giving a pale little girl with glasses a piano lesson. The boy sat quietly in the gloom of the kitchen, carelessly playing with some unrecognizable object. Impression of great ease. Especially in contrast to the bustling about of the tall housemaid, who was washing dishes in a tub.

December 15. Didn't work at all. For two hours now have been looking through new company applications for the office. The afternoon at B.'s. He was somewhat offensive and rude. Empty talk in consequence of my debility, blankness and stupidity almost; was inferior to him in every respect; it is a long time now since I have had a purely private conversation with him, was happy to be alone again. The joy of lying on the sofa in the silent room without a headache, calmly breathing in a manner befitting a human being.

The defeats in Serbia, the stupid leadership.

December 19. Yesterday wrote "The Village Schoolmaster" [26] almost without knowing it, but was afraid to go on writing later than a quarter to two; the fear was well founded, I slept hardly at all, merely suffered through perhaps three short dreams and was then in the office in the condition one would expect. Yesterday Father's reproaches on account of the factory: "You talked me into it." Then went home and calmly wrote for three hours in the consciousness that my guilt is beyond question, though not so great as Father pictures it. Today, Saturday, did not come to dinner, partly in fear of Father, partly in order to use the whole night for working; yet I wrote only one page that wasn't very good.

The beginning of every story is ridiculous at first. There seems no hope that this newborn thing, still incomplete and tender in every joint, will be able to keep alive in the completed organization of the world, which, like every completed organization, strives to close itself off. However, one should not forget that the story, if it has any justification to exist, bears its complete organization within itself even before it has been fully formed; for this reason despair over the beginning of a story is unwarranted; in a like case parents should have to despair of their suckling infant, for they had no intention of bringing this pathetic and ridiculous being into the world. Of course, one never knows whether the despair one feels is warranted or unwarranted. But reflecting on it can give one a certain support; in the past I have suffered from the lack of this knowledge.

December 20. Max's objection to Dostoevsky, that he allows too many mentally ill persons to enter. Completely wrong. They aren't ill. Their illness is merely a way to characterize them, and moreover a very delicate and fruitful one. One need only stubbornly keep repeating of a person that he is simple-minded and idiotic, and he will, if he has the Dostoevskian core inside him, be spurred on, as it were, to do his very best. His characterizations have in this respect about the same significance as insults among friends. If they say to one another, "You're a blockhead," they don't mean that the other is really a blockhead who has disgraced them by his friendship; rather there is generally mixed in it an infinite number of intentions, if the insult isn't merely a joke, or even if it is. Thus, the father of the Karamazovs, though a wicked creature, is by no means a fool but rather a very clever man, almost the equal of Ivan, and in any case much cleverer than his cousin, for example, whom the novelist doesn't attack, or his nephew, the landowner, who feels so superior compared to him.

December 23. Read a few pages of Herzen's "Fogs of London." Had no idea what it was all about, and yet the whole of the unconscious man emerged, purposeful, self-tormenting, having himself firmly in hand and then going to pieces again.

December 26. In Kuttenberg with Max and his wife. How I counted on the four free days, how many hours I pondered how best to spend them, and now perhaps disappointed after all. Tonight wrote almost nothing and am in all likelihood no longer capable of going on with "The Village Schoolmaster," which I have been working at for a week now, and which I should certainly have completed in three free nights, perfect and with no external defect; but now, in spite of the fact that I am still virtually at the beginning, it already has two irremediable defects and in addition is stunted.—New schedule from now on! Use the time even better! Do I make my laments here only to find salvation here? It won't come out of this notebook, it will come when I'm in bed and it will put me on my back so that I lie there beautiful and light and bluish-white; no other salvation will come.

Hotel in Kuttenberg Moravetz, drunken porter, tiny, roofed court with a skylight. The darkly outlined soldier leaning against the railing on the second floor of the building across the court. The room they offered me; its window opened upon a dark, windowless corridor. Red sofa, candle light. Jacobskirche, the devout soldiers, the girls' voices in the choir.

December 27. A merchant was greatly dogged by misfortune. He bore it for a long time, but finally was convinced that he could not bear it any longer, and went to one learned in the law. He intended to ask his advice and learn what he might do to ward off misfortune or to acquire the strength to bear it. Now the scripture always lay open before this sage, that he might study it. It was his custom to receive everyone who sought advice from him with these words: "I am just now reading of your case," at the same time pointing with his finger to a passage of the page in front of him. The merchant, who had heard of this custom, did not like it; it is true that in this way the sage both asserted the possibility of his helping the supplicant, and relieved him of the fear that he had been visited with a calamity which worked in darkness, which he could share with no one and with which no one else could sympathize; but the incredibility of such a statement was after all too great and had in fact deterred the merchant from calling sooner on the man learned in the law. Even now he entered his house with hesitation, halting in the open doorway.

December 31. Have been working since August, in general not little and not badly, yet neither in the first nor in the second respect to the limit of my ability, as I should have done, especially as there is every indication (insomnia, headaches, weak heart) that my ability won't last much longer. Worked on, but did not finish: *The Trial*, "Memoirs of the Kalda Railroad," "The Village Schoolmaster," "The Assistant Attorney," [27] and the beginnings of various little things. Finished only: "In the Penal Colony" and a chapter of "Der Verschollene," [28] both during the two-week vacation. I don't know why I am drawing up this summary, it's not at all like me!

January 4. Great desire to begin another story; didn't yield to it. It is all pointless. If I can't pursue the stories through the nights, they break away and disappear, as with "The Assistant Attorney" now. And tomorrow I go to the factory, shall perhaps have to go there every afternoon after P. joins up. With that, everything is at an end. The thought of the factory is my perpetual Day of Atonement.

January 6. For the time being abandoned "Village Schoolmaster" and "The Assistant Attorney." But almost incapable too of going on with *The Trial*. Thinking of the girl from Lemberg.[29] A promise of some kind of happiness resembles the hope of an eternal life. Seen from a certain distance it holds its ground, and one doesn't venture nearer.

January 17. Yesterday for the first time dictated letters in the factory. Worthless work (an hour), but not without satisfaction. Horrible afternoon previously. Continual headaches, so that I had constantly to hold my hand to my head to calm myself (condition in the Café Arco), and heart pains on the sofa at home.

Read Ottla's letter to E. I have really kept her down, and indeed ruthlessly, because of carelessness and incompetence on my part. F. is right about it. Happily, Ottla is strong enough, once she is alone in a strange city, to recover from my influence. How much of her talent for

getting on with people lies unexploited because of me!
She writes that she felt unhappy in Berlin. Untrue!

Realized that I have by no means made satisfactory use
of the time since August. My constant attempts, by sleeping a great deal in the afternoon, to make it possible for
myself to continue working late into the night were absurd; after the first two weeks I could already see that
my nerves would not permit me to go to bed after one
o'clock, for then I can no longer fall asleep at all, the
next day is insupportable and I destroy myself. I lay down
too long in the afternoon, though I seldom worked later
than one o'clock at night, and always began about eleven
o'clock at the earliest. That was a mistake. I must begin at eight or nine o'clock; the night is certainly the
best time (vacation!), but beyond my reach.

Saturday I shall see F. If she loves me, I do not deserve
it. Today I think I see how narrow my limits are in everything, and consequently in my writing too. If one feels
one's limits very intensely, one must burst. It is probably
Ottla's letter that has made me aware of this. I have been
very self-satisfied of late and knew a variety of arguments
by which to defend and assert myself against F. A pity
I had no time to write them down, today I should be unable
to do it.

Strindberg's *Black Flags*. On faraway influences: You
were certain that others disapproved of your behavior
without their having expressed their disapproval. In solitude you felt a quiet sense of well-being without having
known why; some faraway person thought well of you,
spoke well of you.

January 18. In the factory until half-past six; as usual, worked, read, dictated, listened, wrote without result. The same meaningless satisfaction after it. Headache, slept badly. Incapable of sustained, concentrated work. Also have been in the open air too little. In spite of that began a new story; I was afraid I should spoil the old ones. Four or five stories now stand on their hindlegs in front of me like the horses in front of Schumann, the circus ringmaster, at the beginning of the performance.

January 19. I shall not be able to write so long as I have to go to the factory. I think it is a special inability to work that I feel now, similar to what I felt when I was employed by the Generali.[30] Immediate contact with the workaday world deprives me—though inwardly I am as detached as I can be—of the possibility of taking a broad view of matters, just as if I were at the bottom of a ravine, with my head bowed down in addition. In the newspaper today, for instance, there is an official statement by Sweden according to which it intends, despite threats by the Triple Entente, unconditionally to preserve its neutrality. At the end it says: The members of the Triple Entente will run their heads against a stone wall in Stockholm. Today I swallow it almost entirely the way it was meant. Three days ago I should have felt to my very marrow that a Stockholm ghost was speaking here, that "threats by the Triple Entente," "neutrality," "official statement by Sweden," were only inspissated things of air of a certain shape, which one can enjoy only with one's eye but can never succeed in touching with one's fingers.

I had agreed to go picnicking Sunday with two friends, but quite unexpectedly slept past the hour when we were

to meet. My friends, who knew how punctual I ordinarily am, were surprised, came to the house where I
lived, waited outside awhile, then came upstairs and
knocked on my door. I was very startled, jumped out of
bed and thought only of getting ready as soon as I could.
When I emerged fully dressed from my room, my friends
fell back in manifest alarm. "What's that behind your
head?" they cried. Since my awakening I had felt something preventing me from bending back my head, and I
now groped for it with my hand. My friends, who had
grown somewhat calmer, had just shouted "Be careful,
don't hurt yourself!" when my hand closed behind my
head on the hilt of a sword. My friends came closer, examined me, led me back to the mirror in my room and
stripped me to the waist. A large, ancient knight's sword
with a cross-shaped handle was buried to the hilt in my
back, but the blade had been driven with such incredible
precision between my skin and flesh that it had caused no
injury. Nor was there a wound at the spot on my neck
where the sword had penetrated; my friends assured me
that there was an opening large enough to admit the blade,
but dry and showing no trace of blood. And when my
friends now stood on chairs and slowly, inch by inch,
drew out the sword, I did not bleed, and the opening on
my neck closed until no mark was left save a scarcely dis-
cernible slit. "Here is your sword," laughed my friends,
and gave it to me. I hefted it in my two hands; it was a
splendid weapon, Crusaders might have used it.

Who tolerates this gadding about of ancient knights in
dreams, irresponsibly brandishing their swords, stabbing
innocent sleepers who are saved from serious injury only
because the weapons in all likelihood glance off living
bodies, and also because there are faithful friends knocking at the door, prepared to come to their assistance?

January 20. The end of writing. When will it catch me up again? In what a bad state I am going to meet F.! The clumsy thinking that immediately appears when I give up my writing, my inability to prepare for the meeting; whereas last week I could hardly shake off all the ideas it aroused in me. May I enjoy the only conceivable profit I can have from it—better sleep.

Black Flags. How badly I even read. And with what malice and weakness I observe myself. Apparently I cannot force my way into the world, but lie quietly, receive, spread out within me what I have received, and then step calmly forth.

January 24. With F. in Bodenbach. I think it is impossible for us ever to unite, but dare say so neither to her nor, at the decisive moment, to myself. Thus I have held out hope to her again, stupidly, for every day makes me older and crustier. My old headaches return when I try to comprehend that she is suffering and is at the same time calm and gay. We shouldn't torment each other again by a lot of writing, it would be best to pass over this meeting as a solitary occurrence; or is it that I believe I shall win freedom here, live by my writing, go abroad or no matter where and live there secretly with F.?

We have found each other quite unchanged in other ways as well. Each of us silently says to himself that the other is immovable and merciless. I yield not a particle of my demand for a fantastic life arranged solely in the interest of my work; she, indifferent to every mute request, wants the average: a comfortable home, an interest on my part in the factory, good food, bed at eleven, central heating; sets my watch—which for the past three months has been an hour and a half fast—right to the minute. And she is right in the end and would continue to be right in the end; she is right when she corrects the bad German I used to the waiter, and I can put nothing right when she speaks of the "personal touch" (it cannot be said any way but gratingly) in the furnishings she intends to have in her home. She calls my two elder sisters "shallow," she doesn't ask after the youngest at all, she asks almost no questions about my work and has no apparent understanding of it. That is one side of the matter.

I am as incompetent and dreary as always and should really have no time to reflect on anything else but the question of how it happens that anyone has the slightest desire even to crook her little finger at me. In rapid succession I have blown upon three different kinds of people with this cold breath. The people from Hellerau, the R. family in Bodenbach, and F. F. said, "How well behaved we've been." I am silent as if my hearing had suddenly failed me during this exclamation. We were alone two hours in the room. Round about me only boredom and despair. We haven't yet had a single good moment together during which I could have breathed freely. With F. I never experienced (except in letters) that sweetness one experiences in a relationship with a woman one loves, such as I had in Zuckmantel and Riva—only unlimited admiration, humility, sympathy, despair and self-contempt. I also read aloud to her, the sentences proceeded in a disgusting confusion, with no relationship to the listener, who lay on the sofa with closed eyes and silently received them. A lukewarm request to be permitted to take a manuscript along and copy it. During the reading of the doorkeeper story, greater attention and good observation. The significance of the story dawned upon me for the first time; she grasped it rightly too, then of course we barged into it with coarse remarks; I began it.

The difficulties (which other people surely find incredible) I have in speaking to people arise from the fact that my thinking, or rather the content of my consciousness, is entirely nebulous, that I remain undisturbed by this, so far as it concerns only myself, and am even occasionally self-satisfied; yet conversation with people demands pointedness, solidity, and sustained coherence, qualities not to be found in me. No one will want to lie in clouds of mist with me, and even if someone did, *I* couldn't expel the mist from my head; when two people come together it dissolves of itself and is nothing.

F. goes far out of her way to come to Bodenbach, goes to the trouble of getting herself a passport, after a night spent in sitting up must bear with me, must even listen to me read aloud, and all of it senseless. Does she feel it to be the same sort of calamity I do? Certainly not, even assuming the same degree of sensitivity. After all, she has no sense of guilt.

What I said was true and was acknowledged to be true: each loves the other person as he is. But doesn't think it possible to live with him as he is.

The group here: Dr. W. tries to convince me that F. deserves to be hated, F. tries to convince me that W. deserves to be hated. I believe them both and love them both, or try to.

January 29. Again tried to write, virtually useless. The past two days went early to bed, about ten o'clock, something I haven't done for a long time now. Free feeling during the day, partial satisfaction, more useful in the office, possible to speak to people.—Severe pain in my knee now.

January 30. The old incapacity. Hardly ten days interrupted in my writing and already cast aside. Once again prodigious efforts stand before me. You have to dive down, as it were, and sink more rapidly than that which sinks in advance of you.

February 7. Complete standstill. Unending torments.

At a certain point in self-knowledge, when other circumstances favoring self-scrutiny are present, it will invariably follow that you find yourself execrable. Every moral standard—however opinions may differ on it—will seem too high. You will see that you are nothing but a rat's nest of miserable dissimulations. The most trifling of your acts will not be untainted by these dissimulations. These dissimulated intentions are so squalid that in the course of your self-scrutiny you will not want to ponder them closely but will instead be content to gaze at them from afar. These intentions aren't all compounded merely of selfishness, selfishness seems in comparison an ideal of the good and beautiful. The filth you will find exists for its own sake; you will recognize that you came dripping into the world with this burden and will depart unrecognizable again—or only too recognizable—because of it. This filth is the nethermost depth you will find; at the nethermost depth there will be not lava, no, but filth. It is the nethermost and the uppermost, and even the doubts self-scrutiny begets will soon grow weak and self-complacent as the wallowing of a pig in muck.

February 9. Wrote a little today and yesterday. Dog story.[31]

Just now read the beginning. It is ugly and gives me a headache. In spite of all its truth it is wicked, pedantic, mechanical, a fish barely breathing on a sandbank. I write my *Bouvard et Pécuchet* prematurely. If the two elements —most pronounced in "The Stoker" and "In the Penal Colony"—do not combine, I am finished. But is there any prospect of their combining?

Finally took a room. In the same house on Bilekgasse.

February 10. First evening. My neighbor talks for hours with the landlady. Both speak softly, the landlady almost inaudibly, and therefore so much the worse. My writing, which has been coming along for the past two days, is interrupted, who knows for how long a time? Absolute despair. Is it like this in every house? Does such ridiculous and absolutely killing misery await me with every land-lady in every city? My class president's two rooms in the monastery. It is senseless, however, to give way at once to despair; rather seek some means, much as—no, it is not contrary to my character, there is still some tough Jewishness in me, but for the most part it helps the other side.

February 14. The infinite attraction of Russia. It is best represented not by a troika but by the image of a vast river of yellowish water on which waves—but not too high ones—are everywhere tossing. Wild, desolate heaths upon its banks, blighted grass. But nothing can represent it; everything rather effaces it.

Saint-Simonism.

February 15. Everything at a halt. Bad, irregular sched-ule. This house spoils everything for me. Today again heard the landlady's daughter at her French lesson.

February 16. Can't see my way clear. As though every-thing I possessed had escaped me, and as though it would hardly satisfy me if it all returned.

February 22. Incapable in every respect, and completely so.

February 25. After days of uninterrupted headaches, finally a little easier and more confident. If I were another person observing myself and the course of my life, I should be compelled to say that it must all end unavail-ingly, be consumed in incessant doubt, creative only in its self-torment. But, an interested party, I go on hoping.

March 1. By a great effort, after weeks of preparation and anxiety, gave notice; not entirely with reason, it is quiet enough, but I simply haven't done any good work yet and so haven't sufficiently tested either the quiet or the lack of it. I gave notice rather because of the lack of quiet in me. I want to torment myself, want continu-ally to change my situation, believe I foresee my salva-tion in the change and in addition believe that by such petty changes, which others make while they doze but I make only after having roused up all my faculties, I shall be able to ready myself for the great change that I probably need. I am certainly changing for a room inferior in many ways. Nevertheless, today was the first (or the second) day on which I should have been able to work well, had I not had a very severe headache. Have written a page in haste.

March 11. How time flies; another ten days and I have achieved nothing. It doesn't come off. A page now and then is successful, but I can't keep it up, the next day I am powerless.

Eastern and Western Jews, a meeting.[32] The Eastern Jews' contempt for the Jews here. Justification for this contempt. The way the Eastern Jews know the reason for their contempt, but the Western Jews do not. For example, the appalling notions, beyond all ridicule, by which Mother tries to comprehend them. Even Max, the inadequacy and feebleness of his speech, unbuttoning and buttoning his jacket. And after all, he is full of the best good will. In contrast a certain W., buttoned into a shabby little jacket, a collar that it would have been impossible to make filthier worn as his holiday best, braying yes and no, yes and no. A diabolically unpleasant smile around his mouth, wrinkles in his young face, wild and embarrassed movements of his arms. But the best one is a little fellow, a walking argument, with a sharp voice impossible to modulate, one hand in his pocket, boring toward the listeners with the other, constantly asking questions and immediately proving what he sets out to prove. Canary voice. Tosses his head. I, as if made of wood, a clothesrack pushed into the middle of the room. And yet hope.

March 13. An evening. At six o'clock lay down on the sofa. Slept until about eight. Couldn't get up, waited for the clock to strike and in my sleepiness missed hearing it. Got up at nine o'clock. Didn't go home for supper, nor to Max's either, where there was a gathering tonight. Reasons: lack of appetite, fear of getting back late in the evening; but above all the thought that I wrote nothing yesterday, that I keep getting further and further from it, and am in danger of losing everything I have laboriously achieved these past six months. Provided proof of this by writing one and a half wretched pages of a new story that I have already decided to discard and then in despair, part of the blame for which my listless stomach certainly shares, read Herzen in the hope that he might somehow carry me on. His happiness the first year after he was married, my horror of seeing myself in a similar happy state; the high life around him; Belinski; Bakunin in bed all day long with his fur coat on.

Occasionally I feel an unhappiness which almost dismembers me, and at the same time am convinced of its necessity and of the existence of a goal to which one makes one's way by undergoing every kind of unhappiness (am now influenced by my recollection of Herzen, but the thought occurs on other occasions too).

March 14. A morning: In bed until half-past eleven. Jumble of thoughts which slowly takes shape and hardens in an incredible fashion. Read in the afternoon (Gogol, essay on the lyric), in the evening a walk, part of the time the defensible but untrustworthy ideas of the morning in my head. Was in Chotek Park. Most beautiful spot in Prague. Birds sang, the Castle with its arcade, the old trees hung with last year's foliage, the dim light. Later Ottla arrived with D.

March 17. Harassed by noise. A beautiful, much more friendly room than the one on Bilekgasse. I am so dependent on the view; there is a beautiful one here, the Teinkirche. But a great deal of noise from the carriages down below; however, I am growing quite used to it. But impossible for me to grow used to the noise in the afternoon.

From time to time a crash in the kitchen or the corridor. Yesterday, in the attic above, perpetual rolling of a ball, as if someone for some incomprehensible reason were bowling, then a piano below me in addition. Yesterday evening a relative silence, worked somewhat hopefully ("Assistant Attorney"), today began with joy, suddenly, next door or below me, a party taking place, loud and fluctuating as though I were in its midst. Contended with the noise awhile, then lay on the sofa with nerves virtually shattered, silence after ten o'clock, but can't work any longer.

March 23. Incapable of writing a line. The feeling of ease with which I sat in Chotek Park yesterday and on the Karlsplatz today with Strindberg's *By the Open Sea*. My feeling of ease in my room today. Hollow as a clamshell on the beach, ready to be pulverized by the tread of a foot.

March 25. Yesterday Max's lecture, "Religion and Nation." Talmudic Eastern Jews. The girl from Lemberg. The Western Jew who has become assimilated to the Hasidim, the plug of cotton in his ear. Steidler, a Socialist, long, shining, neatly cut hair. The delight with which the Eastern European Jewesses take sides. The group of Eastern Jews beside the stove. G. in a caftan, the matter-of-fact Jewish life. My confusion.

April 9. Torments of my apartment. Boundless. Worked well a few evenings. If I had been able to work at night! Today kept from sleep, from work, from everything by the noise.

April 14. The Homer class for the Galician girls. The one in the green blouse, sharp, severe face; when she raised her hand she held it straight out in front of her; quick movements when she put on her coat; if she raised her hand and was not called on, she felt ashamed and turned her face aside. The sturdy young girl in green at the sewing machine.

April 27. In Nagy Mihály with my sister.[33] Incapable of living with people, of speaking. Complete immersion in myself, thinking of myself. Apathetic, witless, fearful. I have nothing to say to anyone—never.

Trip to Vienna. The much-traveled, all-knowing, all-judging Viennese, tall, blond-bearded, legs crossed, was reading *Az Est;* obliging, yet, as Elli and I (both of us equally on the watch) noted, reserved. I said, "How much you must have traveled!" (He knew all the train connections I needed—as it turned out later, however, the particulars weren't entirely correct—knew all the trolley lines in Vienna, advised how to telephone in Budapest, knew what the baggage arrangements were, knew that it was cheaper to take a taxi with your luggage.) He made no reply to this but sat motionless with bowed head. The girl from Žižkov, sentimental, talkative but seldom able to make herself heard, a poor, anemic, undeveloped body no longer able to develop. The old woman from Dresden with a face like Bismarck's, let it be known later that she was a Viennese. The fat Viennese woman, wife of one of the editors of *Die Zeit;* knew all about newspapers, spoke clearly; to my extreme disgust usually expressed the very opinions I hold. I for the most part silent, had nothing to say; among such people the war doesn't call forth in me the slightest opinion worth expressing.

Vienna–Budapest. The two Poles, the lieutenant and the lady, soon got off, whispered at the window; she was pale, not quite young, almost hollow-cheeked, her hands often on her tight-skirted hips, smoked a great deal. The two Hungarian Jews; the one at the window, who resembles Bergmann, cushioned the head of the other, who was asleep, on his shoulder. Throughout the morning, from five on, talk about business, accounts and letters passing from hand to hand, samples of every kind of article were taken out of a handbag. Across from me a Hungarian lieutenant, in sleep a vacant, ugly face, open mouth, funny nose; earlier, when he had been describing Budapest, full of animation, bright-eyed; lively voice into which his whole personality entered. Near by in the compartment the Jews from Bistritz who were returning home. A man was accompanying several women. They learned that Körös Mesö had just been closed to civilians. They will have to travel twenty hours or more by car. They told a story of a man who stayed in Radautz until the Russians were so close that it was impossible for him to escape except by climbing onto the last Austrian piece of cannon that went through.

Budapest. Very contradictory reports about connections with Nagy Mihály; I didn't believe the unfavorable ones, which then turned out to be true. At the railroad station the hussar in the laced fur jacket danced and shifted his feet like a show horse. Was bidding goodbye to a lady going away. Chatted easily and uninterruptedly with her, if not by words then by dancing motions and manipulations of the hilt of his saber. Once or twice, in fear lest the train be about to leave, escorted her up the steps to the car, his hand almost under her shoulder. He was of medium height, large, strong, healthy teeth, the cut and accentuated waist-line of his fur jacket gave his appearance a somewhat feminine quality. He smiled a great deal in every direction, a really unwitting, meaningless smile, mere proof of the matter-of-fact, complete and eternal harmony of his being which his honor as an officer almost demanded.

The old couple weeping as they said goodbye. Innumerable kisses senselessly repeated, just as when one despairs, one keeps picking up a cigarette over and over again without being aware of it. They behaved as if at home, without paying any attention to their surroundings. So it is in every bedroom. I couldn't make out her features at all, a homely old woman; if you looked at her face more closely, if you attempted to look at it more closely, it dissolved, so to speak, and only a faint recollection of some sort of homely little ugliness remained, the red nose or several pockmarks, perhaps. He had a gray mustache, a large nose and real pockmarks. Cycling coat and cane. Had himself well under control, though he was deeply moved. In sorrowful jest chucked the old woman under the chin. What magic there is in chucking an old woman under the chin. Finally they looked tearfully into each other's eyes. They didn't mean this, but it could be interpreted to mean: Even this wretched little happiness, the union of us two old people, is destroyed by the war.

The huge German officer, hung with every kind of accouterment, marched first through the railroad station, then through the train. His height and military bearing made him stiff; it was almost surprising that he could move; the firmness of his waist, the breadth of his shoulders, the slimness of his body made one's eyes open in surprise in order to be able to take it all in at once.

Two Hungarian Jewesses in the compartment, mother and daughter. They resembled each other, and yet the mother was decent-looking, the daughter a miserable if self-conscious remnant. Mother—well-proportioned face, a fuzzy beard on her chin. The daughter was shorter;

pointed face, bad complexion, blue dress, a white jabot over her pathetic bosom.

Red Cross nurse. Very certain and determined. Traveled as if she were a whole family sufficient to itself. She smoked cigarettes and walked up and down the corridor like a father; like a boy she jumped up on the seat to get something out of her knapsack; like a mother she carefully sliced the meat, the bread, the orange; like a flirtatious girl —what she really was—she showed off her pretty little feet, her yellow boots and the yellow stockings on her trim legs against the opposite seat. She would have had no objections to being spoken to, and in fact began herself to ask about the mountains one could see in the distance, gave me her guidebook so that I could find the mountains on the map. Dejectedly I lay in my corner, a reluctance to ask her questions, as she expected me to, grew stronger, in spite of the fact that I rather liked her. Strong brown face of uncertain age, coarse skin, arched lower lip, traveling clothes with the nurse's uniform under them, soft peaked hat crushed carelessly over her tightly twisted hair. Since no one asked her a question, she herself started telling fragments of stories. My sister, who, as I learned later, didn't like her at all, helped her out a bit. She was going to Satvralja Ujhel, where she was to learn her ultimate destination; she preferred being where there was most to do because the time passed more quickly (my sister concluded from this that she was unhappy; I, however, didn't think so). You have all sorts of things happen to you; one man, for example, was snoring insufferably, they woke him, asked him to have some consideration for the other patients, he promised, but hardly had his head touched the pillow again when there was the horrible snoring again. It was very funny. The other patients threw their slippers at him, his bed stood in the corner of the room and he was a target impossible to miss. You have to be strict with sick people, otherwise you get nowhere, yes is yes, no is no, just don't be an easy mark.

At this point I made a stupid remark, but one very characteristic of me—servile, sly, irrelevant, impersonal, unsympathetic, untrue, fetched from far off, from some ultimate diseased tendency, influenced in addition by the Strindberg performance of the night before—to the effect that it must do a woman good to be able to treat men in that way. She did not hear the remark, or ignored it. My sister naturally understood it quite in the sense in which I made it, and by laughing made it her own. More stories of a tetanus case who simply wouldn't die. The Hungarian station master who got on later with his little boy. The nurse offered the boy an orange. He took it. Then she offered him a piece of marzipan, touched it to his lips, but he hesitated. I said: He can't believe it. The nurse repeated this word for word. Very pleasant.

Outside the window Theiss and Bodrog with their huge spring floods. Lake views. Wild ducks. Mountains with Tokay vines. Suddenly, near Budapest, among plowed fields, a semicircular fortified position. Barbed-wire entanglements, carefully sand-bagged shelters with benches, looked like models. The expression that was a riddle to me: "adapted to the terrain." To know the terrain requires the instinct of a quadruped.

Filthy hotel in Ujhel. Everything in the room threadbare. The cigar ashes left by the previous occupant of the bed still on the night table. The beds freshly made only in appearance. Attempted to get permission to travel on a military train, first from the squad headquarters, then from the rear headquarters. Each located in a pleasant room, especially the latter. Contrast between the military and the bureaucracy. Proper estimate of paper work: a table with inkwell and pen. The door to the balcony and the window open. Comfortable sofa. In a curtained compartment on the balcony facing the yard, the clatter of dishes. Lunch was being served. Someone—the first lieutenant, as it later turned out—raised the curtain to see who was waiting. With the words, "After all, you have to earn your salary," he interrupted his lunch and approached me. I got nowhere, in spite of the fact that I had to go back to the hotel to fetch my other identification card. All I had written on my identification card was military permission to use the next day's mail train, permission that was entirely superfluous.

The neighborhood around the railroad station like a village, neglected Ringplatz (Kossuth memorial; coffeehouses with gypsy music; pastry shop; an elegant shoe store; newsboys crying the *Az Est*, a one-armed soldier proudly walking around with exaggerated movements; whenever, in the course of the last twenty-four hours, I passed by a crude colored poster announcing a German victory, there was a crowd gathered closely scrutinizing it; met P.), the suburbs cleaner. Evening in the coffeehouse; only civilians from Ujhel, simple people and yet strange, partly suspect, suspect not because there was a war on but because no one could make them out. An army chaplain sitting by himself was reading newspapers.

In the morning the handsome young German soldier in the tavern. Had a great quantity of food served him, smoked a fat cigar, then wrote. Sharp, stern, but youthful eyes; clear, regular, clean-shaven face. Then pulled on his knapsack. Saw him again later saluting someone, but don't remember where.

May 3. Completely indifferent and apathetic. A well gone dry, water at an unattainable depth and no certainty it is there. Nothing, nothing. Don't understand the life in Strindberg's *Separated;* what he calls beautiful, when I relate it to myself, disgusts me. A letter to F., all wrong, impossible to mail it. What is there to tie me to a past or a future? The present is a phantom state for me; I don't sit at the table but hover round it. Nothing, nothing. Emptiness, boredom, no, not boredom, merely emptiness, meaninglessness, weakness. Yesterday in Dobřichovice.[34]

May 4. In a better state because I read Strindberg (*Separated*). I don't read him to read him, but rather to lie on his breast. He holds me on his left arm like a child. I sit there like a man on a statue. Ten times I almost slip off, but at the eleventh attempt I sit there firmly, feel secure, and have a wide view.

Reflection on other people's relationship to me. Insignificant as I may be, nevertheless there is no one here who understands me in my entirety. To have someone possessed of such understanding, a wife perhaps, would mean to have support from every side, to have God. Ottla understands many things, even a great many; Max, Felix, many things; others, like E., understand only details, but with dreadful intensity; F. in all likelihood understands nothing, which, because of our undeniable inner relationship, places her in a very special position. Sometimes I thought she understood me without realizing it; for instance, the time she waited for me at the subway station—I had been longing for her unbearably, and in my passion to reach her as quickly as possible almost ran past her, thinking she would be at the top of the stairs, and she took me quietly by the hand.

May 5. Nothing, dull slight headache. Chotek Park in the afternoon, read Strindberg, who sustains me.

The long-legged, black-eyed, yellow-skinned, childlike girl, merry, pert and lively. Saw a friend who was carrying her hat in her hand. "Do you have two heads?" Her friend immediately understood the joke, in itself a rather feeble one, but alive with the voice and all of the little personality that had been put into it. Laughing, she repeated it to another friend whom she met a few steps farther on: "She asked me whether I have two heads!"

Met Miss R.[35] in the morning. Really an abysmal ugliness, a man could never change so. Clumsy body, limp as if still asleep; the old jacket that I knew; what she was wearing under the jacket was as indeterminable as it was suspect, probably only her slip; and apparently she was disturbed by being discovered in this state, but she did the wrong thing—instead of concealing what it was that had given rise to her embarrassment, she reached as if guiltily inside the neck of her jacket and jerked it into place. Heavy down on her upper lip, but only in one spot; an exquisitely ugly impression. In spite of it all, I like her very much, even in all her undoubted ugliness; the beauty of her smile hasn't changed, the beauty of her eyes has suffered from the falling-off of the whole. As for the rest, we are continents apart, I certainly don't understand her; she on the other hand was satisfied with the first superficial impression she got of me. In all innocence she asked me for a bread card.

Read a chapter of "The New Christians" [36] in the evening.

Old father and his elderly daughter. He reasonable,

slightly stooped, with a pointed beard, a little cane held behind his back. She broad-nosed, with a strong lower jaw, round, distended face; turned clumsily on her broad hips. "They say I don't look well. But I do look well."

May 14. Lost all regularity in writing. In the open a great deal. Walk to Troja with Miss St., to Dobřichovice, Častalice with Miss R., her sister, Felix, his wife and Ottla. As though on the rack. Church services on Teingasse today, then Tuchmachergasse, then the soup kitchen. Read old portions of "The Stoker" today. A strength that seems unattainable (is already unattainable) today. Afraid I am unfit because of a bad heart.

May 27. A great deal of unhappiness in the last entry. Going to pieces. To go to pieces so pointlessly and unnecessarily.

September 13. Eve of Father's birthday, new diary. I don't need it as much as I used to, I mustn't upset myself, I'm upset enough, but to what purpose, when will it come, how can one heart, one heart not entirely sound, bear so much discontent and the incessant tugging of so much desire?

Distractedness, weak memory, stupidity!

September 14. With Max and Langer [37] at the wonder-rabbi's on Saturday. Žižkov,[38] Harantova street. A lot of children on the sidewalk and stairs. An inn. Completely dark upstairs, groped blindly along with my hands for a few steps. A pale, dim room, whitish-gray walls, several small women and girls standing around, white kerchiefs on their heads, pale faces, slight movements. An impression of lifelessness. Next room. Quite dark, full of men and young people. Loud praying. We squeezed into a corner. We had barely looked round a bit when the prayer was over, the room emptied. A corner room, windows on both sides, two windows each. We were pushed toward a table on the rabbi's right. We held back. "You're Jews too, aren't you?" A nature as strongly paternal as possible makes a rabbi. All rabbis look like savages, Langer said. This one was in a silk caftan, trousers visible under it. Hair on the bridge of his nose. Furred cap which he kept tugging back and forth. Dirty and pure, a characteristic of people who think intensely. Scratched in his beard, blew his nose through his fingers, reached into the food with his fingers; but when his hand rested on the table for a moment you saw the whiteness of his skin, a whiteness such as you remembered having seen before only in your childhood imaginings—when one's parents too were pure.

September 16. Humiliation at X.'s. Wrote the first line of a letter to him because a dignified letter had taken shape in my head. Nonetheless gave up after the first line. In the past I was different. Besides, how lightly I bore the humiliation, how easily I forgot it, how little impression even his indifference made on me. I could have floated unperturbed down a thousand corridors, through a thousand offices, past a thousand former friends now grown indifferent, without lowering my eyes. Imperturbable but also unawakable. And in one office Y. could have been sitting, in another Z., etc.

A new headache of a kind unknown so far. Short, painful stab above and to the right of my eye. This morning for the first time, more frequently since.

The Polish Jews going to Kol Nidre. The little boy with prayer shawls under both arms, running along at his father's side. Suicidal not to go to temple.

Opened the Bible. The unjust Judges. Confirmed in my own opinion, or at least in an opinion that I have already encountered in myself. But otherwise there is no significance to this, I am never visibly guided in such things, the pages of the Bible don't flutter in my presence.

Between throat and chin would seem to be the most rewarding place to stab. Lift the chin and stick the knife into the tensed muscles. But this spot is probably rewarding only in one's imagination. You expect to see a magnificent gush of blood and a network of sinews and little bones like you find in the leg of a roast turkey.

Read *Förster Fleck in Russland*. Napoleon's return to the battlefield of Borodino. The cloister there. It was blown up.

September 28. Completely idle. Memoirs of General Marcellin de Marbot, and Holzhausen, *Leiden der Deutschen 1812*.

Pointless to complain. Stabbing pains in my head by way of reply.

A little boy lay in the bathtub. It was his first bath at which—as he had so long wished—neither his mother nor the maid was present. In obedience to the command now and then called out to him from the next room by his mother, he hastily passed the sponge over his body; then he stretched out and enjoyed his immobility in the warm water. The gas flame steadily hummed and in the stove the dying fire crackled. It had long been quiet now in the next room, perhaps his mother had already gone away.

Why is it meaningless to ask questions? To complain means to put a question and wait for the answer. But questions that don't answer themselves at the very moment of their asking are never answered. No distance divides the interrogator from the one who answers him. There is no distance to overcome. Hence meaningless to ask and wait.

September 29. All sorts of vague resolves. That much I can do successfully. By chance caught sight on Ferdinand-strasse of a picture not entirely unconnected with them. A poor sketch of a fresco. Under it a Czech proverb, something like: Though dazzled you desert the winecup for the maid, you shall soon come back the wiser.

Slept badly, miserably, tormenting headaches in the morning, but a free day.

Many dreams. A combination of Marschner the director and Pimisker the servant appeared. Firm red cheeks, waxed black beard, thick unruly hair.

At one time I used to think: Nothing will destroy you, not this tough, clear, really empty head; you will never, either unwittingly or in pain, screw up your eyes, wrinkle your brow, twitch your hands, you will never be able to do more than act such a role.

How could Fortinbras say that Hamlet had prov'd most royally?

In the afternoon I couldn't keep myself from reading

what I had written yesterday, "yesterday's filth"; didn't do any harm, though.

September 30. Saw to it that Felix didn't disturb Max. Then at Felix's.

Rossmann and K., the innocent and the guilty, both executed without distinction in the end, the guilty one with a gentler hand, more pushed aside than struck down.[39]

October 1. Volume III, Memoirs of General Marcellin de Marbot. Polotsk—Beresina—Leipzig—Waterloo.

Mistakes Napoleon made:

1. Decision to wage the war. What did he wish to achieve by that? Strict enforcement of the Continental Blockade in Russia. That was impossible. Alexander I could not comply without endangering his own position. His father, Paul I, had in fact been assassinated because of the alliance with France and the war with England, which had injured Russia's trade immeasurably. Yet Napoleon hoped Alexander would comply. He intended to march to the Niemen only in order to extort Alexander's compliance.

2. He could have known what awaited him. Lieutenant Colonel de Pouthon, who had spent several years on military duty with the Russians, begged him on his knees to give it up. The obstacles he cited were: the apathy and lack of co-operation to be expected from the Lithuanian provinces, which had been subjugated by Russia many years ago; the fanaticism of the Muscovites; the lack of food and forage; the desolate countryside; roads that the lightest rain made impassable to artillery; the severity of the winter; the impossibility of advancing in the snow, which fell as early as the beginning of October.— Napoleon

allowed himself to be influenced in the contrary direction by Maret, the Duke of Bassano and Davout.

3. He failed to appoint the Prussian Crown Prince to his headquarters' staff, despite his having been asked to do so. He should have weakened Austria and Prussia as much as possible by demanding large contingents of additional troops from them, instead asked only 30,000 men from each. He should have used them in the front ranks, instead placed them on his flanks, the Austrians under Schwarzenberg facing Volhynia, the Prussians under Macdonald at the Niemen; in this way they were spared and he made it possible for them to block, or at least to endanger, his retreat, which is what actually happened—in November, after England had arranged peace between Russia and Turkey, so freeing Chichekov's army for service elsewhere, the Austrians permitted it to move north through Volhynia unmolested, and this was responsible for the disaster at the Beresina.

4. In each corps were included great numbers of the untrustworthy allies (Badenese, Mecklenburgers, Hessians, Bavarians, Württembergers, Saxons, Westphalians, Spaniards, Portuguese, Illyrians, Swiss, Croats, Poles, Italians) and in that way the corps' unity was weakened. Good wine spoiled by mixing it with murky water.

5. He set his hopes on Turkey, Sweden and Poland. The first made peace because England paid it to do so. The treacherous Bernadotte deserted him and with England's aid concluded an alliance with Russia; Sweden, it is true, lost Finland, but was promised Norway in return—Norway would be taken from the Danes, who remained devoted to Napoleon. The Poles: Lithuania was too closely tied to them by its forty years' annexation to the Russian state. The Austrian and Prussian Poles did go with him, but

without enthusiasm; they feared for the devastation of their country; only what was now the Saxon Grand Duchy of Warsaw could be counted upon to some extent.

6. From Vilna he wanted to organize conquered Lithuania to his own advantage. He might perhaps have received assistance, 300,000 men, if he had proclaimed a Kingdom of Poland (including Galicia and Posen)—a national assembly in Warsaw had in fact already issued proclamations to that effect—but that would have meant war with Prussia and Austria (and would have made peace with Russia more difficult). Besides, even then the Poles would probably have been undependable. The Vilna district mustered only twenty men as bodyguard for Napoleon. Napoleon chose the middle road, promised a kingdom if they co-operated, and so achieved nothing. In any case Napoleon would not have been able to equip a Polish army, for he had had no supplies of weapons and clothing sent to the Niemen after him.

7. He gave Jerome Bonaparte, who had no military experience, the command of an army of 60,000 men. Immediately upon entering Russia Napoleon had split the Russian army. Czar Alexander and Field Marshal Barclay marched north along the Dvina. Bagration's corps was still at Mir on the lower Niemen. Davout had already occupied Minsk, and he threw Bagration, who sought to pass north that way, back toward Bobruisk in the direction of Jerome. If Jerome had co-operated with Davout—but he did not find that compatible with his royal dignity—Bagration would have been destroyed or forced to capitulate. Bagration escaped, Jerome was sent to Westphalia, Junot replaced him, only shortly to commit a serious error too.

8. He appointed the Duke of Bassano civil governor and General Hogendorp military governor of the province of

Lithuania. Neither knew how to create a reserve force for the army. The Duke was a diplomat, understood nothing of administration; Hogendorp was unacquainted with French customs and military regulations. He spoke French very badly, thus found sympathy neither with the French nor with the local nobility.

9. He spent nineteen days in Vilna, seventeen in Vitebsk, until August 13th, thus lost thirty-six days (a reproach that other writers make against him, not Marbot). But it can be explained: he had still hoped to come to terms with the Russians, wanted to hold a central position from which to command the corps occupying the country behind Bagration, and wanted to spare his troops. Difficulties of supply developed too; every evening, at the end of their day's march, the troops were compelled to fetch their own provisions, often over very great distances. Only Davout had a supply train and cattle for his corps.

10. Unnecessarily great losses at the siege of Smolensk, 12,000 men. Napoleon had expected no such energetic defense. If they had by-passed Smolensk and pressed along Barclay de Tolly's line of retreat, they could have taken it without a struggle.

11. He has been reproached for his failure to act during the Battle of Borodino (September 7th). He walked back and forth in a gully all day long, only twice climbing to a hilltop. In Marbot's opinion this was no error; Napoleon had been ill that day, had had severe migraine. On the evening of the 6th he had received reports from Portugal. Marshal Marmont, one of the generals in whom Napoleon had been mistaken, had been badly defeated by Wellington at Salamanca.

12. In principle the retreat from Moscow had been quickly decided upon. Many things made it necessary: the

fires, the fighting in Kaluga, the cold, the desertions, the menace to his line of retreat, the situation in Spain, a conspiracy that was uncovered in Paris—but in spite of all this Napoleon remained in Moscow from September 15th until October 19th, still hoping to come to terms with Alexander. Kutusov did not even reply to his last offer to negotiate.

13. He tried to withdraw by way of Kaluga, though that meant taking the roundabout route. He hoped to get provisions there, his line of retreat through Mozhaisk extended a great distance on either side. After a few days, however, he realized that he could not continue along this route without giving battle to Kutusov. He therefore turned back along the former line of retreat.

14. The big bridge across the Beresina was covered by a fort and protected by a Polish regiment. Confident that he would be able to use the bridge, Napoleon had all the pontoons burned to lighten and speed the march. But meanwhile Chichekov had taken the fort and burned the bridge. In spite of the extreme cold the river had not frozen. The lack of pontoons was one of the chief causes of the disaster.

15. The crossing over the two bridges thrown across at Studzianka was badly organized. The bridges were thrown across on November 26th, at noon. (If they had had pontoons they could have begun the crossing at daybreak.) They were unmolested by the Russians until the morning of the 28th. Nevertheless, only part of the corps had crossed by then and thousands of stragglers had been left two days on the left bank. The French lost 25,000 men.

16. The line of retreat was not protected. Except at Vilna and Smolensk, there were no garrisoned towns, no depots, no hospitals, from the Niemen to Moscow. The Cossacks were roving all through the intervening country-

side. Nothing could reach or leave the army without running the danger of capture. And for that reason not one of the approximately 100,000 Russian prisoners of war was brought across the frontier.

17. Scarcity of interpreters. The Partouneaux division lost its way on the road from Borisov to Studzianka, ran into Wittgenstein's army and was destroyed. They simply could not understand the Polish peasants who should have served as guides.

Paul Holzhausen, *Die Deutschen in Russland 1812.* Wretched condition of the horses, their great exertions; their fodder was wet green straw, unripe grain, rotten roof thatchings. Diarrhea, loss of weight, constipation. Used smoking tobacco for enemas. One artillery officer said his men had to ram the length of their arms into the horses' rumps to relieve them of the mass of excrement accumulated in their bowels. Their bodies were bloated from the green fodder. Galloping them could sometimes cure it. But many succumbed; there were hundreds with burst bellies on the bridges of Pilony. "They lay in ditches and holes with dim, glassy eyes and weakly struggled to climb out. But all their efforts were in vain; seldom did one of them get a foot up on the road, and when it did, its condition was only rendered worse. Unfeelingly, service troops and artillery men with their guns drove over it; you heard the leg being crushed, the hollow sound of the animal's scream of pain, and saw it convulsively lift up its head and neck in fear and terror, fall back again with all its weight and immediately bury itself in the thick ooze."

Despair even when they set out. Heat, hunger, thirst, disease. A non-commissioned officer who was exhorted to set an example. The next day a Württemberger first lieutenant, after a dressing-down by the regimental commander, tore a bayonet out of the hands of the nearest soldier and ran himself through the breast.

Objection to the tenth mistake. Because of the sorry condition of the cavalry and the lack of scouts, the fords about the city were discovered too late.

October 6. Various types of nervousness. I think noises can no longer disturb me, though to be sure I am not doing any work now. Of course, the deeper one digs one's pit, the quieter it becomes, the less fearful one becomes, the quieter it becomes.

Langer's stories: A Zaddik is to be obeyed more than God. The Baal Shem once commanded a favorite disciple to have himself baptized. He was baptized, earned great esteem, became a bishop. Then the Baal Shem had him come to him and gave him his permission to return to Judaism. Again he obeyed and did great penance for his sin. The Baal Shem explained his command by saying that, because of his exceptional qualities, his disciple had been greatly set upon by the Evil One, whom it was the purpose of the baptism to divert. The Baal Shem himself cast the disciple into the midst of evil; it was not the disciple's own fault that he took this step, but because he was commanded to do so, and there seemed nothing more the Evil One could do.

Every hundred years a supreme Zaddik appears, a Zaddik Hador. He need not be a wonder-rabbi, nor even be known, and yet he is supreme. The Baal Shem was not the Zaddik Hador of his day; it was rather an unknown merchant of Drohobycz. The latter heard that the Baal Shem inscribed amulets—as did other Zaddiks too—and suspected him of being an adherent of Sabbatai Zvi and of inscribing his name on amulets. Therefore, from afar, without knowing him personally, he took away from him the power to bestow amulets. The Baal Shem at once perceived the lack of power in his amulets—he had never inscribed anything but his own name on them—and after some time also learned that the man in Drohobycz was the cause of it. Once, when the man from Drohobycz came to the Baal Shem's town—it was on a Monday—the Baal Shem caused him to sleep an entire day without his being aware of it; as a result the man from Drohobycz fell behind one day in his estimation of the time. Friday evening—he thought it was Thursday—he wanted to depart in order to spend the holiday at home. Then he saw the people going to temple and realized his error. He resolved to remain where he was and asked to be taken to the Baal Shem. Early in the afternoon already, the latter had instructed his wife to prepare a meal for thirty people. When the man from Drohobycz arrived, he sat down to eat immediately after prayers and in a short time finished all the food that had been prepared for thirty people. But he had not eaten his fill, and demanded more food. The Baal Shem said: "I expected an angel of the first rank, but was not prepared for an angel of the second rank." Everything in the house that could be eaten he now had brought in, but even that was insufficient.

The Baal Shem was not the Zaddik Hador, but was even higher. Witness for this is the Zaddik Hador himself. For one evening the latter came to the place where lived the future wife of the Baal Shem. He was a guest in the house of the girl's parents. Before going up to the attic to sleep he asked for a light, but there was none in the house. He went up therefore without a light, but later, when the girl looked up from the yard, his room was as bright as a ballroom. Whereupon she recognized that he was an unusual guest, and asked him to take her for his wife. This she was permitted to ask, for her exalted destiny was revealed by her having recognized him. But the Zaddik Hador said: "You are destined for one even higher." This is proof that the Baal Shem was higher than a Zaddik Hador.

October 7. Was a long time with Miss R. in the lobby of the hotel yesterday. Slept badly. Headaches.

I frightened Gerti by limping; the horror in a clubfoot.[40]

Yesterday a fallen horse with a bloody knee on Niklasstrasse. I looked away and uncontrollably grimaced in the broad daylight.

Insoluble problem: Am I broken? Am I in decline? Almost all the signs speak for it (coldness, apathy, state of my nerves, distractedness, incompetence on the job, headaches, insomnia); almost nothing but hope speaks against it.

November 3. Went about a great deal lately, fewer headaches. Walks with Miss R. With her at *Er und seine Schwester*, played by Girardi. ("Have you talent then?"—"Permit me to intervene and answer for you: Oh yes, oh yes.") In the municipal reading room. Saw the flag at her parents'.

The two wonderful sisters, Esther and Tilka; they are like the contrast between a light on and a light off. Tilka especially is beautiful; olive-brown, lowered, curving eyelids, heart of Asia. Both with shawls drawn about their shoulders. They are of average height, short even, and appear as erect and tall as goddesses; one on the round cushion of the sofa, Tilka in a corner on some unrecognizable seat, perhaps on a box. Half asleep, I had a long vision of Esther,

who, with the passion she impresses me as having for everything spiritual, had the knot of a rope firmly between her
teeth and swung energetically back and forth in the empty
room like the clapper of a bell (a movie poster I remember).

The two L.'s. The little devil of a teacher whom I also
saw in my half-sleep; how she flew furiously along in a
dance, a Cossack-like but floating dance, up and down
over a somewhat sloping, rough, dark brown brick pavement lying there in the twilight.

November 4. I remember a corner in Brescia where, on
a like pavement but in broad daylight, I distributed *soldi*
to the children. And a church in Verona I forlornly and
reluctantly went into, only because of the slight compulsion of duty that a tourist feels, and the heavy compulsion
of a man expiring of futility; saw an overgrown dwarf
stooped under the holy water font, walked around a bit,
sat down; and as reluctantly went out again, as if just such
a church as this one, built door to door with it, awaited me
outside.

The recent departure of the Jews from the railroad station. The two men carrying a sack. The father loading his
possessions on his many children, the smallest one as well,
in order to mount the platform more quickly. The strong,
healthy, young but already shapeless woman sitting on a
trunk holding a suckling infant, surrounded by acquaintances in lively conversation.

November 5. State of excitement in the afternoon. Began
with my considering if and how many war bonds I should
buy. Twice went to the office to give the necessary order

and twice returned without having gone in. Feverishly computed the interest. Then asked my mother to buy a thousand kronen worth of bonds, but raised the amount to two thousand kronen. In the course of all this it was revealed that I knew nothing of an investment I possessed amounting to some three thousand kronen, and that it had almost no effect at all on me when I learned of it. There was nothing in my head save my doubts about the war bonds, which didn't cease plaguing me even after a half-hour's walk through the busiest streets. I felt myself directly involved in the war, weighed the general financial prospects, at least according to what information I possessed, increased or diminished the interest that would some day come to me, etc. But gradually my excitement underwent a transformation, my thoughts turned to writing, I felt myself up to it, wanted nothing save the opportunity to write, considered what nights in the near future I could set aside for it, with pains in my heart crossed the stone bridge at a run, felt what I had already experienced so often, the unhappy sense of a consuming fire inside me that was not allowed to break out, made up a sentence—"Little friend, pour forth"—incessantly sang it to a special tune, and squeezed and released a handkerchief in my pocket in accompaniment as if it were a bagpipe.

November 6. View of the antlike movements of the crowd in front of and in the trench.[41]

At the home of Oskar Pollak's [42] mother. His sister made a good impression on me. Is there anyone, by the way, to whom I don't bow down? Take Grünberg,[43] for instance, who in my opinion is a very remarkable person and almost universally depreciated for reasons which are beyond me—

if it were a question, let's say, of which of the two of us should have to die immediately (no great improbability in his case, for they say he is in an advanced stage of tuberculosis), and the decision lay with me as to which it should be, then I should find the question a preposterous one, so long as it was looked at merely theoretically; for as a matter of course Grünberg, a far more valuable person than I, should have to be spared. Grünberg too would agree with me. But in the final desperate moment I should, as everyone else would have done long before, invent arguments in my favor, arguments that at any other time, because of their crudity, nakedness and falsity, would have made me vomit. And these final moments I am surely undergoing now, though no one is forcing a choice upon me; they are those moments when I put off all external distracting influences and try really to look into myself.

"Silently the 'black ones' sit around the fire. The light of the flames flickers on their somber, fanatic faces."

November 19. Days passed in futility, powers wasting away in waiting, and in spite of all this idleness, throbbing, gnawing pains in my head.

Letter from Werfel. Reply.

At Mrs. M.-T.'s, my defenselessness against everything. My malicious remarks at Max's. Disgusted by them the next morning.[44]

With Miss F.R. and Esther.

In the Altneu Synagogue at the Mishnah lecture. Home

with Dr. Jeiteles.[45] Greatly interested in certain contro-
versial issues.

Self-pity, because it is cold, because of everything. Now,
at half-past nine at night, someone in the next apartment is
hammering a nail into the wall between us.

November 21. Complete futility. Sunday. A more than
ordinarily sleepless night. In bed in the sunshine until a
quarter past eleven. Walk. Lunch. Read the paper, leafed
through some old catalogues. Walk, Hybernerstrasse, City
Park, Wenzelsplatz, Ferdinandstrasse, then in the direction
of Podol. Laboriously stretched out to two hours. Now
and then felt severe pains in my head, once a really burning pain. Had supper. Now at home. Who on high could
behold all this with open eyes from beginning to end?

December 25. Open the diary only in order to lull myself
to sleep. But see what happens to be the last entry and could
conceive of thousands of identical ones I might have entered over the past three or four years. I wear myself out
to no purpose, should be happy if I could write, but don't.
Haven't been able to get rid of my headaches lately. I have
really wasted my strength away.

Yesterday spoke frankly to my boss; my decision to
speak up and my vow not to shrink from it had made it
possible for me to enjoy two—if restless—hours of sleep the
night before last. Put four possibilities to him: (1) Let
everything go on as it has been going this last tortured
week, the worst I've undergone, and end up with brain
fever, insanity or something of the like; (2) out of some
kind of sense of duty I don't want to take a vacation, nor
would it help; (3) I can't give notice now because of my
parents and the factory; (4) only military service remains.

KAFKA SKETCH

Answer: One week's vacation and hematogen treatment, which my boss intends to take with me. He himself is apparently very sick. If I went too, the department would be deserted.

Relief to have spoken frankly. For the first time, almost caused an official convulsion in the atmosphere of the office with the word "notice."

Nevertheless, hardly slept at all today.

Always this one principal anguish: If I had gone away in 1912, in full possession of all my forces, with a clear head, not eaten by the strain of keeping down living forces!

With Langer: He will only be able to read Max's book thirteen days from now. He could have read it Christmas Day—according to an old custom you are not allowed to read Torah on Christmas (one rabbi made a practice of cutting up his year's supply of toilet paper on that evening), but this year Christmas fell on Saturday. In thirteen days, however, the Russian Christmas will be here, he'll read it then. According to a medieval tradition you may take an interest in belles lettres and other worldly knowledge only after your seventieth year, according to a more liberal view only after your fortieth year. Medicine was the only science in which you were allowed to take an interest. Today not even in that, since it is now too closely joined with the other sciences.— You are not allowed to think of the Torah in the toilet, and for this reason you may read worldly books there. A very pious man in Prague, a certain K., knew a great deal of the worldly sciences, he had studied them all in the toilet.

April 19. He attempted to open the door to the corridor, but it resisted. He looked up and down but could not discover what the obstacle was. Nor was the door locked; the key was in the lock on the inside, if anyone had tried to lock it from the outside the key would have been pushed out. And after all, who could have locked it? He pushed against the door with his knee, the frosted glass rang but the door stuck fast. How odd.

He went back into the room, stepped out on the balcony and looked down into the street. But before he had given a thought to the usual afternoon activity below, he again returned to the door and once more attempted to open it. This time, however, it proved more than an attempt, the door immediately opened, hardly any pressure was needed, the draft blowing in from the balcony made it fly right open; he gained entry into the corridor as effortlessly as a child who is playfully allowed to touch the latch at the same time actually that an older person presses it down.

I shall have three weeks to myself. Do you call that inhuman treatment?

A short time ago this dream: We were living on the Graben near the Café Continental. A regiment turned in from Herrengasse on its way to the railroad station. My father: "That's something to look at as long as one can"; he swings himself up on the sill (in Felix's brown bathrobe, the figure in the dream was a mixture of the two) and with outstretched arms sprawls outside on the broad, sharply sloping window ledge. I catch hold of him by the two little loops through which the cord of his bathrobe passes. Maliciously, he leans even farther out, I exert all my strength to hold him. I think how good it would be if I could fasten my feet by ropes to something solid so that my father could not pull me out. But to do that I should have to let go of

my father, at least for a short time, and that's impossible.
Sleep—my sleep, especially—cannot withstand all this tension and I wake up.

April 20. The landlady came down the corridor toward
him with a letter. He scrutinized the old lady's face, not
the letter, as he opened it. Then he read:

"My dear Sir: For several days you have been living
across the way from me. Your close resemblance to an
old friend of mine attracted my attention. Do me the
honor of paying me a visit this afternoon. With best
regards, Louise Halka."

"All right," he said, as much to the landlady, who had
not budged, as to the letter. It was a welcome opportunity
to make what might perhaps be a useful acquaintance in
this city where he was still a complete stranger.

"Do you know Mrs. Halka?" asked the landlady, as he
reached for his hat.

"No," he said, questioningly.

"The girl who delivered the letter is her maid," the landlady said, as though in apology.

"That may well be," he said, annoyed at her interest,
and hurried to leave the house.

"She is a widow," the landlady breathed after him from
the threshold.

A dream: Two groups of men were fighting each other.
The group to which I belonged had captured one of our
opponents, a gigantic naked man. Five of us clung to him,
one by the head, two on either side by his arms and legs.
Unfortunately we had no knife with which to stab him,

we hurriedly asked each other for a knife, no one had one. But since for some reason there was no time to lose and an oven stood nearby whose extraordinarily large cast-iron door was red-hot, we dragged the man to it, held one of his feet close to the oven until the foot began to smoke, pulled it back again until it stopped smoking, then thrust it close to the door again. We monotonously kept this up until I awoke, not only in cold sweat but with my teeth actually chattering.

Hans and Amalia, the butcher's two children, were playing marbles near the wall of the big warehouse—a large old fortress-like stone building with a double row of heavily barred windows—which extended a great distance along the riverbank. Hans took careful aim, intently regarding the marble, the path it must follow, and the hole, before he made his shot; Amalia squatted beside the hole, impatiently striking her little fists against the ground. But suddenly they both left off their play, slowly stood up and looked at the nearest window of the warehouse. They heard a sound as if someone were trying to wipe the dirt off one of the many small dim panes into which the window was divided; but the attempt failed and the pane was broken through, a thin face, smiling for no apparent reason, indistinctly appeared in the small rectangle; it seemed to be a man and he said, "Come in, children, come in. Have you ever seen a warehouse?"

The children shook their heads, Amalia looked up in excitement at the man, Hans glanced behind him to see if anyone were near by, but saw only a man with bent back pushing a heavily laden wheelbarrow along the railing of the wharf, oblivious to everything. "Then it will certainly be a surprise to you," the man said very eagerly, as though

by his eagerness he might overcome the unfortunate circumstance of the wall, bars and window that separated
him from the children. "But come in now. It's getting
late."

"How shall we come in?" asked Amalia.

"I'll show you the door," the man said. "Just follow
me, I'm going to the right now and will knock on every
window." Amalia nodded and ran to the next window,
there was really a knock there and at all the others too.
But while Amalia heeded the strange man and thought-
lessly ran after him as one might run after a hoop, Hans
merely trailed slowly after her. He felt uneasy; the warehouse, which it had never before occurred to him to visit,
was certainly very much worth seeing, but an invitation
from any stranger you please by no means proved that
you were really allowed inside it. It was unlikely, rather,
for were it permissible, his father would surely have
taken him there already, wouldn't he?—his father not only
lived close by but even knew all the people a great distance round about, who bade him good day and treated
him with respect. And it now occurred to Hans that this
might also be the case with the stranger; he ran after
Amalia to confirm this, catching up with her just as she,
and the man with her, stopped at a small, low, galvanized
iron door level with the ground. It looked like a large
oven door.

Again the man broke out a small pane in the last window
and said, "Here is the door. Wait a moment, I'll open the
inner doors."

"Do you know our father?" Hans at once asked, but
the face had already disappeared and Hans had to wait
with his question. Now they in fact heard the inner doors
opening. At first the grating of the key in the lock was

hardly audible, but it grew louder and louder as each successive door was opened. The aperture in the thick masonry at this point seemed to be filled by a great number of doors, one set closely behind the other. The last door finally opened inward, the children lay down on the ground to peer inside, and there in the gloom was the man's face. "The doors are open, come along! Be quick though, quick!" With his arm he pushed all the doors against the wall.

As if the pause outside the door had made her recollect somewhat, Amalia now slipped behind Hans, not wanting to go first, but at the same time she pushed him forward in her eagerness to go with him into the warehouse. Hans was very close to the doorway, he felt the chill air that came through it; he had no desire to go inside, not inside to that strange man, behind all those doors which could be clapped together after him, not inside the huge, cold old building. He asked, only because he already lay in front of the opening: "Do you know our father?"

"No," the man replied, "but come on in, will you? I am not allowed to leave the doors open so long."

"He doesn't know our father," Hans said to Amalia, and stood up; he felt relieved, now he would certainly not go in.

"But of course I know him," said the man, poking his head farther forward in the aperture; "naturally I know him, the butcher, the big butcher near the bridge, I sometimes get meat there myself; do you think I should let you into the warehouse if I didn't know your family?"

"Then why did you first say that you didn't know him?" asked Hans, who, with his hands in his pockets, had already turned his back on the warehouse.

"Because here, in this position, I don't want to carry

on any long discussions. First come inside, then we can talk everything over. Besides, boy, you don't have to come in at all; on the contrary, with your bad manners I should prefer you to stay outside. But your sister now, she's more reasonable, she shall come in and is entirely welcome." And he held out his hand to Amalia.

"Hans," Amalia said, reaching out her hand to the stranger's—without taking it, however—"why don't you want to go in?"

Hans, who after the man's last reply could give no definite reason for his disinclination, merely said softly to Amalia, "He hisses so." The stranger in fact did hiss, not only when he spoke but even when he was silent.

"Why do you hiss?" asked Amalia, who wished to intercede between Hans and the stranger.

"I will answer you, Amalia," the stranger said. "My breathing is heavy, it is the result of having been here in this damp warehouse for so long; and I shouldn't advise you to stay here too long either, though for a little while it's quite extraordinarily interesting."

"I'm going," Amalia said with a laugh, she was now won over completely; "but," she then added, more slowly again, "Hans must come too."

"Of course," the stranger said and, lunging forward with the upper part of his body, grabbed Hans, who was taken completely unawares, by the hands so that he tumbled down at once, and with all his strength the man pulled him into the hole. "This way in, my dear Hans," he said, and dragged the struggling, screaming boy inside, heedless of the fact that one of Hans' sleeves was being torn to shreds on the sharp edges of the doors.

"Mali," Hans suddenly cried out—his feet had already vanished within the hole, it went so quickly despite all the resistance he put up—"Mali, get Father, get Father, I can't get out, he's pulling me so hard!"

But Mali, completely disconcerted by the stranger's rude onslaught—and with some feeling of guilt besides, for to a certain extent she had provoked the offense, though in the final analysis also quite curious, as she had been from the very beginning—did not run away but held on to Hans's feet and let——

It soon became known, of course, that the rabbi was working on a clay figure. Every door of every room in his house stood open night and day, it contained nothing whose presence was not immediately known to everybody. There were always a few disciples, or neighbors, or strangers wandering up and down the stairs of the house, looking into all the rooms and—unless they happened to encounter the rabbi himself—going anywhere they pleased. And once, in a washtub, they found a large lump of reddish clay.

The liberty the rabbi allowed everyone in his house had spoiled people to such a degree that they did not hesitate to touch the clay. It was hard, even when one pressed it one's fingers were hardly stained by it, its taste—the curious even had to touch their tongue to it— was bitter. Why the rabbi kept it in the washtub they could not understand.

Bitter, bitter, that is the most important word. How do I intend to solder fragments together into a story that will sweep one along?

A faint grayish-white smoke was lightly and continuously wafted from the chimney.

The rabbi, his sleeves rolled up like a washerwoman, stood in front of the tub kneading the clay which already bore the crude outline of a human form. The rabbi kept constantly before him the shape of the whole even while he worked on the smallest detail, the joint of a finger, perhaps. Though the figure obviously seemed to be acquiring a human likeness, the rabbi behaved like a madman —time and again he thrust out his lower jaw, unceasingly passed one lip over the other, and when he wet his hands in the bucket of water beside him, thrust them in so violently that the water splashed to the ceiling of the bare vault.

May 11. And so gave the letter to the Director. The day before yesterday. Asked either for a long leave later on, without pay of course, in the event that the war should end by fall; or, if the war goes on, for my exemption to be canceled. It was a complete lie. It would have been half a lie if I had asked for a long leave at once, and, if it were refused, for my dismissal. It would have been the truth if I had given notice. I dared neither, hence the complete lie.

Pointless discussion today. The Director thought I wanted to extort the usual three weeks of vacation, which in my exempted status I am not entitled to, offered me them accordingly without further ado, claimed he had decided on it even before the letter. He said nothing at all of the army, as though there had been nothing in my letter about it. When I mentioned it he didn't hear me. He seemed to find a long leave without pay funny, cautiously referred to it in that tone. Urged me to take the three weeks' vacation at once. Made incidental remarks in the role of a lay psychiatrist, as does everyone. After all,

I don't have to bear the responsibilities he does, a position like his could really make one ill. And how hard he had had to work even before, when he was preparing for his bar examination and at the same time working in the Institute. Eleven hours a day for nine months. And then the chief difference—have I ever in any way had to be afraid of losing my job? But he had had to worry about that. He had had enemies in the Institute who had tried everything possible, even, as he had said, to deprive him of his means of livelihood, to throw him on the junk heap.

Remarkably enough, he did not speak of my writing.

I was weak, though I knew that it was almost a life-and-death matter for me. But insisted that I wanted to join the army and that three weeks were not enough. Whereupon he put off the rest of the discussion. If he were only not so friendly and concerned!

I will stick to the following: I want to join the army, to give in to a wish I've suppressed for two years; I should prefer to have a long leave for various reasons that have nothing to do with me personally. But because of office as well as military considerations, it is probably impossible. By a long leave I understand—the official is ashamed to say it, the invalid is not—a half or an entire year. I want no pay because it is not a matter of an organic illness that can be established beyond a doubt.

All this is a continuation of the lie; but if I am consistent in it, approximates the truth in its effect.

June 2. What a muddle I've been in with girls, in spite of all my headaches, insomnia, gray hair, despair. Let me count them: there have been at least six since the summer. I can't resist, my tongue is fairly torn from my mouth if I don't give in and admire anyone who is admirable and love her until admiration is exhausted. With all six my guilt is almost wholly inward, though one of the six did complain of me to someone.

From *Das Werden des Gottesglaubens* by N. Söderblom, Archbishop of Upsala; quite scientific, without his being personally or religiously involved.

The primordial divinity of the Mesai: how he lowered the first cattle down from heaven on a leather strap to the first kraal.

The primordial divinity of some Australian tribes: he came out of the west in the guise of a powerful medicine man, made men, animals, trees, rivers, mountains, instituted the sacred ceremonies and determined from which clan a member of another clan was to take his wife. His task completed, he went away. The medicine men could climb up to him on a tree or a rope and receive their power from him.

Other tribes: during their creative wanderings from place to place they also performed the sacred dances and rites for the first time.

Others: in primordial times men themselves created their totem animals by their ceremonies. The sacred rites thus of themselves begot the object of their veneration.

The Bimbiga near the coast tell of two men who in primordial times created springs, forests and ceremonies in the course of their wanderings.

June 19. Forget everything. Open the windows. Clear the room. The wind blows through it. You see only its emptiness, you search in every corner and don't find yourself.

With Ottla. Called for her at the English teacher's. Home by way of the quay, the stone bridge, a short stretch of the Kleinseite, the new bridge. Was excited by the statues of saints on the Karlsbrücke. The remarkable light of the summer evening together with the nocturnal emptiness of the bridge.

Joy over Max's liberation. I had believed in its possibility, but now see the reality as well. But again see no possibility for myself.

And they heard the voice of the Lord God walking in the garden toward the cool of the day.
The calm of Adam and Eve.
And the Lord God made for Adam and for his wife garments of skins, and clothed them.
God's rage against the human race. The two trees, the unexplained prohibition, the punishment of all (snake, woman, man), the favor granted Cain, who is nevertheless provoked by God's speaking to him.
My spirit shall not always strive with man.
Then began men to call upon the name of the Lord.
And Enoch walked with God, and he was not; for God took him.

July 3. First day in Marienbad with F. Door to door, keys on either side.

Three houses adjoined each other, forming a little yard. There were also two workshops under sheds in this yard, and in one corner stood a high pile of small boxes. One very stormy night—the wind drove the rain in sheets over the lowest of the houses into the yard—a student still sitting over his books in an attic room heard a loud groan in the yard. He jumped up and listened, but there was silence, unbroken silence. "I was probably mistaken," the student told himself, and resumed his reading.

"Not mistaken," this, after a moment, was what the letters in his book seemed to spell out.

"Mistaken," he repeated, and moved his index finger along the lines to calm their restlessness.

July 4. I awoke to find myself imprisoned in a fenced enclosure which allowed no room for more than a step in either direction. Sheep are folded into pens of this kind, though theirs are not so narrow. The direct rays of the sun beat down on me; to shield my head I pressed it against my breast and squatted down with hunched back.

What are you? I am miserable. I have two little boards screwed against my temples.

July 5. The hardships of living together. Forced upon us by strangeness, pity, lust, cowardice, vanity, and only deep down, perhaps, a thin little stream worthy of the name of love, impossible to seek out, flashing once in the moment of a moment.

Poor F.

July 6. Unhappy night. Impossible to live with F. Intolerable living with anyone. I don't regret this; I regret the impossibility for me of not living alone. And yet how absurd it is for me to regret this, to give in, and then finally to understand. Get up from the ground. Hold to the book. But then I have it all back again: insomnia; headaches; jump out of the high window but onto the rain-soaked ground where the fall won't be fatal. Endless tossing with eyes closed, exposed to any random glance.

Only the Old Testament knows—say nothing yet on it.

Dreamed of Dr. H.—he sat behind his desk, somehow leaning back and bending forward at the same time; limpid eyes; slowly and precisely, as is his way, pursuing an orderly train of thought to its end; even in the dream hear almost nothing of his words, simply follow the logic by which it is carried on. Then found myself beside his wife, who was carrying a lot of luggage and (what was astonishing) playing with my fingers; a patch was torn out of the thick felt of her sleeve, her arms took up only a small part of the sleeve, which was filled with strawberries.

That they laughed at him troubled Karl not a whit. What kind of fellows were they and what did they know? Smooth American faces having only two or three wrinkles, but these two or three tumid and deeply graven in their brows or down one side of their nose and mouth. Native Americans, in order to know them for what they were it would almost suffice to hammer on their stony brows. What did they know——

A man lay in bed, seriously ill. The doctor sat at the little table that had been pushed next to the bed and watched the sick man, who looked at him in return. "No help," said the sick man, not as if he were asking but as if he were answering a question. The doctor partly opened a large medical work lying on the edge of the little table, hurriedly glanced into it from afar and, clapping the book shut, said, "Help is coming from Bregenz." When the sick man, with an effort, squinted his eyes, the doctor added: "Bregenz in Vorarlberg."

"That is far away," the sick man said.

Receive me into your arms, they are the depths, receive me into the depths; if you refuse me now, then later.

Take me, take me, web of folly and pain.

The Negroes came out of the thicket. They leaped into a dance which they performed around a wooden stake encircled by a silver chain. The priest sat to one side, a little rod raised above the gong. The sky was overcast and silent; no rain fell.

I have never yet been intimate with a woman apart from that time in Zuckmantel. And then again with the Swiss girl in Riva. The first was a woman, and I was ignorant; the second a child, and I was utterly confused.

July 13. Then open yourself. Let the human person come forth. Breathe in the air and the silence.

It was an open-air restaurant in a spa. The afternoon had been rainy, not one customer had put in an appearance. The sky cleared only toward evening, the rain gradually stopped and the waitresses began to wipe off the tables. The manager stood under the arch of the gate and looked out for customers. And in fact one was already coming up the path through the woods. He wore a long-fringed plaid over his shoulders, his head was bowed down on his breast and at every step his outstretched arm brought his stick down on the ground far in front of him.

July 14. Isaac denies his wife before Abimelech, as Abraham earlier had denied his wife.

Confusion of the wells in Gerar. Verse repeated.
Jacob's sins. Esau's predestination.

A clock strikes gloomily. Listen to it as you enter the
house.

July 15. He ran to the woods to look for help, he
crossed the first hill almost in a bound, he sped up to the
sources of the downward-flowing brooks, he beat the air
with his hands, his breath came thickly through his nose
and mouth.

July 19.

Träume und weine, armes Geschlecht,
findest den Weg nicht, hast ihn verloren.
Wehe! ist dein Gruss am Abend. Wehe! am Morgen.

Ich will nichts, nur mich entreissen
Händen der Tiefe, die sich strecken,
mich Ohnmächtigen hinabzunehmen.
Schwer fall ich in die bereiten Hände.

Tönend erklang in der Ferne der Berge
langsame Rede. Wir horchten.

Ach, sie trugen, Larven der Hölle,
verhüllte Grimassen, eng an sich gedrückt den Leib.

Langer Zùg, langer Zug trägt den Unfertigen.[46]

A singular judicial procedure. The condemned man is
stabbed to death in his room by the executioner with no
other person present. He is seated at his table finishing

a letter in which he writes: O loved ones, O angels, at what height do you hover, unknowing, beyond the reach of my earthly hand——

July 20. A small bird flew out of a nearby chimney, perched on its edge, looked about, soared and flew away. It is no ordinary bird that flies out of a chimney. From a window on the first floor a girl looked up at the sky, saw the bird's upward flight, and cried: "There it goes, quick, there it goes!" and two children at once crowded to her side to see the bird.

Have mercy on me, I am sinful in every nook and cranny of my being. But my gifts were not entirely contemptible; I had some small talents, squandered them, unadvised creature that I was, am now near my end just at a time when outwardly everything might at last turn out well for me. Don't thrust me in among the lost. I know it is my ridiculous love of self that speaks here, ridiculous whether looked at from a distance or close at hand; but, as I am alive, I also have life's love of self, and if life is not ridiculous its necessary manifestations can't be either.—Poor dialectic!

If I am condemned, then I am not only condemned to die, but also condemned to struggle till I die.

Sunday morning, shortly before I left, you seemed to want to help me. I hoped. Until today a vain hope.

And no matter what my complaint, it is without conviction, even without real suffering; like the anchor of a lost ship, it swings far above the bottom in which it could catch hold.

Let me only have rest at night—childish complaint.

July 21. They called. The weather was fine. We stood up, a mixed lot of people, and assembled in front of the house. The street was silent as it always is in the early morning. A baker's boy put down his basket and watched us. All of us came running down the stairs at each other's heels, all the people living on the six floors were mingled indiscriminately together, I myself helped the merchant on the first floor put on the overcoat he had until then been dragging behind him. This merchant was our leader; that was only right, he had more experience of the world than any of us. First he arranged us in an orderly group, admonished the most restive of us to be quiet, took away the hat the bank clerk insisted on swinging and threw it across the street; each child's hand was taken by an adult.

July 22. A singular judicial procedure. The condemned man is stabbed to death in his cell by the executioner without any other person being permitted to be present. He is seated at the table finishing a letter or his last meal. A knock is heard, it is the executioner.

"Are you ready?" he asks. The content and sequence of his questions and actions are fixed for him by regulation, he cannot depart from it. The condemned man, who at first jumped up, now sits down again and stares straight before him or buries his face in his hands. Having received no reply, the executioner opens his instrument case on the cot, chooses the daggers and even now attempts to touch up their several edges here and there. It is very dark by now, he sets up a small lantern and lights it. The condemned man furtively turns his head toward the executioner, but shudders when he sees what he is doing, turns away again and has no desire to see more.

"Ready," the executioner says after a little while.

"Ready?" screams the condemned man, jumps up and now, however, looks directly at the executioner. "You're not going to kill me, not going to put me down on the cot and stab me to death, you're a human being after all, you can execute someone on a scaffold, with assistants and in the presence of magistrates, but not here in this cell, one man killing another!" And when the executioner, bent over his case, says nothing, the condemned man adds, more quietly: "It is impossible." And when the executioner even now says nothing, the condemned man goes on to say: "This singular judicial procedure was instituted just because it is impossible. The form is to be preserved, but the death penalty itself is no longer carried out. You will take me to another jail; I shall probably have to stay there a long time, but they will not execute me."

The executioner loosens a new dagger from its cotton sheath and says: "You are probably thinking of those fairy tales in which a servant is commanded to expose a child but does not do so and instead binds him over as apprentice to a shoemaker. Those are fairy tales; this, though, is not a fairy tale."——

August 21. For the collection: "All the beautiful phrases about transcending nature prove ineffectual in face of the primordial forces of life" (Essays against Monogamy).

August 27. Final conclusion after two dreadful days and nights: you can thank your official's vices—weakness, parsimony, vacillation, calculation, caution, etc.—that you haven't sent F. the card. It is possible that you might not have retracted it, that, I grant, is possible. What would have been the result? Some decisive action on your part, a revival? No. You have acted decisively several times already and nothing was improved by it. Don't try to explain it; I am sure you can explain the past, down to the last detail, considering that you are too timid to embark upon a future without having it thoroughly explained in advance—which is plainly impossible. What seems a sense of responsibility on your part, and honorable as such, is at bottom the official's spirit, childishness, a will broken by your father. Change this for the better, this is what to work at, this is what you can do at once. And that means, not to spare yourself (especially at the expense of a life you love, F.'s), for sparing yourself is impossible; this apparent sparing of yourself has brought you today to the verge of your destruction. It is not only the sparing of yourself so far as concerns F., marriage, children, responsibility, etc.; it is also the sparing of yourself so far as concerns the office you mope about in, the miserable room you don't stir out of. Everything. Then put a stop to all that. One cannot spare oneself, cannot calculate things in advance. You haven't the faintest idea of what would be better for you.

Tonight, for example, two considerations of equal strength and value battled in you at the expense of your brain and heart, you were equally worried on both their accounts; hence the impossibility of making calculations. What is left? Never again degrade yourself to the point where you become the battleground of a struggle that goes on with no regard as it were for you, and of which you feel nothing but the terrible blows of the warriors. Rise up, then. Mend your ways, escape officialdom, start seeing what you are instead of calculating what you should become. There is no question of your first task: become a soldier. Give up too those nonsensical comparisons you like to make between yourself and a Flaubert, a Kierkegaard, a Grillparzer. That is simply infantile. As a link in the chain of calculation, they undoubtedly serve as useful examples—or rather useless examples, for they are part of the whole useless chain of calculation; all by themselves, however, the comparisons are useless right off. Flaubert and Kierkegaard knew very clearly how matters stood with them, were men of decision, did not calculate but acted. But in your case—a perpetual succession of calculations, a monstrous four years' up and down. The comparison with Grillparzer is valid, perhaps, but you don't think Grillparzer a proper one to imitate, do you? an unhappy example whom future generations should thank for having suffered for them.

October 8. Förster: Wants the social relations that exist in school life to be made a subject of instruction.

The bringing up of children as a conspiracy on the part of adults. We lure them from their unconstrained rompings into our narrow dwelling by pretenses in which we perhaps believe, but not in the sense we pretend. (Who would not like to be a nobleman? Shut the door.)

The incompensable value of giving free rein to one's vices consists in this, that they rise into view in all their strength and size, even if, in the excitement of indulgence, one catches only a faint glimpse of them. One doesn't learn to be a sailor by exercising in a puddle, though too much training in a puddle can probably render one unfit to be a sailor.

October 16. Among the four conditions that the Hussites proposed to the Catholics as basis for an agreement, there was one that made all mortal sins—by which they meant "gluttony, drunkenness, unchastity, lying, perjury, usury, fee-taking for confessions and mass"—punishable by death. One faction even wanted to grant each and every individual the right to exact the death penalty on the spot whenever he saw anyone besmirching himself with one of these sins.

Is it possible that reason and desire first disclose the bare outlines of the future to me, and that I actually move step by step into this same future only under their tugs and blows?

We are permitted to crack that whip, the will, over us with our own hand.

October 18. From a letter to F.:
The matter is not so simple that I can accept without correction what you say of your mother, parents, flowers, the New Year, and the dinner company. You say that for you too it "would not be the greatest of pleasures to sit at table at home with your whole family." Of course, you merely express your own opinion when you say this, and are perfectly right not to consider whether or not it pleases me. Well, it doesn't please me. But it would certainly please me even less had you written the contrary. Please tell me as plainly as you can in what this unpleasantness consists and what you regard as its reasons. I know that we have already often spoken of the matter from my side, but it is difficult to grasp even a little of the truth of the matter.

Baldly put—hence with a harshness that doesn't quite correspond to the truth—my position is about as follows: I, who for the most part have been a dependent creature, have an infinite yearning for independence and freedom in all things. Rather put on blinkers and go my way to the limit than have the familiar pack mill around me and distract my gaze. For that reason it is easy for every word I say to my parents or they to me to become a stumbling block under my feet. Every relationship that I don't create or conquer by myself, even though it be in part to my own detriment, is worthless, it hinders my walking, I hate it or am close to hating it. The way is long, my strength is little, there is abundant reason for such hatred. However, I am descended from my parents, am linked to them and my sisters by blood, am sensible of it neither in my everyday affairs nor, as a result of their inevitable familiarity to me, in my special concerns, but at bottom have more respect for it than I realize. Sometimes this bond of blood too is the target of my hatred; the sight of the double bed at home, the used sheets, the nightshirts carefully laid out, can exasperate me to the point of nausea, can turn me inside out; it is as if I had not been definitively born, were continually born anew into the world out of the stale life in that stale room, had constantly to seek confirmation of myself there, were indissolubly joined with all that loathsomeness, in part even if not entirely, at least it still clogs my feet which want to run, they are still stuck fast in the original shapeless pulp. That is how it sometimes is.

But at other times again, I know that they are my parents after all, indispensable elements of my own being from whom I constantly draw strength, essential parts of me, not only obstacles. At such times I want them to be the best parents one could wish for: if I, in all my viciousness, rudeness, selfishness, and lack of affection, have nevertheless always trembled in front of them (and in fact do so today—such habits aren't broken), and if they again, Father from one side, Mother from the other, have inevitably almost broken my spirit, then I want them at least to be worthy of their victory. They have cheated me of what is mine and yet, without going insane, I can't revolt against the law of nature—and so hatred again and only hatred. (At times Ottla seems to me to be what I should want a mother to be: pure, truthful, honest, consistent. Humility and pride, sympathetic understanding and distance, devotion and independence, vision and courage in unerring balance. I mention Ottla because Mother is in her too, though it is impossible to discern.) Very well then, I want them to be worthy of it.

You belong to me, I have made you mine. I can't believe that there was ever a woman in a fairy tale fought for harder and more desperately than I have fought for you within myself, from the beginning, and always anew, and perhaps forever. You belong to me then, and so my relation to your people is similar to my relation to my own, although incomparably less intense, of course, both for good and for bad. They constitute a tie that hinders me (hinders me even if I should never exchange a word with them), and they are not—in the sense I have used the word above—worthy. I speak as frankly to you as I should to myself; don't take it amiss or look for arrogance in it, it isn't there, at least not where you might look for it.

When you are here, sitting at my parents' table, my vulnerability to what is hostile to me in my father and mother is of course much greater. My connection with the whole family seems to them to have grown much stronger (but it hasn't and shouldn't); I seem to them part of the chain one link of which is the bedroom near by (but I am not);

they hope to have found an accomplice in you against my opposition (they haven't found one); and they appear more ugly and contemptible in my eyes in the degree that I expect more from them under such circumstances.

If all this is as I say, then why don't I rejoice at your remark? Because I confront my family unceasingly flailing about me in a circle with knives, as it were, in order simultaneously to injure and defend them. Let me be entirely your representative in this, without your representing me in the same sense to your family. Is this too great a sacrifice for you, darling? It is a tremendous one, I know, and will be made easier for you only by the knowledge that my nature is such that I must take it from you by force if you do not voluntarily make me it. But if you do make it, then you have done a great deal for me. I will purposely refrain from writing to you for a day or two so that you can think it over undisturbed by me and give me your reply. A single word—so great is my confidence in you—will serve as answer.

October 20. Two gentlemen in the paddock were discussing a horse whose hindquarters a stable boy was rubbing down. "I haven't," said the white-haired elder man, squinting one eye somewhat as he gently gnawed his lower lip, "I haven't seen Atro for a week now, one's memory for horses is an uncertain thing no matter how much practice one has had. I miss qualities in Atro now that I distinctly remember him to have had. It is the total impression I speak of—the details, I am sure, are correct, though I do notice a flabbiness of his muscles here and there. Look here and here." His lowered head moved from side to side in scrutiny and his hands groped in the air.[47]

April 6. Today, in the tiny harbor where save for fishing boats only two ocean-going passenger steamers used to call, a strange boat lay at anchor. A clumsy old craft, rather low and very broad, filthy, as if bilge water had been poured over it, it still seemed to be dripping down the yellowish sides; the masts disproportionately tall, the upper third of the mainmast split; wrinkled, coarse, yellowish-brown sails stretched every which way between the yards, patched, too weak to stand against the slightest gust of wind.

I gazed in astonishment at it for a time, waited for someone to show himself on deck; no one appeared. A workman sat down beside me on the harbor wall. "Whose ship is that?" I asked; "this is the first time I've seen it."

"It puts in every two or three years," the man said, "and belongs to the Hunter Gracchus."

July 29. Court jester. Essay on court jesters.

The great days of the court jesters are probably gone never to return. Everything points in another direction, it cannot be denied. I at least have thoroughly delighted in the institution, even if it should now be lost to mankind.

My place was always far in the rear of the shop, completely in the dark, often you had to guess what it was that you held in your hand; in spite of this every bad stitch brought you a blow from the master.

Our King made no display of pomp; anyone who did not know him from his pictures would never have recognized him as the King. His clothes were badly made, not in our shop, however, of a skimpy material, his coat forever unbuttoned, flapping and wrinkled, his hat crumpled, clumsy, heavy boots, broad, careless movements of his arms, a strong face with a large, straight, masculine nose, a short mustache, dark, somewhat too sharp eyes, a powerful, well-shaped neck. Once he stopped in passing in the doorway of our shop, put his right hand up against the lintel of the door, and asked, "Is Franz here?" He knew everyone by name. I came out of my dark corner and made my way through the journeymen. "Come along," he said, after briefly glancing at me. "He's moving into the castle," he said to the master.

July 30. Miss K. Coquetry that ill suits the kind of person she is. She spreads, points, pouts her lips as if her fingers were invisibly shaping them. Makes sudden, probably nervous, though controlled movements which always take one by surprise—the way she arranges her skirt over her knees, for instance, or changes her seat. Her conversation contains a minimum of words and ideas, is unassisted by other people, is chiefly produced by turns of her head, gesticulations, various pauses, lively glances; if necessary, by clenching her little fists.

He disengaged himself from their midst. Mist blew about him. A round clearing in the woods. The phoenix in the underbrush. A hand continually making the sign of the cross on an invisible face. A cool, perpetual rain, a changing song, as if from a heaving breast.

A useless person. A friend? If I attempt to summon to mind what those attributes are which he possesses, what remains, even after the most charitable verdict, is only his voice, somewhat deeper than mine. If I cry out, "Saved!"— I mean if I were Robinson Crusoe and cried out, "Saved!"

—he would echo it in his deeper voice. If I were Korah and cried out, "Lost!" he would promptly be there with his deeper voice to echo it. One eventually grows weary of perpetually leading this bass fiddler around with one. He himself by no means does this cheerfully, he echoes me only because he must and can do nothing else. Occasionally, during a vacation, when for once I have time to turn my attention to such personal matters, I consult with him, in the garden perhaps, as to how I might get rid of him.

July 31. Sit in a train, forget the fact, and live as if you were at home; but suddenly recollect where you are, feel the onward-rushing power of the train, change into a traveler, take a cap out of your bag, meet your fellow travelers with a more sovereign freedom, with more insistence, let yourself be carried toward your destination by no effort of your own, enjoy it like a child, become a darling of the women, feel the perpetual attraction of the window, always have at least one hand extended on the window sill. Same situation, more precisely stated: Forget that you forgot, change in an instant into a child traveling by itself on an express train around whom the speeding, trembling car materializes in its every fascinating detail as if out of a magician's hand.

August 1. Dr. O.'s stories at the swimming pool of old Prague. The wild speeches Friedrich Adler [48] made against the rich during his student days, which everyone laughed at so; later he made a wealthy match and spoke no more.— When Dr. O. was a little boy and came from Amschelberg to attend the Gymnasium at Prague, he lived with a Jewish scholar whose wife was a saleswoman in a secondhand clothing store. Meals were brought in from a tavern. At half-past five every day, O. was awakened for prayers.—He provided for the education of all his younger brothers and sisters; it caused him a great deal of labor but gave him confidence and satisfaction. A certain Dr. A., who later became a treasury official and has long been retired (a great egoist), once advised him at that time to go away, hide, simply run away from his family, for otherwise they would be the ruin of him.

I tighten the reins.

August 2. Usually the one whom you are looking for lives next door. This isn't easy to explain, you must simply accept it as a fact. It is so deeply founded that there is nothing you can do about it, even if you should make an effort to. The reason is that you know nothing of this neighbor you are looking for. That is, you know neither that you are looking for him nor that he lives next door, in which case he very certainly lives next door. You may of course know this as a general fact in your experience; only such knowledge doesn't matter in the least, even if you expressly keep it forever in mind. I'll tell you of one such case——

Pascal arranges everything very tidily before God makes his appearance, but there must be a deeper, uneasier skepticism than that of a man cutting himself to bits with—indeed—wonderful knives, but still, with the calm of a butcher. Whence this calm? this confidence with which the knife is wielded? Is God a theatrical triumphal chariot that (granted the toil and despair of the stagehands) is hauled onto the stage from afar by ropes?

August 3. Once more I screamed at the top of my voice into the world. Then they shoved a gag into my mouth, tied my hands and feet and blindfolded me. I was rolled back and forth a number of times, I was set upright and knocked down again, this too several times, they jerked at my legs so that I jumped with pain; they let me lie quietly for a moment, but then, taking me by surprise, stabbed deep into me with something sharp, here and there, at random.

For years I have been sitting at the great intersection, but tomorrow, because the new Emperor is arriving, I intend to leave my post. As much on principle as from disinclination, I meddle in nothing that goes on around me. For a long time now I have even stopped begging; old passers-by give me something out of habit, out of loyalty, out of friendship, and the newcomers follow their example. I have a little basket beside me, and everybody tosses as much as he thinks proper into it. But for that very reason, because I bother with no one and in the tumult and absurdity of the street preserve the calmness of my outlook and the calmness of my soul, I understand better than anyone else everything that concerns me, my position, and what is rightfully my due. There can be no dispute about these questions, here only my opinion is of consequence. And therefore when a policeman, who naturally knows me very well but whom I just as naturally never noticed, halted beside me this morning and said, "Tomorrow the Emperor will arrive; see to it that you're not here tomorrow," I replied by asking him, "How old are you?"

The term "literature," when uttered in reproach, is a conversational catch-all for so much, that—there was probably some such intention in its usage from the very first—

it has gradually become a catch-all for ideas as well; the term deprives one of right perspective and causes the reproach to fall short and wide of its mark.

The alarm trumpets of the void.

A: I want to ask your advice.

B: Why mine?

A: I have confidence in you.

B: Why?

A: I have often seen you at our gatherings. And among us it is ultimately always a matter of gathering together to seek advice. We agree on that, don't we? No matter what sort of gathering it may be, whether we want to put on theatricals, or drink tea, or raise up spirits, or help the poor, it is always ultimately a matter of seeking advice. So many people with no one to advise them! And even more than would appear, for those who proffer advice at meetings of this kind do so only with their voices, in their hearts they desire to be advised themselves. Their double is always among the listeners, their words are particularly aimed at him. But he, more than anyone else, departs unsatisfied, disgusted, and drags his adviser after him to other meetings and the same game.

B: That's how it is?

A: Certainly, you see it yourself, don't you? But there is no particular merit in your discernment; all the world sees it, and its plea is so much the more insistent.

August 5. The afternoon in Radešovicz with Oskar. Sad, weak, made frequent efforts to keep track of the main question.

A: Good day.

B: You've been here once before? Right?

A: You recognize me? How surprising.

B: Several times already I've spoken to you in my thoughts. Now what was it you wanted the last time we met?

A: To ask your advice.

B: Correct. And was I able to give it to you?

A: No. Unfortunately, we couldn't agree even on how to put the question.

B: So that's how it was.

A: Yes. It was very unsatisfactory, but only for the moment, after all. One can't just get at the thing all at once. Couldn't we repeat the question once again?

B: Of course. Fire away.

A: Well then, my question is—

B: Yes?

A: My wife—

B: Your wife?

A: Yes, of course.

B: I don't understand. You have a wife?

A: ——

August 6.

A: I am not satisfied with you.

B: I won't ask why. I know.

A: And?

B: I am so powerless. I can change nothing. Shrug my shoulders and screw up my mouth, that's all; I can't do more.

A: I'll take you to my Master. Will you go?

B: I feel ashamed. How will he receive me? Go straight to the Master! It's not right.

A: Let me bear the responsibility. I'm taking you. Come. (*They go along a corridor.* A *knocks on a door. A voice calls out,* "*Come in.*" B *wants to run away, but* A *catches hold of him and they enter.*)

C: Who is the Master?

A: I thought— At his feet! throw yourself at his feet!

A: No way out, then?

B: I've found none.

A: And you're the one who knows the neighborhood best of all.

B: Yes.

August 7.

A: You're always hanging around the door here. Now what do you want?

B: Nothing, thank you.

A: Really! Nothing? Besides, I know you.

B: You must be mistaken.

A: No, no. You are B and went to school here twenty years ago. Yes or no?

B: All right, yes. I didn't dare introduce myself.

A: You do seem to have grown timid with the years. You weren't then.

B: Yes, then I wasn't. I repent me of everything as if I had done it this very hour.

A: You see, everything is paid for in this life.

B: Alas!

A: I told you so.

B: You told me so. But it *isn't* so. Things aren't paid for directly. What does my employer care if I chattered in school. That was no obstacle to my career, no.

The explorer felt too tired to give commands or to do anything. He merely took a handkerchief from his pocket, gestured as if he were dipping it in the distant bucket, pressed it to his brow and lay down beside the pit. He was found in this position by the two men the Commandant had sent out to fetch him. He jumped up when they spoke to him as if revived. With his hand on his heart he said, "I am a cur if I allow that to happen." But then he took his own words literally and began to run around on all fours. From time to time, however, he leaped erect, shook the fit off, so to speak, threw his arms around the neck of one of the men and tearfully exclaimed, "Why does all this happen to me!" and then hurried back to his post.[49]

August 8. And even if everything remained unchanged, the spike was still there, crookedly protruding from his shattered forehead as if it bore witness to some truth.[50]

As though all this were making the explorer aware that what was still to follow was solely his and the dead man's affair, he dismissed the soldier and the condemned man with a gesture of his hand; they hesitated, he threw a stone at them, and when they still deliberated, he ran up to them and struck them with his fists.

"What?" the explorer suddenly said. Had something been forgotten. A last word? A turn? An adjustment? Who can penetrate the confusion? Damned, miasmal tropical air, what are you doing to me? I don't know what is happening. My judgment has been left back at home in the North.

"What?" the explorer suddenly said. Had something been forgotten? A word? A turn? An adjustment? Very likely. Very probably. A gross error in the calculation, a fundamental misconception, the whole thing is going wrong. But who will set it right? Where is the man who will set it right? Where is the good old miller back home in the North who would stick these two grinning fellows between his millstones?

"Prepare the way for the snake!" came the shout. "Prepare the way for the great Madame!"

"We are ready," came the answering shout, "we are ready!" And we who were to prepare the way, renowned stone-crushers all, marched out of the woods. "Now!" our Commandant called out, blithely as always, "go to it, you snake-fodder!" Immediately we raised our hammers and for miles around the busiest hammering began. No pause was allowed, only a change from one hand to the other. The arrival of our snake was promised for the evening, by then everything had to be crushed to dust, our snake could not stand even the tiniest of stones. Where is there another snake so fastidious? She is a snake without peer, she has been thoroughly pampered by our labor and by now there is no one to compare with her. We do not understand, we deplore the fact that she still calls herself a snake. She should call herself Madame at least—though as Madame she is of course without peer too. But that is no concern of ours; our job is to make dust.

Hold the lamp up high, you up front there! The rest of you without a sound behind me! All in single file! And quiet! That was nothing. Don't be afraid, I'm responsible. I'll lead you out.

August 9. The explorer made a vague movement of his

hand, abandoned his efforts, again thrust the two men away from the corpse and pointed to the colony where they were to go at once. Their gurgling laughter indicated their gradual comprehension of his command; the condemned man pressed his face, which had been repeatedly smeared with grease, against the explorer's hand, the soldier slapped the explorer on the shoulder with his right hand—in his left hand he waved his gun—all three now belonged together.

The explorer had forcibly to ward off the feeling coming over him that in this case a perfect solution had been effected. He was stricken with fatigue and abandoned his intention of burying the corpse now. The heat, which was still on the increase—the explorer was unwilling to raise his head toward the sun only lest he grow dizzy—the sudden, final silence of the officer, the sight of the two men opposite staring strangely at him, and with whom every connection had been severed by the death of the officer, and lastly, the smooth, automatic refutation which the officer's contention had found here, all this—the explorer could no longer stand erect and sat down in the cane chair.

If his ship had slithered to him across this trackless sand to take him aboard—that he would have preferred to everything. He would have climbed aboard, except that from the ladder he would have once more denounced the officer for the horrible execution of the condemned man. "I'll tell them of it at home," he would have said, raising his voice so that the captain and the sailors bending in curiosity over the rail might hear him. "Executed?" the officer would have asked, with reason. "But here he is," he would have said, pointing to the man carrying the explorer's baggage. And in fact it was the condemned man, as the explorer proved to himself by looking sharply at him and scrutinizing his features.

"My compliments," the explorer was obliged to say, and said it gladly. "A conjuring trick?" he asked.

"No," the officer said, "a mistake on your part; I was executed, as you commanded." The captain and the sailors now listened even more attentively. And all saw together how the officer passed his hand across his brow to disclose a spike crookedly protruding from his shattered forehead.

It was during the period of the last great battles that the American government had to wage against the Indians. The fort deepest in Indian territory—it was also the best fortified—was commanded by General Samson, who had often distinguished himself in this place and possessed the unswerving confidence of the population and his soldiers. The shout, "General Samson!" was almost as good as a rifle against a single Indian.

One morning a scouting party out in the woods captured a young man, and in accordance with the standing order of the General—he took a personal interest even in the most trivial matters—brought him to headquarters. As the General was in conference at that moment with several farmers from the border district, the stranger was first brought before the adjutant, Lieutenant Colonel Otway.

"General Samson!" I cried, and staggered back a step. It was he who stepped out of the tall thicket. "Be quiet!" he said, pointing behind him. An escort of about ten men stumbled after him.

August 10. I was standing with my father in the lobby of a building; outside it was raining very hard. A man was about to hurry into the lobby from the street when he noticed my father. That made him stop. "Georg," he said slowly, as though he had gradually to bring old memories to the surface, and, holding out his hand, approached my father from the side.

"No, let me alone! No, let me alone!" I shouted without pause all the way along the streets, and again and again she laid hold of me, again and again the clawed hands of the siren struck at my breast from the side or across my shoulder.

Sept. 15.[51] You have the chance, as far as it is at all possible, to make a new beginning. Don't throw it away. If you insist on digging deep into yourself, you won't be able to avoid the muck that will well up. But don't wallow in it. If the infection in your lungs is only a symbol, as you say, a symbol of the infection whose inflammation is called F. and whose depth is its deep justification; if this is so then the medical advice (light, air, sun, rest) is also a symbol. Lay hold of this symbol.

O wonderful moment, masterful version, garden gone to seed. You turn the corner as you leave the house and the goddess of luck rushes toward you down the garden path.

Majestic presence, prince of the realm.

The village square abandoned to the night. The wisdom of the children. The primacy of the animals. The women. Cows moving across the square in the most matter-of-fact way.

September 18. Tear everything up.

September 19. Instead of the telegram—Very Welcome Michelob Station Feel Splendid Franz Ottla—which Mařenka twice took to Flöhau claiming not to have been able to send it because the post office had closed shortly before she arrived, I wrote a farewell letter and once again, at one blow, suppressed the violent beginnings of torment. Though the farewell letter is ambiguous, like my feelings.

It is the age of the infection rather than its depth and festering which makes it painful. To have it repeatedly ripped open in the same spot, though it has been operated on countless times, to have to see it taken under treatment again—that is what is bad.

The frail, uncertain, ineffectual being—a telegram knocks it over, a letter sets it on its feet, reanimates it, the silence that follows the letter plunges it into a stupor.

The cat's playing with the goats. The goats resemble: Polish Jews, Uncle S., I., E.W.

The manservant H. (who today left without dinner or saying goodbye; it is doubtful whether he will come tomorrow), the young woman and Mařenka are unapproachable in different but equally severe ways. I really feel constrained in their presence, as in the presence of animals in stalls when you tell them to do something and, surprisingly, they do it. Their case is the more difficult only because they so often seem approachable and understandable for a moment.

Have never understood how it is possible for almost everyone who writes to objectify his sufferings in the very midst of undergoing them; thus I, for example, in the midst of my unhappiness, in all likelihood with my head still smarting from unhappiness, sit down and write to someone: I am unhappy. Yes, I can even go beyond that and with as many flourishes as I have the talent for, all of which seem to have nothing to do with my unhappiness, ring simple, or contrapuntal, or a whole orchestration of changes on my theme. And it is not a lie, and it does not still my pain; it is simply a merciful surplus of strength at a moment when suffering has raked me to the bottom of my being and plainly exhausted all my strength. But then what kind of surplus is it?

Yesterday's letter to Max. Lying, vain, theatrical. A week in Zürau.

In peacetime you don't get anywhere, in wartime you bleed to death.

Dreamed of Werfel: He was saying that in Lower Austria, where he is stopping at present, by accident he lightly jostled against a man on the street, whereupon the latter swore at him shamefully. I have forgotten the precise words, I remember only that one of them was "barbarian" (from the World War), and that it ended with "you proletarian Turch." An interesting combination: "Turch" is a dialect word for "Turk"; "Turk" is a curse word apparently still part of a tradition deriving from the old wars against the Turks and the sieges of Vienna, and added to that the new epithet, "proletarian." Excellently characterizes the simplicity and backwardness of his insulter, for today neither "proletarian" nor "Turk" is a real curse word.

September 21. F. was here, traveled thirty hours to see

me; I should have prevented her. As I see it, she is suffering the utmost misery and the guilt is essentially mine. I myself am unable to take hold of myself, am as helpless as I am unfeeling, think of the disturbance of a few of my comforts and, as my only concession, condescend to act my part. In single details she is wrong, wrong in defending what she calls—or what are really—her rights, but taken all together, she is an innocent person condemned to extreme torture; I am guilty of the wrong for which she is being tortured, and am in addition the torturer.— With her departure (the carriage in which she and Ottla are riding goes around the pond, I cut across and am close to her once more) and a headache (the last trace in me of my acting), the day ends.

A dream about my father: There was a small audience (to characterize it, Mrs. Fanta was there) before which my father was making public for the first time a scheme of his for social reform. He was anxious to have this select audience, an especially select one in his opinion, undertake to make propaganda for his scheme. On the surface he expressed this much more modestly, merely requesting the audience, after they should have heard his views, to let him have the address of interested people who might be invited to a large public meeting soon to take place. My father had never yet had any dealings with these people, consequently took them much too seriously, had even put on a black frock coat, and described his scheme with that extreme solicitude which is the mark of an amateur. The company, in spite of the fact that they weren't at all prepared for a lecture, recognized at once that he was offering them, with all the pride of originality, what was nothing more than an old, outworn idea that had been thoroughly debated long ago. They let my father feel this. He had anticipated the objection, however, and, with magnificent conviction of its futility (though it often appeared to tempt even him), with a faint bitter smile, put his case even more emphatically. When he had finished, one could perceive from the general murmur of annoyance that he had convinced them neither of the originality nor the practicability of his scheme. Not many were interested in it. Still, here and there someone was to be found who, out of kindness, and perhaps because he knew me, offered him a few addresses. My father, completely unruffled by the general mood, had cleared away his lecture notes and picked up the piles of white slips that he had ready for writing down the few addresses. I could hear only the name of a certain Privy Councillor Střižanowski, or something similar.

Later I saw my father sitting on the floor, his back against the sofa, as he sits when he plays with Felix.[52] Alarmed, I asked him what he was doing. He was pondering his scheme.

September 22. Nothing.

September 25. On the way to the woods. You have destroyed everything without having really possessed it. How do you intend to put it together again? What strength still remains to the roving spirit for the greatest of all labors?

Das neue Geschlecht by Tagger—miserable, loudmouthed, lively, skilful, well written in spots, with faint tremors of amateurishness. What right has he to make a big stir? At bottom he is as miserable as I and everybody else.

Not entirely a crime for a tubercular to have children.

Flaubert's father was tubercular. Choice: either the child's lungs will warble (very pretty expression for the music the doctor puts his ear to one's chest to hear), or it will be a Flaubert. The trembling of the father while off in the emptiness the matter is being discussed.

I can still have passing satisfaction from works like *A Country Doctor*, provided I can still write such things at all (very improbable). But happiness only if I can raise the world into the pure, the true, and the immutable.

The whips with which we lash each other have put forth many knots these five years.

September 28. Outline of my conversations with F.
I: This, then, is what I have come to.
F.: This is what *I* have come to.
I: This is what I have brought you to.
F.: True.

I would put myself in death's hands, though. Remnant of a faith. Return to a father. Great Day of Atonement.[53]

From a letter to F., perhaps the last (October 1):
If I closely examine what is my ultimate aim, it turns out that I am not really striving to be good and to fulfil the demands of a Supreme Judgment, but rather very much the contrary: I strive to know the whole human and animal community, to recognize their basic predilections, desires, moral ideals, to reduce these to simple rules and as quickly as possible trim my behavior to these rules in order that I may find favor in the whole world's eyes; and, indeed (this is the inconsistency), so much favor that in the end I could openly perpetrate the iniquities within me without alienat-

ing the universal love in which I am held—the only sinner who won't be roasted. To sum up, then, my sole concern is the human tribunal, which I wish to deceive, moreover, though without practicing any actual deception.

October 8. In the meantime: letter of complaint from F.; G.B. threatens me with writing a letter. Disconsolate state (lumbago). Feeding the goats; field tunneled by mice; digging potatoes ("How the wind blows up our arses"); picking hips; the peasant F. (seven girls, one of them short, a sweet look, a white rabbit on her shoulder); a picture in the room, "Emperor Franz Josef in the Capuchin Tomb"; the peasant K. (a powerful man; loftily recited the whole history of his farm, yet friendly and kind). General impression given one by peasants: noblemen who have escaped into agriculture, where they have arranged their work so wisely and humbly that it fits perfectly into everything and they are protected against all insecurity and worry until their blissful death. True dwellers on this earth.— The boys who ran over the broad fields in the evening in pursuit of the fleeing, scattered herds of cattle, and who at the same time had to keep yanking round a young fettered bull that refused to follow.

Dickens' *Copperfield*. "The Stoker" a sheer imitation of Dickens, the projected novel even more so. The story of the trunk, the boy who delights and charms everyone, the menial labor, his sweetheart in the country house, the dirty houses, *et al.*, but above all the method. It was my intention, as I now see, to write a Dickens novel, but enhanced by the sharper lights I should have taken from the times and the duller ones I should have got from myself. Dickens' opulence and great, careless prodigality, but in consequence passages of awful insipidity in which he wearily works over effects he has already achieved. Gives one a barbaric impression because the whole does not make sense, a barbarism that I, it is true, thanks to my weakness and wiser for my epigonism, have been able to avoid. There is a heartlessness behind his sentimentally overflowing style. These rude characterizations which are artificially stamped on everyone and without which Dickens would not be able to get on with his story even for a moment. (Walser resembles him in his use of vague, abstract metaphors.)

October 9. At the peasant Lüftner's. The great hall. All of it quite theatrical. His nervous hee-hee and ha-ha, banged on the table, raised his arms, shrugged his shoulders and lifted his beer glass like one of Wallenstein's men. His wife beside him, an old woman whom he married ten years ago when he was her hired hand. Is a passionate hunter, neglects the farm. Two huge horses in the stable, Homeric figures in a fleeting ray of sunshine coming through the stable windows.

October 15. On the highway to Oberklee in the evening; went because the housekeeper and two Hungarian soldiers were sitting in the kitchen.

The view from Ottla's window in the twilight, yonder a house and immediately behind it the open fields.

K. and his wife in their fields on the slope opposite my window.

October 21. Beautiful day, sunny, warm, no wind.

Most dogs bark pointlessly, even if someone is just walking by in the distance; but some, perhaps not the best watchdogs, yet rational creatures, quietly walk up to a stranger, sniff at him, and bark only if they smell something suspicious.

November 6. Sheer impotence.

November 10. I haven't yet written down the decisive thing, I am still going in two directions. The work awaiting me is enormous.

Dreamed of the battle of the Tagliamento. A plain, the river wasn't really there, a crowd of excited onlookers ready to run forward or backward as the situation changed. In front of us a plateau whose plainly visible edge was alternately bare and overgrown with tall bushes. Upon the plateau and beyond Austrians were fighting. Everyone was tense; what would be the outcome? By way of diversion you could from time to time look at isolated clumps on the dark slope, from behind which one or two Italians were firing. But that had no importance, though we did take a few steps backward in flight. Then the plateau again: Austrians ran along the bare edge, pulled up abruptly behind the bushes, ran again. Things were apparently going badly, and moreover it was incomprehensible how they could ever go well; how could one merely human being ever conquer other human beings who were imbued with a will to defend themselves? Great despair, there will have to be a general retreat. A Prussian major appeared who had been watching the battle with us all the while; but when he calmly stepped forward into the suddenly deserted terrain, he seemed a new apparition. He put two fingers of each hand into his mouth and whistled the way one whistles to a dog, though affectionately. This was a signal to his detachment, which had been waiting close by and now marched forward. They were Prussian Guards, silent young men, not many, perhaps only a company, all seemed to be officers, at least they carried long sabers and their uniforms were dark. When they marched by us, with short steps, slowly, in close order, now and then looking at us, the matter-of-factness of their death march was at once stirring, solemn and a promise of victory. With a feeling of relief at the intercession of these men, I woke up.*

June 27. A new diary, really only because I have been reading the old ones. A number of reasons and intentions, now, at a quarter to twelve, impossible to ascertain.

June 30. Was in Rieger Park. Walked up and down with J.[54] beside the jasmine bushes. False and sincere, false in my sighs, sincere in my feeling of closeness to her, in my trustfulness, in my feeling of security. Uneasy heart.

July 6. The same thought continually, desire, anxiety. Yet calmer than usual, as if some great development were going forward the distant tremor of which I feel. Too much said.

December 5. Again pulled through this terrible, long, narrow crack; it can only be forced through in a dream. On purpose and awake, one could certainly never do it.

December 8. Spent Monday, a holiday, in the park, the restaurant and the Gallerie. Sorrow and joy, guilt and innocence, like two hands indissolubly clasped together; one would have to cut through flesh, blood and bones to part them.

December 9. A lot of Eleseus.[55] But wherever I turn, the black wave rushes down on me.

* Final entry of 1917. There are no entries for 1918.

December 11. Thursday. Cold. With J. in Rieger Park, said not a word. Seduction on the Graben. All this is too difficult. I am not sufficiently prepared. It is the same thing, in a certain sense, as twenty-six years ago my teacher Beck saying, of course without realizing the prophetic joke he was making: "Let him continue in the fifth grade for a while, he still isn't strong enough; rushing him in this way will have its consequences later on." And in fact such has been my growth, like a shoot forced too soon and forgotten; there is a certain hothouse delicacy in the way in which I shrink from a puff of wind, if you like, even something affecting in it, but that is all. Like Eleseus and his spring trips to the cities. By the way, he is not to be underestimated: Eleseus could have become the hero of the book, and in Hamsun's youth such would probably have happened.

January 6. His every action seems extraordinarily new to him. If it had not this fresh and living quality, of itself it would inevitably be something out of the old swamp of hell, this he knows. But this freshness deceives him: it allows him to forget his knowledge, or be heedless of it, or, though he see through the freshness, see without pain.

Today is undoubtedly the day, is it not, on which progress prepares to progress farther?

January 9. Superstition and principle and what makes life possible: Through a heaven of vice a hell of virtue is reached. So easily? So dirtily? So unbelievably? Superstition is easy.

A segment has been cut out of the back of his head. The sun, and the whole world with it, peep in. It makes him nervous, it distracts him from his work, and moreover it irritates him that just he should be the one to be debarred from the spectacle.

It is no disproof of one's presentiment of an ultimate liberation if the next day one's imprisonment continues on unchanged, or is even made straiter, or if it is even expressly stated that it will never end. All this can rather be the necessary preliminary to an ultimate liberation.[56]

October 15. About a week ago gave M.[57] all the diaries. A little freer? No. Am I still able to keep a diary? It will in any case be a different kind of diary, or rather it will hide itself away, there won't be any diary at all; only with the greatest of effort could I note something down on Hardt, for example, though I was rather taken with him. It is as if I had already written everything there was to write about him long ago, or, what is the same thing, as if I were no longer alive. I could probably write about M., but would not willingly do it, and moreover it would be aimed too directly at myself; I no longer need to make myself so minutely conscious of such things, I am not so forgetful as I used to be in this respect, I am a memory come alive, hence my insomnia.

October 16. Sunday. The misery of having perpetually to begin, the lack of the illusion that anything is more than, or even as much as, a beginning, the foolishness of those who do not know this and play football, for example, in order at last "to advance the ball," one's own foolishness buried within one as if in a coffin, the foolishness of those who think they see a real coffin here, hence a coffin that one can transport, open, destroy, exchange.

Among the young women up in the park. No envy. Enough imagination to share their happiness, enough judgment to know I am too weak to have such happiness, foolish enough to think I see to the bottom of my own and their situation. Not foolish enough; there is a tiny crack there, the wind whistles through it and spoils the full effect.

Should I greatly yearn to be an athlete, it would probably be the same thing as my yearning to go to heaven and to be permitted to be as despairing there as I am here.

No matter how sorry a constitution I may have, even if—"given the same circumstances"—it be the sorriest in the world (particularly in view of my lack of energy), I must do the best I can with it (even in my sense of the word)—it is hollow sophistry to argue that there is only one thing to be done with such a constitution, which must perforce be its best, and that that one thing is to despair.

October 17. There may be a purpose lurking behind the fact that I never learned anything useful and—the two are connected—have allowed myself to become a physical wreck. I did not want to be distracted, did not want to be distracted by the pleasures life has to give a useful and healthy man. As if illness and despair were not just as much of a distraction!

There are several ways in which I could complete this thought and so reach a happy conclusion for myself, but don't dare, and don't believe—at least today, and most of the time as well—that a happy solution exists.

I do not envy particular married couples, I simply envy all married couples together; and even when I do envy one couple only, it is the happiness of married life in general, in all its infinite variety, that I envy—the happiness to be found in any one marriage, even in the likeliest case, would probably plunge me into despair.

I don't believe people exist whose inner plight resembles mine; still, it is possible for me to imagine such people—but that the secret raven forever flaps about their heads as it does about mine, even to imagine that is impossible.

It is astounding how I have systematically destroyed myself in the course of the years, it was like a slowly widening breach in a dam, a purposeful action. The spirit that brought it about must now be celebrating triumphs; why doesn't it let me take part in them? But perhaps it hasn't yet achieved its purpose and can therefore think of nothing else.

October 18. Eternal childhood. Life calls again.

It is entirely conceivable that life's splendor forever lies in wait about each one of us in all its fulness, but veiled from view, deep down, invisible, far off. It *is* there, though, not hostile, not reluctant, not deaf. If you summon it by the right word, by its right name, it will come. This is the essence of magic, which does not create but summons.

October 19. The essence of the Wandering in the Wilderness. A man who leads his people along this way with a shred (more is unthinkable) of consciousness of what is happening. He is on the track of Canaan all his life; it is incredible that he should see the land only when on the verge of death. This dying vision of it can only be intended to illustrate how incomplete a moment is human life, incomplete because a life like this could last forever and still be nothing but a moment. Moses fails to enter Canaan not because his life is too short but because it is a human life. This ending of the Pentateuch bears a resemblance to the final scene of the *Education sentimentale*.

Anyone who cannot come to terms with his life while he is alive needs one hand to ward off a little his despair over his fate—he has little success in this—but with his other hand he can note down what he sees among the ruins, for he sees different (and more) things than do the others; after all, dead as he is in his own lifetime, he is the real survivor. This assumes that he does not need both hands, or more hands than he has, in his struggle against despair.

October 20. In the afternoon Langer, then Max, who read *Franzi* aloud.

A short dream, during an agitated, short sleep, in agitation clung to it with a feeling of boundless happiness. A dream with many ramifications, full of a thousand connections that became clear in a flash; but hardly more than the basic mood remains: My brother had committed a crime, a murder, I think, I and other people were involved in the crime; punishment, solution and salvation approached from afar, loomed up powerfully, many signs indicated their ineluctable approach; my sister, I think, kept calling out these signs as they appeared and I kept greeting them with insane exclamations, my insanity increased as they drew nearer. I thought I should never be able to forget my fragmentary exclamations, brief sentences merely, because of their succinctness, and now don't clearly remember a single one. I could only have uttered brief exclamations be-

cause of the great effort it cost me to speak—I had to puff
out my cheeks and at the same time contort my mouth as
if I had a toothache before I could bring a word out. My
feeling of happiness lay in the fact that I welcomed so
freely, with such conviction and such joy, the punishment
that came, a sight that must have moved the gods, and I felt
the gods' emotion almost to the point of tears.

October 21. It had been impossible for him to enter the
house, for he had heard a voice saying to him: "Wait till I
lead you in!" And so he continued to lie in the dust in
front of the house, although by now, probably, everything
was hopeless (as Sarah would say).

All is imaginary—family, office, friends, the street, all
imaginary, far away or close at hand, the woman; the truth
that lies closest, however, is only this, that you are beating
your head against the wall of a windowless and doorless
cell.

October 22. A connoisseur, an expert, someone who
knows his field, knowledge, to be sure, that cannot be im-
parted but that fortunately no one seems to stand in need
of.

October 23. A film about Palestine in the afternoon.

October 25. Ehrenstein yesterday.

My parents were playing cards; I sat apart, a perfect
stranger; my father asked me to take a hand, or at least to
look on; I made some sort of excuse. What is the meaning
of these refusals, oft repeated since my childhood? I could

have availed myself of invitations to take part in social, even, to an extent, public life; everything required of me I should have done, if not well at least in middling fashion; even card-playing would probably not have bored me overmuch—yet I refused. Judging by this, I am wrong when I complain that I have never been caught up in the current of life, that I never made my escape from Prague, was never made to learn a sport or trade, and so forth—I should probably have refused every offer, just as I refused the invitation to play cards. I allowed only absurd things to claim my attention, my law studies, the job at the office, and later on such senseless additional occupations as a little gardening, carpentering, and the like; these later occupations are to be looked on as the actions of a man who throws a needy beggar out the door and then plays the benefactor by himself by passing alms from his right hand to his left.

I always refused, out of general weakness, probably, and in particular out of weakness of will—it was rather a long time before I understood as much. I used to consider this refusal a good sign (misled by the vague great hopes I cherished for myself); today only a remnant of this benevolent interpretation remains.

October 29. A few evenings later I did actually join in, to the extent of keeping score for my mother. But it begot no intimacy, or whatever trace there was of it was smothered under weariness, boredom and regret for the wasted time. It would always have been thus. I have seldom, very seldom crossed this borderland between loneliness and fellowship, I have even been settled there longer than in loneliness itself. What a fine bustling place was Robinson Crusoe's island in comparison!

October 30. In the afternoon to the theater, Pallenberg.

The possibilities within me, I won't say to act or write *The Miser*, but to be the miser himself. It would need only a sudden determined movement of my hands, the entire orchestra gazes in fascination at the spot above the conductor's stand where the baton will rise.

Feeling of complete helplessness.

What is it that binds you more intimately to these impenetrable, talking, eye-blinking bodies than to any other thing, the penholder in your hand, for example? Because you belong to the same species? But you don't belong to the same species, that's the very reason why you raised this question.

The impenetrable outline of human bodies is horrible.

The wonder, the riddle of my not having perished already, of the silent power guiding me. It forces one to this absurdity: "Left to my own resources, I should have long ago been lost." My own resources.

November 1. Werfel's *Goat Song*.

Free command of the world at the expense of its laws. Imposition of the law. The happiness in obeying the law.

But the law cannot merely be imposed upon the world, and then everything left to go on as before except that the new lawgiver be free to do as he pleases. Such would be not law, but arbitrariness, revolt against law, self-defeat.

November 2. Vague hope, vague confidence.

An endless, dreary Sunday afternoon, an afternoon swallowing down whole years, its every hour a year. By turns walked despairingly down empty streets and lay quietly on the couch. Occasionally astonished by the leaden, meaningless clouds almost uninterruptedly drifting by. "You are reserved for a great Monday!" Fine, but Sunday will never end.

November 7. This inescapable duty to observe oneself: if someone else is observing me, naturally I have to observe myself too; if none observes me, I have to observe myself all the closer.

I envy the ease with which all those who fall out with me, or grow indifferent, or find me a nuisance, can shake me off—provided, probably, that it is not a life-and-death matter for me; once, with F., when it seemed to be a matter of life and death, it was not easy to shake me off, though of course I was young then, and strong, with strong desires.

December 1. After paying four calls on me, M. left; she goes away tomorrow. Four calmer days in the midst of tormented ones. I feel no sorrow at her departure, no real sorrow; it is a long way from this unconcern to the point where her departure would cause me endless sorrow. Sorrow, I confess it, is not the greatest evil.

December 2. Writing letters in my parents' room—the forms my decline takes are inconceivable! This thought lately, that as a little child I had been defeated by my father and because of ambition have never been able to quit the battlefield all these years despite the perpetual defeats I suffer.— Always M. or not M.—but a principle, a light in the darkness!

December 6. From a letter: "During this dreary winter I warm myself by it." Metaphors are one among many things which make me despair of writing. Writing's lack of independence of the world, its dependence on the maid who tends the fire, on the cat warming itself by the stove; it is even dependent on the poor old human being warming himself by the stove. All these are independent activities ruled by their own laws; only writing is helpless, cannot live in itself, is a joke and a despair.

Two children, alone in their house, climbed into a large trunk; the cover slammed shut, they could not open it, and suffocated.

December 20. Suffered much in my thoughts.

I was startled out of a deep sleep. By the light of a candle I saw a strange man sitting at a little table in the center of the room. Broad and heavy, he sat in the dim light, his un-buttoned winter coat making him appear even broader.

Don't forget:

Raabe, while dying, when his wife stroked his forehead: "How pleasant."

The toothless mouth of the grandfather laughing at his grandchild.

Undeniably, there is a certain joy in being able calmly to write down: "Suffocation is inconceivably horrible." Of course it is inconceivable—that is why I have written noth-ing down.

December 23. Again sat over *Náš Skautík*.[58] Ivan Ilyich.[59]

January 16. This past week I suffered something very like a breakdown; the only one to match it was on that night two years ago; apart from then I have never experienced its like. Everything seemed over with, even today there is no great improvement to be noticed. One can put two interpretations on the breakdown, both of which are probably correct.

First: breakdown, impossible to sleep, impossible to stay awake, impossible to endure life, or, more exactly, the course of life. The clocks are not in unison; the inner one runs crazily on at a devilish or demoniac or in any case inhuman pace, the outer one limps along at its usual speed. What else can happen but that the two worlds split apart, and they do split apart, or at least clash in a fearful manner. There are doubtless several reasons for the wild tempo of the inner process; the most obvious one is introspection, which will suffer no idea to sink tranquilly to rest but must pursue each one into consciousness, only itself to become an idea, in turn to be pursued by renewed introspection.

Second: This pursuit, originating in the midst of men, carries one in a direction away from them. The solitude that for the most part has been forced on me, in part voluntarily sought by me—but what was this if not compulsion too?—is now losing all its ambiguity and approaches its denouement. Where is it leading? The strongest likelihood is, that it may lead to madness; there is nothing more to say, the pursuit goes right through me and rends me asunder. Or I can—can I?—manage to keep my feet somewhat and be carried along in the wild pursuit. Where, then, shall I be brought? "Pursuit," indeed, is only a metaphor. I can also say, "assault on the last earthly frontier," an assault, moreover, launched from below, from mankind, and since this too is a metaphor, I can replace it by the metaphor of an assault from above, aimed at me from above.

All such writing is an assault on the frontiers; if Zionism

had not intervened, it might easily have developed into a new secret doctrine, a Kabbalah. There are intimations of this. Though of course it would require genius of an unimaginable kind to strike root again in the old centuries, or create the old centuries anew and not spend itself withal, but only then begin to flower forth.

January 17. Hardly different.

January 18. A moment of thought: Resign yourself, learn (learn, forty-year-old) to rest content in the moment (yes, once you could do it). Yes, in the moment, the terrible moment. It is not terrible, only your fear of the future makes it so. And also looking back on it in retrospect. What have you done with your gift of sex? It was a failure, in the end that is all that they will say. But it might easily have succeeded. A mere trifle, indeed so small as not to be perceived, decided between its failure and success. Why are you surprised? So it was with the greatest battles in the history of the world. Trifles decide trifles.

M. is right: fear means unhappiness but it does not follow from this that courage means happiness; not courage, which possibly aims at more than our strength can achieve (there were perhaps only two Jews in my class possessed of courage, and both shot themselves while still at school or shortly after); not courage, then, but fearlessness with its calm, open eye and stoical resolution. Don't force yourself to do anything, yet don't feel unhappy that you force yourself, or that if you were to do anything, you would have to force yourself. And if you don't force yourself, don't hanker after the possibilities of being forced. Of course, it is never as clear as all that, or rather, it is; it is always as clear as all that; for instance: sex keeps gnawing at me, hounds me day and night, I should have to conquer **fear** and shame and probably sorrow too to satisfy it; yet on the other hand I am certain that I should at once take advantage, with no feeling of fear or sorrow or shame, of the first opportunity to present itself quickly, close at hand, and willingly; according to the above, then, I am left with the law that fear, etc. should not be conquered (but also that one should not continually dally with the idea of conquest), but rather take advantage of opportunities as they come (and not complain if none should come). It is true that there is a middle ground between "doing" and the "opportunity to do," namely this, to make, to tempt one's "opportunities" to one, a practice I have unfortunately followed not only in this but everything. As far as the "law" is concerned, there is hardly anything to be said against this, though this "tempting" of opportunities, especially when it makes use of ineffectual expedients, bears a considerable resemblance to "dallying with the idea of conquest," and there is no trace in it of calm, open-eyed fearlessness. Despite the fact that it satisfies the "letter" of the "law," there is something detestable in it which must be unconditionally shunned. To be sure, one would have to force oneself to shun it—and so I shall never have done with the matter.

January 19. What meaning have yesterday's conclusions today? They have the same meaning as yesterday, are true, except that the blood is oozing away in the chinks between the great stones of the law.

The infinite, deep, warm, saving happiness of sitting beside the cradle of one's child opposite its mother.

There is in it also something of this feeling: matters no

longer rest with you, unless you wish it so. In contrast, this feeling of those who have no children: it perpetually rests with you, whether you will or no, every moment to the end, every nerve-racking moment, it perpetually rests with you, and without result. Sisyphus was a bachelor.

Evil does not exist; once you have crossed the threshold, all is good. Once in another world, you must hold your tongue.

The two questions: [60]
Because of several piddling signs I am ashamed to mention, it was my impression that your recent visits were indeed kind and noble as ever but somewhat tiresome to you nevertheless, somewhat forced, too, like the visits one pays an invalid. Is my impression correct?
Did you find in the diaries some final proof against me?

January 20. A little calmer. How needed it was. No sooner is it a little calmer with me than it is almost too calm. As though I have the true feeling of myself only when I am unbearably unhappy. That is probably true too.

Seized by the collar, dragged through the streets, pushed through the door. In abstract, that is how it is; in reality, there are counterforces, only a trifle less violent than the forces they oppose—the trifle that keeps life and torment alive. I the victim of both.

This "too calm." It is as if the possibility of a calm creative life—and so creativity in general—were somehow closed to me because of physical reasons, because of year-long physical torments (confidence! confidence!)—for torment has no meaning for me beyond itself, is closed off against everything.

The torso: seen in profile, from the top of the stocking up, knee, thigh and hip of a dark woman.

Longing for the country? It isn't certain. The country calls forth the longing, the infinite longing.

M. is right about me: "All things are glorious, only not for me, and rightly so." I say rightly, and show that I am sanguine at least to this extent. Or am I? For it is not really "rightness" that I am thinking of; life, because of its sheer power to convince, has no room in it for right and wrong. As in the despairing hour of death you cannot meditate on right and wrong, so you cannot in the despairing hour of life. It is enough that the arrows fit exactly in the wounds that they have made.

On the other hand, there is no trace in me of a general condemnation of my generation.

January 21. As yet, it is not too calm. In the theater suddenly, when I see Florestan's prison, the abyss opens. Everything—singers, music, audience, neighbors, everything—more remote than the abyss.

No one's task was as difficult, so far as I know. One might say that it is not a task at all, not even an impossible one, it is not even impossibility itself, it is nothing, it is not even as much of a child as the hope of a barren woman. But nevertheless it is the air I breathe, so long as I shall breathe at all.

I fell asleep past midnight, awoke at five, a remarkable

achievement for me, remarkable good fortune; apart from that I still felt sleepy. My good fortune, however, proved my misfortune, for now the inevitable thought came: you don't deserve so much good fortune; all the venging furies flung themselves upon me, I saw their enraged chieftain wildly spread her fingers and threaten me, or horribly strike cymbals. The excitement of the two hours until seven o'clock not only devoured what benefit I had got from sleep but made me tremulous and uneasy all day.

Without forebears, without marriage, without heirs, with a fierce longing for forebears, marriage and heirs. They all of them stretch out their hands to me: forebears, marriage and heirs, but too far away for me.

There is an artificial, miserable substitute for everything, for forebears, marriage and heirs. Feverishly you contrive these substitutes, and if the fever has not already destroyed you, the hopelessness of the substitutes will.

January 22. Nocturnal resolve.

The remark about "bachelors remembered from our youth" was clairvoyant, though of course under very favorable circumstances.[61] My resemblance to Uncle Rudolf, however, is even more disconcerting: both of us quiet (I less so), both dependent on our parents (I more so), at odds with our fathers, loved by our mothers (he in addition condemned to the horror of living with his father, though of course his father was likewise condemned to live with him), both of us shy, excessively modest (he more so), both regarded as noble, good men—there is nothing of these qualities in me and, so far as I know, very little in him (shyness, modesty, timidity are accounted noble and good because they offer little resistance to other people's aggressive impulses)—both hypochondriacal at first, then really ill, both, for do-nothings, kept fairly well by the world (he, because he was less of a do-nothing, kept much more poorly, so far as it is possible to make a comparison now), both officials (he a better one), both living the most unvarying lives, with no trace of any development, young to the end of our days ("well-preserved" is a better expression), both on the verge of insanity; he, far away from Jews, with tremendous courage, with tremendous vitality (by which one can measure the degree of the danger of insanity) escaped into the church where, so far as one could tell, his tendencies to madness were somewhat held in check, he himself had probably not been able for years to hold himself in check. One difference in his favor, or disfavor, was his having had less artistic talent than I, he could therefore have chosen a better path in life for himself in his youth, was not inwardly pulled apart, not even by ambition. Whether he had had to contend (inwardly) with women I do not know, a story by him that I read would indicate as much; when I was a child, moreover, they spoke of something of the sort. I know much too little about him, I don't dare ask about it. Besides, up to this point I have been writing about him as irreverently as if he were alive. It isn't true that he was not good, I never found a trace of niggardliness, envy, hate or greed in him; he was probably too unimportant a person to be able to help others. He was infinitely more innocent than I, there is no comparison. In single details he was my caricature, in essentials I am his.

January 23. A feeling of fretfulness again. From what did it arise? From certain thoughts which are quickly forgotten but leave my fretfulness unforgettably behind. Sooner than the thoughts themselves I could list the places in which they occurred to me; one, for example, on the little path that passes the Altneu Synagogue. Fretful too because of a certain sense of contentment that now and then drew near me, though timidly enough and sufficiently far off. Fretful too that my nocturnal resolve remains merely a resolve. Fretful that my life till now has been merely marking time, has progressed at most in the sense that decay progresses in a rotten tooth. I have not shown the faintest firmness of resolve in the conduct of my life. It was as if I, like everyone else, had been given a point from which to prolong the radius of a circle, and had then, like everyone else, to describe my perfect circle round this point. Instead, I was forever starting my radius only constantly to be forced at once to break it off. (Examples: piano, violin, languages, Germanics, anti-Zionism, Zionism, Hebrew, gardening, carpentering, writing, marriage attempts, an apartment of my own.) The center of my imaginary circle bristles with the beginnings of radii, there is no room left for a new attempt; no room means old age and weak nerves, and never to make another attempt means the end. If I sometimes prolonged the radius a little farther than usual, in the case of my law studies, say, or engagements, everything was made worse rather than better just because of this little extra distance.

Told M. about the night, unsatisfactory. Accept your symptoms, don't complain of them; immerse yourself in your suffering.

Heart oppression.

The second opinion kept in reserve. The third opinion: already forgotten.

January 24. How happy are the married men, young and old both, in the office. Beyond my reach, though if it were within my reach I should find it intolerable, and yet it is the only thing with which I have any inclination to appease my longing.

Hesitation before birth. If there is a transmigration of souls then I am not yet on the bottom rung. My life is a hesitation before birth.

Steadfastness. I don't want to pursue any particular course of development, I want to change my place in the world entirely, which actually means that I want to go to another planet; it would be enough if I could exist alongside myself, it would even be enough if I could consider the spot on which I stand as some other spot.

My development was a simple one. While I was still contented I wanted to be discontented, and with all the means that my time and tradition gave me, plunged into discontent—and then wanted to turn back again. Thus I have always been discontented, even with my contentment. Strange how make-believe, if engaged in systematically enough, can change into reality. Childish games (though I was well aware that they were so) marked the beginning of my intellectual decline. I deliberately cultivated a facial tic, for instance, or would walk across the Graben with arms crossed behind my head. A repulsively childish but successful game. (My writing began in the same way; only later on its development came to a halt, unfortunately.)

If it is possible so to force misfortune upon oneself, it is possible to force anything upon oneself. Much as my development seems to contradict me, and much as it contradicts my nature to think it, I cannot grant that the first beginnings of my unhappiness were inwardly necessitated; they may have indeed had a necessity, but not an inward one—they swarmed down on me like flies and could have been as easily driven off.

My unhappiness on the other shore would have been as great, greater probably (thanks to my weakness); after all, I have had some experience of it, the lever is still trembling somewhat from the time when I last tried to shift it—why then do I add to the unhappiness that this shore causes me by longing to cross over to the other?

Sad, and with reason. My sadness depends on this reason. How easy it was the first time, how difficult now! How helplessly the tyrant looks at me: "Is that where you are taking me!" And yet no peace in spite of everything; the hopes of the morning are buried in the afternoon. It is impossible amicably to come to terms with such a life; surely there has never been anyone who could have done so. When other people approached this boundary—even to have approached it is pitiful enough—they turned back; I cannot. It even seems to me as if I had not come by myself but had been pushed here as a child and then chained to this spot; the consciousness of my misfortune only gradually dawned on me, my misfortune itself was already complete; it needed not a prophetic but merely a penetrating eye to see it.

In the morning I thought: "There is a possibility that I could go on living in this fashion, only guard such a way of life against women." Guard it against women—why, they are already lurking in the "in-this-fashion."

It would be very unjust to say that you deserted me; but that I *was* deserted, and sometimes terribly so, is true.

Even in the sense of my "resolve" I have a right to despair boundlessly over my situation.

January 27. Spindelmühle. I must be above such mixtures of bad luck and clumsiness on my own part as the mistake with the sled, the broken trunk, the rickety table, the poor light, the impossibility of having quiet in the hotel during the afternoon, etc. Such superiority cannot be got by not caring, for one cannot remain indifferent to such things; it can only be got by summoning up new strength. Here, indeed, surprises await one, this the most despairing person will allow; experience proves that something can come of nothing, that the coachman and his horses can crawl out of the tumble-down pigpen.[62]

My strength crumbling away during the sleigh ride. One cannot make a life for oneself as a tumbler makes a handstand.

The strange, mysterious, perhaps dangerous, perhaps saving comfort that there is in writing: it is a leap out of murderers' row; it is a seeing of what is really taking place. This occurs by a higher type of observation, a higher, not a keener type, and the higher it is and the less within reach of the "row," the more independent it becomes, the more obedient to its own laws of motion, the more incalculable, the more joyful, the more ascendant its course.

Despite my having legibly written down my name, despite their having correctly written to me twice already, they have Joseph K.[63] down in the directory. Shall I enlighten them, or shall I let them enlighten me?

January 28. A little dizzy, tired from the tobogganing; weapons still exist for me, however seldom I may employ them; it is so hard for me to lay hold of them because I am ignorant of the joys of their use, never learned how when I was a child. It is not only "Father's fault" that I never learned their use, but also my wanting to disturb the "peace," to upset the balance, and for this reason I could not allow a new person to be born elsewhere while I was bending every effort to bury him here. Of course, in this too there is a question of "fault," for why did I want to quit the world? Because "he" would not let me live in it, in his world. Though indeed I should not judge the matter so precisely, for I am now a citizen of this other world, whose relationship to the ordinary one is the relationship of the wilderness to cultivated land (I have been forty years wandering from Canaan); I look back at it like a foreigner, though in this other world as well— it is the paternal heritage I carry with me—I am the most insignificant and timid of all creatures and am able to keep alive thanks only to the special nature of its arrangements; in this world it is possible even for the humblest to be raised to the heights as if with lightning speed, though they can also be crushed forever as if by the weight of the seas. Should I not be thankful despite everything? Was it certain that I should find my way to this world? Could not "banishment" from one side, coming together with rejection from this, have crushed me at the border? Is not Father's power such that nothing (not I, certainly) could have resisted his decree? It is indeed a kind of Wandering in the Wilderness in reverse that I am undergoing: I think that I am continually skirting the wilderness and am full of childish hopes (particularly as regards women) that "perhaps I shall keep in Canaan after all"—when all the while I have been decades in the wilderness and these hopes are merely mirages born of despair, especially at those times when I am the wretchedest of creatures in the desert too, and Canaan is perforce my only Promised Land, for no third place exists for mankind.

January 29. Suffered some attacks on the road through the snow in the evening. There are conflicting thoughts always in my head, something like this: My situation in this world would seem to be a dreadful one, alone here in Spindelmühle, on a forsaken road, moreover, where one keeps slipping in the snow in the dark, a senseless road, moreover, without an earthly goal (to the bridge? Why there? Besides, I didn't even go that far); I too forsaken in this place (I cannot place a human, personal value on the help the doctor gives me, I haven't earned it; at bottom the fee is my only relationship to him), incapable of striking up a friendship with anyone, incapable of tolerating a friendship, at bottom full of endless astonishment when I see a group of people cheerfully assembled together (here in the hotel, indeed, there is little that is cheerful; I won't go so far as to say that I am the cause of this, in my character, perhaps, as "the man with the too-great shadow," though my shadow in this world *is* too great—with fresh astonishment I observe the capacity for resistance some people have, who, "in spite of everything," want to live under this shadow, directly under it; but there is much more than this to be said on the matter), or especially when I see parents with their children; forsaken, moreover, not only here but in general, even in Prague, my "home," and what is more, forsaken not by people (that would not be the worst thing, I could run after them as long as I was alive), but rather by myself vis-à-vis people, by my strength vis-à-vis people; I am fond of lovers but I cannot love, I am too far away, am banished, have—since I am human after all and my roots want nourishment—my proxies "down" (or up) there too, sorry, unsatisfactory comedians who can satisfy me (though indeed they don't satisfy me at all and it is for this reason that I am so forsaken) only because I get my principal nourishment from other roots in other climes, these roots too are sorry ones, but nevertheless better able to sustain life.

This brings me to the conflict in my thoughts. If things were only as they seem to be on the road in the snow, it would be dreadful; I should be lost, lost not in the sense of a dreadful future menacing me but in the sense of a present execution. But I live elsewhere; it is only that the attraction of the human world is so immense, in an instant it can make one forget everything. Yet the attraction of my world too is strong; those who love me love me because I am "forsaken"—not, I feel sure, on the principle of a Weissian vacuum, but because they sense that in happy moments I enjoy on another plane the freedom of movement completely lacking to me here.

If M., for example, should suddenly come here, it would be dreadful. Externally, indeed, my situation would at once seem comparatively brighter. I should be esteemed as one human being among others, I should have words spoken to me that were more than merely polite. I should sit at the actors' table (less erect, it is true, than now, when I am sitting here alone, though even now I am slumped

down); outwardly, I should be almost a match in con-
viviality for Dr. H.—yet I should be plunged into a world
in which I could not live. It only remains to solve the
riddle of why I had fourteen days of happiness in Marienbad, and why, consequently, I might perhaps also be able
to be happy here with M. (though of course only after
a painful breaking down of barriers). But the difficulties
would probably be much greater than in Marienbad, my
opinions are more rigid, my experience larger. What used
to be a dividing thread is now a wall, or a mountain
range, or rather a grave.

January 30. Waiting for pneumonia. Afraid, not so
much of the illness, as for and of my mother, my father,
the director and all the others. Here it would seem clear
that the two worlds do exist and that I am as ignorant in
face of the illness, as detached, as fearful, as, say, in face
of a headwaiter. And moreover the division seems to
me to be much too definite, dangerous in its definiteness,
sad, and too tyrannical. Do I live in the other world,
then? Dare I say that?

Someone makes the remark: "What do I care about
life? It is only on my family's account that I don't want
to die." But it is just the family that is representative of
life, and so it is on life's account that he wants to stay
alive. Well, so far as my mother is concerned, this would
seem to be the case with me as well, though only lately.
But is it not gratitude and compassion that have brought this
change about in me? Yes, gratitude and compassion, because
I see how, with what at her age is inexhaustible strength,
she bends every effort to compensate me for my isolation
from life. But gratitude too is life.

January 31. This would mean that it is on my mother's account that I am alive. But it cannot be true, for even if I were much more important than I am, I should still be only an emissary of Life, and, if by nothing else, joined to it by this commission.

The Negative alone, however strong it may be, cannot suffice, as in my unhappiest moments I believe it can. For if I have gone the tiniest step upward, won any, be it the most dubious kind of security for myself, I then stretch out on my step and wait for the Negative, not to climb up to me, indeed, but to drag me down from it. Hence it is a defensive instinct in me that won't tolerate my having the slightest degree of lasting ease and smashes the marriage bed, for example, even before it has been set up.

February 1. Nothing, merely tired. The happiness of the truck driver, whose every evening is as mine has been today, and even finer. An evening, for example, stretched out on the stove. A man is purer than in the morning; the period before falling wearily asleep is really the time when no ghosts haunt one; they are all dispersed; only as the night advances do they return, in the morning they have all assembled again, even if one cannot recognize them; and now, in a healthy person, the daily dispersal of them begins anew.

Looked at with a primitive eye, the real, incontestable truth, a truth marred by no external circumstance (martyrdom, sacrifice of oneself for the sake of another), is only physical pain. Strange that the god of pain was not the chief god of the earliest religions (but first became so in the later ones, perhaps). For each invalid his household god, for the tubercular the god of suffocation. How can one bear his approach if one does not partake of him in advance of the terrible union?

February 2. Struggle on the road to Tannenstein in the morning, struggle while watching the ski-jumping contest. Happy little B. in all his innocence somehow shadowed by my ghosts, at least in my eyes, his aimless wandering glance, his aimless talk. In this connection it occurs to me—but this is already forced—that toward evening he wanted to go home with me.

The "struggle" would probably be horrible if I were to learn a trade.

The Negative having been in all probability greatly strengthened by the "struggle," a decision between insanity and security is imminent.

The happiness of being with people.

February 3. Almost impossible to sleep; plagued by dreams, as if they were being scratched on me, on a stubborn material.

There is a certain failing, a lack in me, that is clear and distinct enough but difficult to describe: it is a compound of timidity, reserve, talkativeness and halfheartedness; by this I intend to characterize something specific, a group of failings that under a certain aspect constitute one single clearly defined failing (which has nothing to do with such grave vices as mendacity, vanity, etc.). This failing keeps me from going mad, but also from making any headway. Because it keeps me from going mad, I cultivate it; out of fear of madness I sacrifice whatever headway I might make and shall certainly be the loser in the bargain, for no bargains are possible at this level. Provided that drowsiness does not intervene and with its nocturnal-diurnal labor break down every obstacle and clear the road. But in that event I shall be snapped up by madness—for to make headway one must want to, and I did not.

February 4. In the terrible cold, my changed face, the incomprehensible faces of the others.

What M. said, without being able completely to understand the truth of it (there is a type of sad conceit that is wholly justified), about the joy of merely talking with people. How can talking delight anyone but me! Too late, probably, and returning by a queer roundabout way to people.

February 5. Escape them. Any kind of nimble leap. At home beside the lamp in the silent room. Incautious to say this. It calls them out of the woods as if one had lit the lamp to help them find the way.

February 6. The comfort in hearing that someone had served in Paris, Brussels, London, Liverpool, had gone up the Amazon on a Brazilian steamer as far as the Peruvian border, with comparative ease had borne the dreadful sufferings of the winter campaign of the Seven Communities [64] because he had been accustomed to hardship since his childhood. The comfort consists not only in the demonstration that such things are possible, but in the pleasure one feels when one realizes that with these achievements on the one level, much at the same time must have necessarily been achieved on the other level, much must have been wrung from clenched fists. It *is* possible, then.

February 7. Shielded and exhausted by K. and H.

February 8. Horribly taken advantage of by both and yet—I surely could not live like that (it is not living, it is a tug-of-war in which the other person keeps straining and winning and yet never pulls me across); I sink into a peaceful numbness, as I did that time with W.

February 9. Two days lost; used the same two days, however, to get settled.

February 10. Can't sleep; have not the slightest relationship with people other than what their initiative creates, which then persuades me for the moment, as does everything they do.

New attack by G. Attacked right and left as I am by overwhelming forces, it is as plain as can be that I cannot escape either to the right or to the left—straight on only, starved beast, lies the road to food that will sustain you, air that you can breathe, a free life, even if it should take you beyond life. Great, tall commander-in-chief, leader of multitudes, lead the despairing through the mountain passes no one else can find beneath the snow. And who is it that gives you your strength? He who gives you your clear vision.

The commander-in-chief stood at the window of the ruined hut and looked outside with wide, unclosing eyes at the column of troops marching by in the snow under the pale moonlight. Now and then it seemed to him that a soldier out of ranks would halt by the window, press his face against the pane, look at him for a moment and then go on. Though always a different soldier, it always seemed to him to be the same one; a big-boned face with fat cheeks, round eyes and coarse sallow skin; each time that the man walked away he would straighten the straps of his pack, shrug his shoulders and skip his feet to get back into step with the mass of troops marching by as always in the background. The commander-in-chief had no intention of tolerating this game any longer; he lay in wait for the next soldier, threw open the window in his face and seized the man by the front of his coat. "Inside with you!" he said, and made him climb through the window. He pushed the man into a corner, stood in front of him and asked: "Who are you?"

"Nobody," the soldier said, fearfully.

"One might have expected as much," the commander-in-chief said. "Why did you look inside?"

"To see if you were still here."

February 12. The gesture of rejection with which I was forever met did not mean: "I do not love you," but: "You cannot love me, much as you would like; you are unhappily in love with your love for me, but your love for me is not in love with you." It is consequently incorrect to say that I have known the words, "I love you"; I have known only the expectant stillness that should have been broken by my "I love you," that is all that I have known, nothing more.

The fear I have tobogganing, my nervousness in walking on the slippery snow; a little story I read today revived in me the long unheeded, ever present question of whether the cause of my downfall was not insane selfishness, mere anxiety for self; not, moreover, anxiety for a higher self, but vulgar anxiety for my well-being; such that it would seem that I have dispatched my own avenger from myself (a special instance of the-right-hand-not-knowing-what-the-left-hand-does). In the Great Account of my life, it is still reckoned as if my life were first beginning tomorrow, and in the meantime it is all over with me.

February 13. The possibility of serving with all one's heart.

February 14. The power comfort has over me, my powerlessness without it. I know no one in whom both are so great. Consequently everything I build is insubstantial, unstable; the maid who forgets to bring me my warm water in the morning overturns my world. At the same time I have been under comfort's constant harassment; it has deprived me not only of the strength to bear up under anything, but also the strength myself to create comfort; it creates itself about me of itself, or I achieve it by begging, crying, renouncing more important things.

February 15. A bit of singing on the floor below, an occasional door slamming in the corridor, and all is lost.

February 16. The story of the crevice in the glacier.

February 18. The theater director who must himself create everything from the ground up, has even first to beget the actors. A visitor is not admitted; the director has important theatrical work in hand. What is it? He is changing the diapers of a future actor.

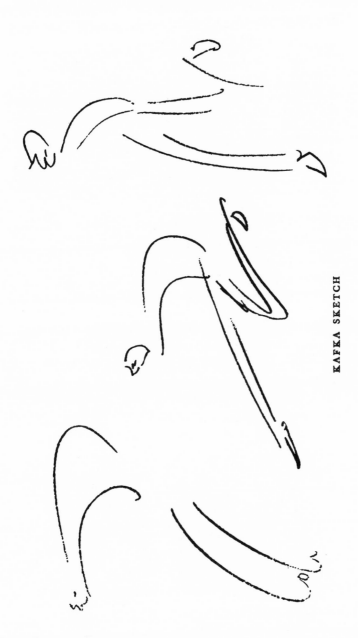

KAFKA SKETCH

February 19. Hopes?

February 20. Unnoticeable life. Noticeable failure.

February 25. A letter.

February 26. I grant—to whom do I grant it? the letter?—that possibilities exist in me, possibilities close at hand
that I don't yet know of; only to find the way to them!
and when I have found it, to dare! This signifies a great
many things: that possibilities do exist; it even signifies
that a scoundrel can become an honest man, a man happy
in his honesty.

Your drowsy fantasies recently.

February 27. Slept badly in the afternoon; everything
is changed; my misery pressing me hard again.

February 28. View of the tower and the blue sky. Calm-
ing.

March 1. *Richard III*. Impotence.

March 5. Three days in bed. A small party of people
at my bedside. A sudden reversal. Flight. Complete surrender. These world-shaking events always going on
within four walls.

March 6. New seriousness and weariness.

March 7. Yesterday the worst night I have had; as if
everything were at an end.

March 9. But that was only weariness; today a fresh
attack, wringing the sweat from my brow. How would
it be if one were to choke to death on oneself? If the pressure of introspection were to diminish, or close off entirely, the opening through which one flows forth into
the world. I am not far from it at times. A river flowing
upstream. For a long time now, that is what for the most
part has been going on.

Mount your attacker's horse and ride it yourself. The only possibility. But what strength and skill that requires! And how late it is already!

Life in the jungle. Jealous of the happiness and inexhaustibility of nature, whose impelling force (like mine) is yet distress, though always satisfying all the demands its antagonist lays upon it. And so effortlessly, so harmoniously.

In the past, when I had a pain and it passed away, I was happy; now I am merely relieved, while there is this bitter feeling in me: "Only to be well again, nothing more."

Somewhere help is waiting and the beaters are driving me there.

March 13. This pure feeling I have and my certainty of what has caused it: the sight of the children, one girl especially (erect carriage, short black hair), and another (blonde; indefinite features, indefinite smile); the rousing music, the marching feet. A feeling of one in distress who sees help coming but does not rejoice at his rescue—nor is he rescued—but rejoices, rather, at the arrival of fresh young people imbued with confidence and ready to take up the fight; ignorant, indeed, of what awaits them, but an ignorance that inspires not hopelessness but admiration and joy in the onlooker and brings tears to his eyes. Hatred too of him whom the fight is against is mingled in it (but little Jewish feeling, or so I think).

March 15. Objections to be made against the book: he

has popularized it, and with a will, moreover—and with magic. How he escapes the dangers (Blüher).[65]

To flee to a conquered country and soon find it insupportable there, for there is nowhere else to flee.

March 16. The attacks, my fear, rats that tear at me and whom my eyes multiply.

March 17. 99.3°.

Still unborn and already compelled to walk around the streets and speak to people.

March 19. Hysteria making me surprisingly and unaccountably happy.

March 20. Yesterday an unsuccessful, today a lost (?) evening. A hard day.

The conversation at dinner on murderers and executions. The placidly breathing breast knows no fear. Knows no difference between murder planned and murder executed.

March 23. In the afternoon dreamed of the boil on my cheek. The perpetually shifting frontier that lies between ordinary life and the terror that would seem to be more real.

March 24. How it lies in wait for me! On the way to the doctor, for example, so often there.

March 29. In the stream.

April 4. How long the road is from my inner anguish to a scene like that in the yard—and how short the road back. And since one has now reached one's home, there is no leaving it again.

April 6. Yesterday an outbreak I had been afraid of for two days; further pursuit; the enemy's great strength. One of the causes: the talk with my mother, the jokes about the future.—Planned letter to Milena.

The three Erinyes. Flight into the grove. Milena.

April 7. The two pictures and the two terra-cotta figures in the exhibition.

Fairy princess (Kubin), naked on a divan, looks out of an open window; the landscape prominently looming up, has a kind of airiness like that in Schwind's picture.

Nude girl (Bruder),[66] German-Bohemian, her unmatchable grace faithfully caught by a lover; noble, convincing, seductive.

Pietsch: Seated peasant girl; luxuriously resting with one leg under her, her ankle bent. Standing girl, her right arm clasping her body across her belly; left hand supporting her head under the chin; broad-nosed, simple and pensive, unique face.

Letter by Storm.

April 10. The five guiding principles on the road to hell (in genetic succession):

1. "The worst lies outside the window." All else is conceded to be angelic either openly or (more often) by silently ignoring it.

2. "You must possess every girl!" not in Don Juan fashion, but according to the devil's expression, "sexual etiquette."

3. "This girl you are not permitted to possess!" and for this very reason cannot. A heavenly fata morgana in hell.

4. "All comes back to mere needs." Since you have needs, resign yourself to the fact.

5. "Needs are all." But how could you have all? Consequently you have not even needs.

As a boy I was as innocent of and uninterested in sexual matters (and would have long remained so, if they had not been forcibly thrust on me) as I am today in, say, the theory of relativity. Only trifling things (yet even these only after they were pointedly called to my attention) struck me, for example that it was just those women on the street who seemed to me most beautiful and best dressed who were supposed to be bad.

April 11. "All that he deserves is the dirty unknown old woman with shrunken thighs who drains his semen in an instant, pockets the money and hurries off to the next room where another customer is already waiting for her."

Eternal youth is impossible; even if there were no other obstacle, introspection would make it impossible.

April 13. Max's grief. Morning in his office.
Afternoon in front of the Thein Church (Easter Sunday).

My fear of being disturbed; my insomnia because of this fear. A nightmare recently because of M.'s letter in my portfolio.

I. Young little girl, eighteen years old; nose, shape

of head, blonde; seen fleetingly in profile; came out of the church.

April 16. Max's grief. A walk with him. Tuesday he leaves.

II. Five-year-old girl; orchard, little path to the main allee; hair, nose, shining face.

April 23. III. Fawn-colored velvet jacket in the distance in the direction of the fruit market.

Helpless days; yesterday evening.

April 27. Yesterday a Makkabi girl in the office of *Selbst-wehr* telephoning: "*Přišla jsem ti pomoct.*" [67] Clear, cordial voice and speech.
Shortly thereafter opened the door to M.

May 8. Work with the plow. It digs in deep and yet goes easily along. Or it just scratches the ground. Or it moves along with the plowshare drawn uselessly up; with it or without it, it is all the same.

The work draws to an end in the way an unhealed wound might draw together.

Would you call it a conversation if the other person is silent and, to keep up the appearance of a conversation, you try to substitute for him, and so imitate him, and so parody him, and so parody yourself.

M. was here, won't come again; probably wise and right in this, yet there is perhaps still a possibility whose locked door we both are guarding lest it open, or rather lest we open it, for it will not open of itself.

Maggid.[68]

May 12. The constant variety of the forms it takes, and once, in the midst of it all, the affecting sight of a momentary abatement in its variations.

From *Pilger Kamanita*, from the Vedas: "O beloved, even as a man brought blindfold from the land of the Gandharians and then set free in the desert will wander east or north or south, for in blindness was he brought there and in blindness was set free; yet after someone has struck the blindfold from his eyes and said to him: 'Thither dwell the Gandharians, go ye thither,' after having asked his way from village to village, enlightened and made wise he comes home to the Gandharians—so too a man who has found a teacher here below knows: 'I shall belong to this earthly coil until I am redeemed, and then I shall return home.' "

In the same place: "Such a one, so long as he dwells in the body, is seen by men and gods; but after his body is fallen to dust, neither men nor gods see him more. And even nature, the all-seeing, sees him no more: he has blinded the eye of nature, he has vanished from the sight of the wicked."

May 19. He feels more deserted with a second person than when alone. If he is together with someone, this second person reaches out for him and he is helplessly delivered into his hand. If he is alone, all mankind reaches out for him—but the innumerable outstretched arms become entangled with one another and no one reaches to him.

May 20. The Freemasons on Altstädter Ring. The possible truth that there is in every discourse and doctrine.

The dirty little barefoot girl running along in her shift with her hair blowing.

May 23. It is incorrect to say of anyone: Things were easy for him, he suffered little; more correct: His nature was such that nothing could happen to him; most correct: He has suffered everything, but all in a single all-embracing moment; how could anything have still happened to him when the varieties of sorrow had been completely exhausted either in actual fact or at his own peremptory command? (Two old Englishwomen in Taine.)

May 25. Day before yesterday "H. K." Pleasant walk today. Everywhere people sitting, wearily standing, dreamily leaning.—Much disturbed.

May 26. The severe "attacks" during the evening walk (resulting from four tiny vexations during the day: the dog in the summer resort; Mars' book; enlistment as a soldier; lending the money through Z.); momentary confusion, helplessness, hopelessness, unfathomable abyss, nothing but abyss; only when I turned in at the front door did a thought come to my assistance—during the entire walk none came to me, apparently because, in my complete hopelessness, I had made no attempt at all to seek it out, though otherwise its possibility is always close at hand.

June 5. Myslbeck's funeral. Talent for "botch work."

June 16. Quite apart from the insuperable difficulties

always presented by Blüher's philosophical and visionary power, one is in the difficult position of easily incurring the suspicion, almost with one's every remark, of wanting ironically to dismiss the ideas of this book. One is suspect even if, as in my case, there is nothing further from one's mind, in face of this book, than irony. This difficulty in reviewing his book has its counterpart in a difficulty that Blüher, from his side, cannot surmount. He calls himself an anti-Semite without hatred, *sine ira et studio*, and he really is that; yet he easily awakens the suspicion, almost with his every remark, that he is an enemy of the Jews, whether out of happy hatred or unhappy love. These difficulties confront each other like stubborn facts of nature, and attention must be called to them lest in reflecting on this book one stumble over these errors and at the very outset be rendered incapable of going on.

According to Blüher, one cannot refute Judaism inductively, by statistics, by appealing to experience; these methods of the older anti-Semitism cannot prevail against Judaism; all other peoples can be refuted in this way, but not the Jews, the chosen people; to each particular charge the anti-Semites make, the Jew will be able to give a particular answer in justification. Blüher makes a very superficial survey, to be sure, of the particular charges and the answers given them.

This perception, insofar as it concerns the Jews and not the other peoples, is profound and true. Blüher draws two conclusions from it, a full and a partial one——

June 23. Plana.[69]

July 27. The attacks. Yesterday a walk with the dog in the evening. Tvrz Sedlec. The row of cherry trees where the woods end; it gives one almost the same sense of seclusion as a room. The man and woman returning from the fields. The girl in the stable door of the dilapidated farmyard seems almost at odds with her big breasts; an innocently attentive animal gaze. The man with glasses who is pulling the heavy cartload of fodder; elderly, somewhat hunchbacked, but nevertheless very erect because of his exertions; high boots; the woman with the sickle, now at his side and now behind him.

September 26. No entries for two months. With some exceptions, a good period thanks to Ottla. For the past few days collapse again. On one of the first days made a kind of discovery in the woods.

November 14. Always 99.6°, 99.9° in the evening. Sit at the desk, get nothing done, am hardly ever in the street. Nevertheless tartuffism to complain of my illness.

December 18. All this time in bed. Yesterday *Either-Or*.

June 12. The horrible spells lately, innumerable, almost without interruption. Walks, nights, days, incapable of anything but pain.

And yet. No "and yet," no matter how anxiously and tensely you look at me; Krizanovskaya on the picture postcard in front of me.

More and more fearful as I write. It is understandable. Every word, twisted in the hands of the spirits—this twist of the hand is their characteristic gesture—becomes a spear turned against the speaker. Most especially a remark like this. And so ad infinitum. The only consolation would be: it happens whether you like or no. And what you like is of infinitesimally little help. More than consolation is: You too have weapons.

TRAVEL DIARIES

I should write the whole night through, so many things occur to me, but all of it rough. What a power this has come to have over me, whereas in the past I was able, so far as I remember, to elude it by a turn, a slight turn which by itself had been enough to make me happy.

A Reichenberg Jew in the compartment called attention to himself by uttering brief exclamations over expresses that are expresses only insofar as the fare is concerned. Meanwhile a very thin passenger was rapidly wolfing down ham, bread and two sausages, the skins of which he kept scraping with a knife until they were transparent; finally he threw all the scraps and paper under the seat behind the steampipe. While eating in all this unnecessary heat and haste (a practice with which I am sympathetic, but cannot successfully imitate), he read through two evening papers that he held up in my direction. Protruding ears. A nose that seemed broad only by comparison. Wiped hair and face with his greasy hands without getting himself dirty, another thing I should not succeed in.

Across from me a deaf gentleman with a piping voice and a pointed beard and mustache laughed derisively at the Reichenberg Jew, silently at first, without betraying himself; after exchanging understanding glances with him, I joined in, always with a certain repugnance but out of some kind of feeling of deference. Later it turned out that this man, who read the *Montagsblatt*, ate something, bought wine at one stop and drank in the way I do, in gulps, was nobody.

Then too a red-cheeked young fellow who spent a great deal of time reading the *Interessantes Blatt*, the pages of which he carelessly cut open with the edge of his hand only finally to fold it up again, as if it were a piece of silk, with that painstaking solicitude people who have nothing to do display and which always arouses my admiration; he folded it together, creased it on the inside, straightened it out on the outside, smoothed the surfaces, and, bulky as it was, stuffed it into his breast pocket. Thus he intended to read it again at home. I don't know where he got off.

The hotel in Friedland. The great entrance hall. I remember a Christ on the Cross that perhaps wasn't there at all.—No water closet; the snowstorm came up from below. For a while I was the only guest. Most of the weddings in the neighborhood take place in the hotel. Very indistinctly I recall glancing into a room the morning after a wedding. It was very cold throughout the entrance hall and corridor. My room was over the hotel entrance; I felt the cold at once, how much more so when I became aware of the reason. In front of my room was a sort of alcove off the entrance hall; there on a table, in vases, were two bouquets left over from a wedding. The window closed top and bottom not with latches but with hooks. I now recollect that once I heard music for a short while. However, there was no piano in the guest room; perhaps there was one in the room where the wedding took place. Every time I went to close the window I saw a grocery store on the other side of the market place. My room was heated by burning logs. Chambermaid with a large mouth; once her throat was bare and her collar open, in spite of the cold; at times she was withdrawn in her manner, at

other times surprisingly friendly; I was always respectful
and embarrassed, as I usually am in the presence of friendly
people. While she was fixing the fire she noticed with
pleasure the brighter light I had had put in so that I could
work in the afternoon and evening. "Of course, it was
impossible to work with the other light," she said. "And
with this one too," I said, after a few jaunty exclamations
of the sort that unfortunately always come into my mouth
when I am embarrassed. And I could think of nothing
else but to express an opinion that electric light is at once
too harsh and too weak. Whereupon she went silently on
with the fire. Only when I said, "Besides, I have only turned
the old lamp up," did she laugh a little, and we were in
accord.

On the other hand, I can do things like the following
very well: I had always treated her like a lady and she
acted accordingly. Once I came back at an unexpected
hour and saw her scrubbing the floor in the cold entrance
hall. It gave me not the slightest difficulty to spare her
whatever embarrassment she may have felt by saying hello
to her and making some request about the heating.

Beside me on the return trip from Raspenau to Friedland the rigid, corpse-like man whose beard came down
over his open mouth and who, when I asked him about a
station, cordially turned toward me and with great animation gave me the information.

The castle in Friedland.[71] The different ways there are
to view it: from the plain, from a bridge, from the park,
through bare trees, from the woods through tall firs. The
castle astonishes one by the way it is built one part above
the other; long after one has entered the yard it still pre-

sents no unified appearance, for the dark ivy, the dark gray walls, the white snow, the ice covering the slate-colored glacis enhance the heterogeneity of its aspect. The castle is really built not on a plateau but around the rather steep sides of a hilltop. I went up by a road, slipping all the time, while the castellan, whom I encountered farther up, came up without difficulty by two flights of stairs. A wide view from a jutting coign. A staircase against the wall came pointlessly to an end halfway up. The chains of the drawbridge dangled in neglect from their hooks.

Beautiful park. Because it is laid out terrace-fashion on the slope, with scattered clumps of trees, but part of it too extending down around the pond below, it was impossible to guess what it looked like in summer. On the icy water of the pond floated two swans, one of them put its head and neck into the water. Uneasy and curious, but also undecided, I followed two girls who kept looking uneasily and curiously back at me; I was led by them along the mountain, over a bridge, a meadow, under a railroad embankment into a rotunda unexpectedly formed by the wooded slope and the embankment, then higher up into a wood with no apparent end to it. The girls walked slowly at first, by the time I began to wonder at the extent of the wood they were walking more quickly, and by then we were already on the plateau with a brisk wind blowing, a few steps from the town.

The Emperor's Panorama, the only amusement in Friedland. Didn't feel quite at ease because I hadn't been prepared for so elegantly furnished an interior as I found inside, had entered with snow-covered boots, and, sitting in front of the glass showcases, touched the rug only with

my boot toes. I had forgotten how such places are arranged and for a moment was afraid I should have to walk
from one chair to another. An old man reading a volume
of the *Illustrierte Welt* at a little table lighted by a lamp
was in charge of everything. After a while he showed
magic-lantern slides for me. Later two elderly ladies arrived, sat down at my right, then another one at my left.
Brescia, Cremona, Verona. People in them like wax dolls,
their feet glued to the pavement. Tombstones; a lady dragging the train of her dress over a low staircase opens a door
part way, looking backward all the while. A family, in
the foreground a boy is reading, one hand at his brow;
a boy on the right is bending an unstrung bow. Statue of
the hero, Tito Speri: his clothes flutter in enthusiastic
neglect about his body. Blouse, broad-brimmed hat.

The pictures more alive than in the cinema because they
offer the eye all the repose of reality. The cinema com·
municates the restlessness of its motion to the things pic·
tured in it; the eye's repose would seem to be more important. The smooth floors of the cathedrals at the tip of our
tongues. Why can't they combine the cinema and stereoscope in this way? Posters reading "Pilsen Wührer," familiar to me from Brescia.[72] The gap between simply hearing about a thing and seeing lantern slides of it is greater
than the gap between the latter and actually seeing the
thing itself. Alteisenmarkt in Cremona. At the end wanted
to tell the old gentleman how much I enjoyed it, did not
dare. Got the next program. Open from ten to ten.

I had noticed the *Literarischen Ratgeber* of the Dürer
society in the window of the bookstore. Decided to buy
it, but changed my mind, then once again returned to my
original decision; while this went on I kept halting in

front of the store window at every hour of the day. The bookstore seemed so forlorn to me, the books so forlorn. It was only here that I felt a connection between Friedland and the world, and it was such a tenuous one. But since all forlornness begets in me a feeling of warmth in return, I at once felt what must be this bookstore's joy, and once I even went in to see the inside. Because there is no need for scientific works in Friedland, there was almost more fiction on its shelves than on those of metropolitan bookstores. An old lady sat under a green-shaded electric light. Four or five copies of *Kunstwart*, just unpacked, reminded me that it was the first of the month. The woman, refusing my help, took the book, of whose existence she was hardly aware, out of the display, put it into my hand, was surprised that I had noticed it behind the frosted pane (I had in fact already noticed it before), and began to look up its price in the ledgers, for she didn't know it and her husband was out. I'll return later on in the evening, I said (it was 5 P.M.), but did not keep my promise.

Reichenberg.

One is completely in the dark as to what real object people have in hurrying through a small town in the evening. If they live outside the town, then they surely have to use the trolley, because the distances are too great. But if they live in the town itself, there are really no great distances to go and thus no reason to hurry. And yet people hurry with lengthened strides across this square which would not be too large for a village and which is made to seem even smaller by the unexpected size of the town hall (its shadow can more than cover the square). At the same time, because the square is so small, one can't quite believe that the town hall is as large as it is, and would like to attribute his first impression of its size to the smallness of the square.

One policeman did not know the address of the work-men's compensation office, another where its exhibition was taking place, a third did not even know where Johan-nesgasse was. This they explained by their having been on the force only a short time. For directions I was obliged to go to the police station, where there were a great many policemen lounging about, all in uniforms whose beauty, newness and color surprised one, for otherwise one saw nothing but dark winter coats on the street.

The narrow streets allowed for the laying of only a single line of track. This is why the trolley going to the rail-road station ran on different streets than the one coming from the railroad station. From the railroad station through Wiener Strasse (where I was living in the Hotel Eiche); to the railroad station through Stückerstrasse.

Went to the theater three times. *Des Meeres und der Liebe Wellen.* I sat in the balcony, an actor who was much too good made too much noise in the part of Naukleros; I had tears in my eyes several times, as at the end of the first act when Hero and Leander could not take their eyes away from one another. Hero stepped out of the temple doorway through which you saw something that could have been nothing else but an icebox. In the second act, forests of the kind you see pictured in old de luxe editions, it was very affecting, creepers twined from tree to tree. Everything mossy and dark green. The backdrop of the wall of the tower chamber turned up again in *Miss Dudelsack* a few evenings later. From the third act on, the play fell off, as though an enemy had been after it.

TRIP TO SWITZERLAND, ITALY, PARIS, AND ERLENBACH

AUGUST–SEPTEMBER, 1911

Departed August 28, 1911. Noon. Our idea a poor one: to describe the trip and at the same time our feelings toward each other during the trip.[73] How impossible it is, proved when a wagon full of peasant women passed by. The heroic peasant woman (Delphic Sibyl). One of them was laughing and another, who had been sleeping in her lap, woke up and waved. If I should describe the way Max waved to them a false enmity would enter the description.

A girl (who later turned out to be Alice R.[74]) got on at Pilsen. (During the trip you ordered coffee from the steward by putting a little green sticker up on the window. However, you didn't have to take the coffee even if there was a sticker on your window, and could get it even if there was none.) At first I couldn't see her because she was sitting next to me. Our first social contact: her hat, which had been put away on the rack above, fell down on Max. Thus do hats come in with difficulty through the carriage doors and fly out with ease through the large windows.

Max probably made it impossible to give a true description of the scene later; he is a married man and had to say something that would deprive the incident of all its risk, and in doing so passed over what was important, emphasized what was didactic and made it all a little ugly.

"Perfect aim!" "Fire away!" "Rate of fall zero point

five"; our joking about the card she'd write in Munich, we agreed to mail it for her, but from Zurich, and it will read: "The expected, alas, has happened . . . wrong train . . . now in Zurich . . . two days of the trip lost." Her delight. But she expected that as gentlemen we should add nothing to it. Automobile in Munich. Rain, fast ride (twenty minutes), a view as if from a basement apartment, the driver called out the names of the invisible sights, the tires hummed on the wet asphalt like a movie projector. My clearest recollection: of the uncurtained window of the Vier Jahreszeiten, the reflections of the lights on the asphalt as if in a river.

Washing hands and face in the men's room in the station in Munich.

Baggage left on the train. A place provided for Alice in a car where a lady (who was more to be feared than we) offered to take her under her protection. Offer enthusiastically accepted. Suspicious.

Max asleep in the compartment. The two Frenchmen, the dark one laughed continually; once because Max left him hardly enough room in which to sit (he was so sprawled out), and then because he seized his opportunity and Max could no longer stretch out. Max under the hood of his ulster. Eating at night. An invasion by three Swiss. One of them was smoking. One, who stayed on after the other two got off, was at first inconspicuous, grew expansive only toward morning. Bodensee.

Switzerland left to itself in the first hours of the morning. I woke Max when I caught sight of such a bridge [75] and then got from it my first strong impression of Switzerland, despite the fact that I had been peering out into the gray daybreak at it for a long time from the inner obscurity of the train.—The impression the houses in St. Gallen give one of standing boldly upright in defiance of any arrangement into streets.—Winterthur.—The man leaning over the porch railing of the lighted villa in Württemberg at two o'clock in the morning. Door to the study open.—The cattle already awake in sleeping Switzerland. —Telegraph poles: cross-sections of clothes-hooks.—The meadows paling under the rising sun.—My recollection of the prison-like station at Cham, with its name inscribed on it with biblical solemnity. The window decorations, despite their meagerness, seemed to be contrary to regulations.

Tramp in the station at Winterthur with cane, song and one hand in his trouser pocket.

Business carried on in villas.

A lot of singing in the station at Lindau during the night.

Patriotic statistics: the area of Switzerland, were it spread out level on a plain.

Foreign chocolate companies.

Zurich. The station loomed up before us like a composite of several stations recently seen.— Max took possession of it for A + x.[76]

The impression foreign soldiers make on one of being out of the past. The absence of it in one's own. Anti-militarist argument.

Marksmen in the station at Zurich. Our fear lest their guns go off when they ran.

Bought a map of Zurich.

Back and forth on a bridge in indecision as to the order in which to have a cold bath, a warm bath and breakfast.

In the direction of Limmat, Urania Observatory.

Main business artery, empty trolley, pyramids of cuffs in the foreground of an Italian haberdasher's window.

Only fancy posters (spas, festival performance of *Marignano* by Wiegand, music by Jermoli).

Enlargement of the premises of a department store. Best advertisement. Watched for years by all the townspeople. (Dufayel.)

Postmen, looked as though they were wearing night-shirts. Carried small boxes in front, in which they sorted their letters like the "planets" [77] at the Christmas Fair. Lake view. If you imagine you live here, a strong sense of its being Sunday. Horseman. Frightened horse. Pedagogic inscription, possibly a relief of Rebecca at the well. The inscription's serenity above the flowing water.

Altstadt: Narrow, steep street which a man in a blue blouse was laboriously descending. Down steps.

I remember the traffic-menaced toilet in front of Saint Roche in Paris.

Breakfast in the temperance restaurant. Butter like egg yolk. *Zürcher Zeitung.*

Large cathedral, old or new? Men are supposed to sit at the sides. The sexton pointed out some better seats to us. We walked after him in that direction, since it was on our way to the door. When we were already at the exit, he apparently thought we couldn't find the seats and came diagonally across the church toward us. We pushed each other out. Much laughter.

Max: Scrambling languages together as the solution for national difficulties; the chauvinist would be at his wits' end.

Swimming pool in Zurich: For men only. One man next to the other. Swiss: German poured out like lead. There

weren't enough lockers for everyone; republican freedom
of undressing in front of your own clothes-hook, as well
as the swimming master's freedom to clear the crowded
solarium with a fire hose. Moreover, clearing the solarium
in this way would be no more senseless than the language
was incomprehensible. Diver: his feet outspread on the
railing, he jumped down on the springboard, thus adding
to his spring.— It's only possible to judge the conveniences
of a bathing establishment after long use. No swimming
lessons. A long-haired nature-healer looking lonesome.
Low banks of the lake.

Free concert by the Officers' Tourist Club. A writer in
the audience, surrounded by companions, was noting something down in a closely written notebook; after one number on the program was finished, he was pulled away by
his companions.

No Jews. Max: The Jews have let this big business slip
from their hands. Began with the *Bersaglieri March*. Ended
with the *Pro Patria March*. In Prague there are no free
concerts for the sake of the music alone (Jardin de Luxem-
bourg); republican, according to Max.

Keller's room closed. Travel Bureau. Bright house behind a dark street. Houses with terraces on the right bank
of the Limmat. Window shutters a brilliant blue-white.
The soldiers walking slowly along serve as policemen. Concert hall. Polytechnic institute not looked for and not
found. City Hall. Lunch on the first floor. Meilen wine.
(Sterilized wine made of fresh grapes.) A waitress from
Lucerne told us what trains run there. Pea soup with sago,
beans with baked potatoes, lemon crême.— Decent-looking
buildings in Arts-and-Crafts style.

Left about three o'clock for Lucerne, going around the
lake. The empty, dark, hilly, wooded shores of the Lake of

Zug with its many peninsulas. Had an American look. During the trip, my distaste for making comparisons with countries not yet seen. To the right of the railroad station a skating rink. We walked into the midst of the hotel employees and called out: Rebstock. A bridge (so Max said) divides the lake from the river, as in Zurich.

Where is the German population that warrants the German signs? Casino. The [German] Swiss you see everywhere in Zurich don't seem to have any aptitude for hotelkeeping; here, where they do run hotels, they have disappeared from view, the hotelkeepers may even be French.

The empty balloon hangar opposite. Hard to imagine how the airship glides in. Roller-skating rink, Berlin-like appearance. Fruit. The dark outlines of the Strand Promenade still clearly apparent under the treetops in the evening. Men with their daughters or prostitutes. Boats rocking so steeply their undermost ribs were visible.

Ridiculous lady receptionist in the hotel; a laughing girl showed people to their rooms; a serious, red-cheeked chambermaid. Small staircase. Bolted, walled-up chest in the room. Happy to be out of the room. Would have liked to dine on fruit. Gotthard Hotel, girls in Swiss costume. Apricot compote, Meilen wine. Two elderly ladies and a gentleman talking about growing old.

Discovered the gambling house in Lucerne. Admission one franc. Two long tables. It is unpleasant to describe anything really worth seeing, people impatiently expect, as it were, to see the thing before them. At each table a croupier in the middle with an observer on either side. Betting limit five francs. "The Swiss are requested to give precedence to foreigners as the game is intended for the entertainment of our visitors." One table with balls, one with toy horses. Croupiers in Prince Alberts. "*Messieurs faites votre jeu.*"—"*Marquez le jeu.*"—"*Les jeux sont faits.*"—"*Sont marqués.*"—"*Rien ne va plus.*" Croupiers with nickeled rakes at the end of wooden sticks. The things they can do with them: rake the money onto the right squares, sort it, draw money to them, catch the money they toss on the winning squares. The influence the different croupiers have on your chances, or rather: you like the croupier with whom you win. Our excitement when we both of us decided to play; you feel entirely alone in the room. The money (ten francs) disappeared down a gently sloping incline. The loss of ten francs was not enough temptation to go on playing, but still, a temptation. Rage at everything. The day prolonged by the gambling.

Monday, August 28. Man in high boots breakfasting against the wall. Second-class steamer. Lucerne in the morning. Poorer appearance of the hotels. A married couple reading letters from home with newspaper clippings about cholera in Italy. The beautiful homes that you could only see from a boat on the lake. Changing shapes of the mountains. Vitznau. Rigi railway. Lake seen through leaves. Feeling of the south. Your surprise when you suddenly catch sight of the broad surface of the Lake of Zug. Woods like at home. Railroad built in '75; look it up in the old copy of *Über Land und Meer*. Old stamping ground for the English, they still wear checks and sideburns here. Telescope. Jungfrau in the distance, rotunda of the Monk, shimmering heat waves lent movement to the picture. The outstretched palm of the Titli. A snow field sliced through like a loaf of bread. False estimates of the altitudes from above as well as from below. Unsettled dispute as to whether the railroad station at Arth-Goldau rested on slanting or on level ground. Table d'hôte. Dark woman, serious, sharp mouth—had already seen her below near the carriage—sat in the hall. English girl at the departure, her teeth even all around. A short Frenchwoman got into the next compartment, with outstretched arm announced that our full compartment was not "complet," and pushed in her father and her older, shorter sister, who looked at once innocent and lewd and who tickled my hips with her elbow. Some more English, toothily spoken by the old lady at Max's right. We tried to guess what part of England. Route from Vitznau to Flüelen—Gersau, Beckenried, Brunnen (nothing but hotels), Schillerstein, Tellplatte, Rütli, two loggias on Axenstrasse (Max imagined there were several of them, because in photographs you always see these two), Urnser Becken, Flüelen. Hotel Sternen.

Tuesday, August 29. This beautiful room with a balcony. The friendliness. Too much hemmed in by mountains. A man and two girls, in raincoats, one behind the other, walked through the hall in the evening carrying alpenstocks; when all of them were already on the steps they were stopped by a question from the chambermaid. They thanked her, they knew about it. In reply to a further question about their mountain excursion: "And it wasn't so easy either, I can tell you that." In the hall they seemed to me to be out of *Miss Dudelsack;* on the staircase they seem to Max to be out of Ibsen, then to me too. Forgotten binoculars. Boys with Swiss flags. Bathing in Lake Lucerne. Married couple. Life preserver. People walking on Axenstrasse. Fisherwoman in light yellow dress.

Boarding the Gotthard train, Reuss. Milky water of our rivers. The Hungarian flower. Thick lips. Exotic curve from the back to the buttocks. The handsome man among the Hungarians. Jesuit general in the railroad station at Göschenen. Italy suddenly, tables placed haphazardly in front of taverns; an excited young man dressed in all colors who couldn't contain himself; the women with high-piled black hair waving their hands in goodbye (a kind of pinching motion) beside a station; bright pink houses, blurred signs. Later the landscape lost its Italian aspect, or the underlying Swiss quality emerged. Ticino Falls, off and on we saw waterfalls everywhere. German Lugano. Noisy palestra. Post office recently built. Hotel Belvedere. Concert in the assembly room. No fruit.

August 30. From four in the evening to eleven at the same table with Max;[78] first in the garden, then in the reading room, then in my room. Bath in the morning and mail.

August 31. The snowcaps on the Rigi rose up into view like the hands of a clock.

Friday, September 1. Left at 10:05 from Place Guglielmo Tell.— Awning frames on the boats like on milk wagons.— Every debarkation an attack.

No luggage on the trip, hand free to prop up my head.

Gandria [near Lugano]: one house stuck behind the other; loggias hung with colored cloths; no bird's-eye view; streets, then no streets. St. Margarita, a fountain on the landing stage. Villa in Oria with twelve cypresses. You cannot, dare not imagine a house in Oria that has a porch in front with Greek pillars. Mamette: medieval magician's cap on a belfry. Earlier, a donkey in the arbored walk, along one side of the harbor. Osteno. The clergyman among the ladies. The shouting more than ordinarily incomprehensible. Child in the window behind the passage to the pissoir. Shivery feeling at the sight of lizards wriggling on a wall. Psyche's falling hair. Soldiers riding by on bicycles and hotel employees dressed up as sailors.

Children on the landing stage at Menaggio; their father;

the pride in her children expressed in the woman's body.

Passers-by in a carriage pointed out the Italian boys to one another.

Statesman with half-opened mouth (Villa Carlotta).

Frenchwoman with my aunt's voice and a straw parasol with a thick fiber edge was writing something down about *montagne*, etc. in a small notebook. Dark man framed by the arching ribs of his boat, bent over the oars. Customs official rapidly examined a little basket, rummaging through it as if it all had been a present for him. Italian on the Porlezza-Menaggio train. Every word of Italian spoken to one penetrates the great void of one's own ignorance and, whether understood or not, lengthily engages one's attention; one's own uncertain Italian cannot prevail against the speaker's fluency and, whether understood or not, is easily disregarded.—Joke about the train going backward at Menaggio, nice matter for a conversation.— On the other side of the street, in front of the villas, decorated stone boathouses. Thriving business in antiques. Boatman: *Peu de commerce.*— Revenue cutter ("Story of Captain Nemo" and *A Journey through Planetary Space*).

September 2. Saturday. My face was twitching on board the small steamer. Draped curtains (brown, edged in white) in front of the stores (Cadenabbia). Bees in the honey. Lonely, peevish, short-waisted woman, a language teacher. The punctiliously dressed gentleman in high-drawn trousers. His forearms were suspended over the table as though he were clasping not the handles of a knife and fork but the end of an arm rest. Children watching the weak rockets: *Encore un*—hiss—arms stretched up.

Bad trip on the steamer, too much a part of the rocking of the boat. Not high enough to smell the fresh air and have an unobstructed view around, somewhat like the situation of the stokers. A passing group: man, cow and woman. She was saying something. Black turban, loose dress.— The heartbeat of lizards.— Host's little boy, without my having spoken to him previously, under the urging of his mother held his mouth up to me for a good-night kiss. I enjoyed it.

Gandria: instead of streets, cellar steps and cellar passageways. A boy was being whipped; the hollow sound of beds being beaten. House overgrown with ivy. Seamstress in Gandria at the window without shutters, curtains or panes. We were so tired we had to hold one another up on the way from the bathing place to Gandria. Solemn procession of boats behind a small black steamer. Young men looking at pictures, kneeling, lounging about on the wharf in Gandria, one of them a rather pale person well known to us as a ladies' man and buffoon.

On the quay in the evening in Porlezza. At the William Tell monument a full-bearded Frenchman we had already forgotten reminded us again of what had been memorable about him.

September 3, Sunday. A German with a gold tooth who because of it would have stuck in the memory of anyone describing him, though the impression he made was otherwise an indeterminate one, bought a ticket for the swimming pool as late as a quarter to twelve, despite its closing at twelve; the swimming master inside immediately called this to his attention in an incomprehensible Italian which for this reason sounded rather stern. Flustered by it even in his own language, the German stammeringly asked why in that case they had sold him a ticket at the entrance booth, complained that they should have sold him a ticket, and protested at its having been sold to him so late. From the Italian reply you could make out that he still had almost a quarter-hour in which to swim and get dressed, didn't he? Tears.— Sat on the barrel in the lake. Hotel Belvedere: "With all due respect to the manager, the food is miserable."

September 4. Cholera reports: travel bureau, *Corriere della Sera*, North German Lloyd, *Berliner Tageblatt*, chambermaid brought us reports from a Berlin doctor; the general character of the reports varied according to the group and one's physical condition; when we left Lugano for Porto Ceresio, at 1:05, they were fairly favorable.— Felt a passing enthusiasm for Paris in the wind blowing on the September 3rd *Excelsior*, which we held open in front of us and ran off to a bench to read. There was still some billboard space to rent out on the bridge across Lake Lugano.

Friday. Three crew members chased us away from the ship's bow on the pretext that the helmsman had to have an unobstructed view forward of the light, and then pushed a bench over and sat down themselves. I should have liked to have sung.

Under the eyes of the Italian who advised us to make the trip to Turin (exposition) and to whom we nodded agreement, we shook hands in confirmation of our common decision not to go to Turin at any price. Praised the cut-rate tickets. Cyclist circling about on the lake terrace of a house in Porto Ceresio. Whip that had only a little tail of horsehair instead of a strap. A cyclist pedaling along with a rope in his hand, leading a horse that trotted beside him.

Milan: Forgot guidebook in a store. Went back and stole it. Ate apple strudel in the courtyard of the Mercanti. Health cake. Teatro Fossati. Every hat and fan in motion. A child laughing up above. An elderly lady in the male or-

chestra. *Poltrone.—Ingresso.—* Pit on a level with the orchestra. All the windows in the back wall open. Tall, vig-
orous actor with delicately painted nostrils; the black of
the nostrils continued to stand out even when the outline of
his upturned face was lost in the light. Girl with a long
slender neck ran off stage with short steps and rigid elbows
—you could guess at the high heels that went with the long
neck. The importance of the laughter exaggerated, for there
is a greater gap between laughter and uncomprehending
gravity than between it and the gravity of an initiated spectator. Significance of every piece of furniture. Five doors
in each of the two plays for any emergency. Nose and
mouth of a girl shadowed by her painted eyes. Man in a
box opened his mouth when he laughed until a gold molar
became visible, then kept it open like that for a while. That
kind of unity of stage and audience which is created for
and against the spectator who does not understand the
language, a unity impossible to achieve in any other way.

Young Italian woman whose otherwise Jewish face became non-Jewish in profile. How she stood up, leaned forward with her hands on the ledge so that only her narrow
body could be seen, her arms and shoulders being concealed; how she extended her arms to either side of the window; how she clung in the breeze with both hands to one
side of the window, as though to a tree. She was reading a
paper-bound detective story that her little brother had
been vainly begging from her for some time. Her father,
near by, had a hooked nose whereas hers, at the same place,
curved gently, was therefore more Jewish. She looked at
me often, curious to see whether I shouldn't finally stop my
annoying staring. Her dress of raw silk. Tall, stout, perfumed woman near me scattering her scent into the air
with her fan. I felt myself shrivel up next to her.— In the

baggage room the tin plate over the gas flame was shaped like a girl's flat-brimmed hat. Pleasant variety of lattice-work on the houses. We had been looking for the Scala right under the arch of its entrance; when we came out on the square and saw its simple, worn façade we were not surprised at the error we had made.

Pleased by the connection a pair of folding doors affords between the two rooms. Each of us can open a door. A good arrangement for married people too, Max thinks.

First write down a thought, then recite it aloud; don't write as you recite, for in that case only the beginning already inwardly pondered will succeed, while what is still to be written will be lost. A discussion of asphyxia and [lethal] heart injection at a little table in a coffeehouse on the Cathedral Square. Mahler asked for a heart injection too. As the discussion went on, I felt the time that we had planned to spend in Milan rapidly dwindling away, in spite of some resistance on my part.— The Cathedral with its many spires is a little tiresome.

Genesis of our decision to go to Paris: the moment in Lugano with the *Excelsior;* trip to Milan in consequence of our not altogether voluntary purchase of the Porto Ceresio–Milan tickets; from Milan to Paris out of fear of the cholera and the desire to be compensated for this fear. In addition, our calculation of the time and money this trip would save us.

I. Rimini–Genoa–Nervi (Prague).

II. Upper Italian lakes, Milan–Genoa (wavering between Locarno and Lugano).

III. Omit Lago Maggiore, Lugano, Milan, trip through the cities as far as Bologna.

IV. Lugano–Paris.

V. Lugano–Milan (several days)–Maggiore.

VI. In Milan: directly to Paris (possibly Fontainebleau).

VII. Got off at Stresa. Here, for the first time, we were at a point in our trip where it was possible to look backward and forward along it; it had passed out of its infant stages and there was something there to take by the waist.

I have never yet seen people looking so small as they did in the Galleria in Milan. Max thought the Galleria was only as high as the other houses you saw outside; I denied it with some objection I have since forgotten, for I will always come to the defense of the Galleria. It had almost no superfluous ornamentation, there was nothing to arrest the sweep of the eye, seemed little because of this, as well as because of its height, but could afford that too. It was shaped like a cross, through which the air blew freely. From the roof of the Cathedral the people seemed to have grown bigger as against the Galleria. The Galleria consoled me completely for the fact that I did not see the ancient Roman ruins.

Transparent inscription deep in the tiles over the brothel: *Al vero Eden.* Heavy traffic between there and the street, mostly single persons. Up and down the narrow streets of the neighborhood. They were clean, some had sidewalks in spite of their narrow width; once we looked from one narrow street down another that ran into it at right angles and saw a woman leaning against the window grating on the top floor of a house. I was lighthearted and unhesitating in everything at the time, and, as always in such moods, felt my body grow heavier. The girls spoke their French like virgins. Milanese beer smells like beer, tastes like wine. Max regrets what he writes only during the writing of it, never afterward. Somewhat apprehensively, Max took a cat for a walk in the reading room.

A girl with a belly that had undoubtedly spread shapelessly over and between her outspread legs under her transparent dress while she had been sitting down; but when she stood up it was pulled in, and her body at last looked something like what a girl's body should. The Frenchwoman whose sweetness, to an analytical eye, chiefly showed in her round, talkative and devoted knees. An imperious and monumental figure that thrust the money she had just earned into her stocking.—The old man who lay one hand atop the other on one knee.—The woman by the door, whose sinister face was Spanish, whose manner of putting her hands on her hips was Spanish and who stretched herself in her close-fitting dress of prophylactic silk.—At home it was with the German bordello girls that one lost a sense of one's nationality for a moment, here it was with the French girls. Perhaps insufficiently acquainted with the conditions here.

My passion for iced drinks punished: one grenadine, two aranciatas in the theater, one in the bar on the Corso Emmanuele, one sherbet in the coffeehouse in the Galleria, one French Thierry mineral water that all at once disclosed what had been the effect of everything that I had had before. Sadly went to bed, looking out from it on a sweeping, very Italianate prospect framed in the shallow bay window of a side wall. Miserably awoke with a dry pressure against the walls of my mouth.—The very unofficial elegance of the police who make their rounds carrying their knit gloves in one hand and their canes in the other.

September 5. Banca Commerciale on Scala Square. Letters from home.—Card to my boss.—Our astonishment when we entered the Cathedral.—Wanted to make an architectural sketch of it; the Cathedral interior was purely architectural, there were no benches for the most part, few statues on the pillars, a few dim pictures on the distant walls; the individual visitors on the Cathedral floor provided a measure of its height, and their walking about provided a measure of its extent. Sublime, but recalled the Galleria too directly.

Inexcusable to travel—or even live—without taking notes. The deathly feeling of the monotonous passing of the days is made impossible.

Climbed to the roof of the Cathedral. A young Italian in front made the climb easier for us by humming a tune, trying to take off his coat, looking through cracks through which only sunlight could be seen, and continually tapping at the numerals that showed the number of steps.— View from the roof: something was wrong with the trolleys down below, they moved so slowly, only the curve of the rails carried them along. A conductor, distorted and foreshortened from where we stood, hurried to his trolley and jumped in. A fountain shaped like a man, spinal column and brain removed to make a passage for the rainwater.— Each of the great stained glass windows was dominated by the color of some one piece of clothing that recurred over and over again in the individual panes.

Max: Toy railroad station in the display of a toy store, rails that formed a circle and led nowhere; is and will remain his strongest impression of Milan. An attempt to show the variety of the stock could account for placing the railroad station and Cathedral side by side in the display.— From the back portal of the Cathedral you looked right into the face of a large clock on a roof.—Teatro Fossati.— Trip to Stresa. The people turning in their sleep in the crowded compartment. The two lovers.—Afternoon in Stresa.

Thursday, September 7. Bath, letters, departure.—Sleeping in public.—

Friday, September 8. Trip [to Paris]. Italian couple. Clergyman. American. The two little Frenchwomen with their fat behinds. Montreux. Your legs parted company on the broad Parisian streets.—Japanese lanterns in the garden restaurants.—The Place de la Concorde is arranged so that its sights are off in the distance, where one's eye can easily find them out, but only if it looks for them.

Ecole Florentine (XVth century), apple scene.—Tintoretto: *Suzanne*.—Simone Martini: (1285, école de Sienne) *Jésus Christ marchant au Calvaire*.—Mantegna: *La Sagesse victorieuse des Vices* 1431–1506, école Vénétienne.—Titian: *Le Concile de Trente* 1477–1576.—Raphael: *Apollo and Marsyas*.—Velasquez: *Portrait de Philippe IV roi d'Espagne* 1599–1660. Jacob Jordaens 1593–1678: *Le concert après le repas*.—Rubens: *Kermesse*.[79]

Confiserie de l'enfant gâté, Rue des Petits Champs. Washerwoman in morning undress.—Rue des Petits Champs so narrow it was entirely in the shade. Le sou du soldat, société anonyme. Capital one mill., Avenue de l'Opéra.—Robert, Samuel. *Ambassadeur:* a roll of the drums followed by brasses (the double *s*), with the *eur* the drumsticks are lifted up in the midst of their flourish and are silent.—Gare de Lyon. The construction workers' substitute for suspenders is a colored sash worn round the waist; here, where sashes have an official meaning, it gives it a democratic effect.

I didn't know whether I was sleepy or not, and the question bothered me all morning on the train. Don't mistake the nursemaids for French governesses of German children.

Prise de Salins, May 17, 1668, par M. Lafarge. In the background a man dressed in red on a white horse and a man in dark clothes on a dark horse catch their breath after the siege of a city by going for a ride while a storm approaches.—*Voyage de Louis XVI à Cherbourg*, 23 juin 1786.—*Bivouak de Napoléon sur le champ de bataille de Wagram, nuit de 5 au 6 juillet 1809.*[80] Napoleon is sitting alone, one leg propped on a low table. Behind him a smoking campfire. The shadows of his right leg and of the legs of the table and camp stool lie in the foreground like rays about him. Peaceful moon. The generals, in a distant semi-circle, look into the fire or at him.

How easy it is for a grenadine and seltzer to get into your nose when you laugh (bar in front of the Opéra Comique).

Platform tickets—that vulgar intrusion on family life—are unknown.

Alone [in Erlenbach [81]] in the reading room with a lady who was hard of hearing; while she looked elsewhere, I vainly introduced myself to her; she considered the rain I pointed to outside as a continuing humidity. She was telling fortunes by cards according to the instructions given in a book beside her, into which she intently peered with her head propped against her fist. There must have been a hundred little miniature cards printed on both sides in her fist that she hadn't used yet. Near by, his back to me, an old gentleman dressed in black was reading the *Münchner Neueste Nachrichten*. A pouring rain. Traveled with a Jewish goldsmith. He was from Cracow, a little more than twenty years old, had been in America two and a half years, had been living in Paris for two months and had had only fourteen days' work. Badly paid (only ten francs a day), no place to do business. When you've just come to a city you don't know what your work is worth. Fine life in

Amsterdam. Full of people from Cracow. Every day you knew what was new in Cracow, for someone was always going there or coming back. There were entire streets where only Polish was spoken. Made a lot of money in New York because the girls earn a lot there and can deck themselves out. Paris wouldn't compare with it, the minute you stepped into the boulevards you could see that. Left New York because his people live here, after all, and because they wrote him: We're here in Cracow and still make a living too; how long are you going to stay in America? Quite right. Enthusiastic over the way the Swiss live. Living out in the country as they do and raising cattle, they must get to be as strong as giants. And the rivers. But the most important thing is, bathe in running water after you get up.—He had long, curly hair, only occasionally ran his fingers through it, very bright eyes, a gently curving nose, hollows in his cheeks, a suit of American cut, a frayed shirt, falling socks. His bag was small, but when he got off he carried it as if it had been a heavy burden. His German was disturbed by an English pronunciation and English expressions; his English was so strong that his Yiddish was given a rest. Full of animation after a night spent in traveling. "You're an Austrian, aren't you? You have one of those raincapes too. All the Austrians have them." By showing him the sleeves I proved that it was not a cape but a coat. He still maintained that every Austrian had a cape. This was how they threw it on. He turned to a third person and showed him how they did it. He pretended to fasten something in back on his shirt collar, bent his body to see whether it held, then pulled this something first over his right then over his left arm, until he was entirely enveloped in it and nice and warm, as you could see. Although he was sitting down, the movements of his legs showed how easily and unconcernedly an Austrian wearing a cape like that could walk. There was almost no mockery in all this, rather it was done as if by someone who had traveled around a bit and seen something of the world. There was a little child-like touch to it all.

My walk in the dark little garden in front of the sanatorium.

Morning setting-up exercises accompanied by the singing of a song from *Wunderhorn* which someone played on the cornet.

The secretary who went for walking trips every winter, to Budapest, southern France, Italy. Barefoot, ate raw food only (whole-wheat bread, figs, dates), lived two weeks with two other people in the region around Nice, mostly naked, in a deserted house.

Fat little girl who was always picking her nose, clever but not especially pretty, had a nose with no expectations, was called Waltraute and, according to a young woman, there was something radiant about her.

I dreaded the pillars of the dining room in advance, because of the pictures (tall, shining, solid marble) I had seen in the prospectus, and cursed myself during the trip across on the little steamer. But they turned out to be made of very unpretentious brick painted in bad imitation of marble, and unusually low.

Lively conversation between a man in the pear tree opposite my window and a girl on the ground floor whom I couldn't see.

A pleasant feeling when the doctor listened over and over again to my heart, kept asking me to change my position and couldn't make up his mind. He tapped the area around my heart for an especially long time; it lasted so long he seemed almost absent-minded.

The quarrel at night between the two women in the compartment, the lamp of which they had covered over. The Frenchwoman lying down screamed out of the darkness, and the elderly woman whom her feet were pressing against the wall and who spoke French badly didn't know what to do. According to the Frenchwoman she should have left the seat, carried all her luggage over to the other side, the back seat, and permitted her to stretch out. The Greek doctor in my compartment said she was definitely in the wrong, in bad, clear French that was apparently based on German. I fetched the conductor, who settled matters between them.

Again encountered the lady, who is a fanatical writer too. She carried with her a portfolio full of stationery, cards, pens and pencils, all of which was an incitement to me.

This place looks like a family group now. Outside it is raining, the mother has her fortune-telling cards in front of her and the son is writing. Otherwise the room is empty. Since she is hard of hearing, I could also call her mother.

In spite of my great dislike for the word "type," I think it is true that nature-healing and everything associated with it is producing a new human type represented in a person such as Mr. Fellenberg (of course, I only know him superficially). People with thin skins, rather small heads, looking exaggeratedly clean, with one or two incongruous little details (in the case of Mr. F., some missing teeth, the beginning of a paunch), a greater spareness than would seem appropriate to the structure of their bodies, that is, every trace of fattiness is suppressed, they treat their health as if it were a malady, or at least something they had acquired by their own merit (I'm not reproaching them), with all the other consequences of an artificially cultivated feeling of good health.

In the balcony at the Opéra Comique. In the front row a man in a frock coat and top hat; in one of the rear rows, a man in his shirt sleeves (with his shirt even turned in in front in order to leave his chest free), all prepared to go to bed.

National quarrels in Switzerland. Biel, a wholly German city a few years ago, is in danger of becoming gallicized because of the heavy immigration of French watchmakers. Ticino, the only Italian canton, wants to secede from Switzerland. An irredenta exists. The reason is that the Italians have no representation in the Federal Council (it has seven members); with their small number (perhaps 180,000) it would need a council of nine members to give them representation. But they don't want to change the number. The St. Gotthard railroad was a private German enterprise, had German officials who founded a German school in Bellinzona; now that it has been taken over by the state the Italians want Italian officials and the suppression of the German school. And education is actually a matter in which only the government of the canton is authorized to make decisions. Total population: two-thirds German, one-third French and Italian.

The ailing Greek doctor who drove me out of the compartment with his coughing during the night can only—so he said—digest mutton. Since he had to spend the night in Vienna, he asked me to write the German word down for him.

Though it was raining and later on I was left completely to myself, though my misery is always present to me, though group games were going on in the dining hall in which I took no part because of my lack of skill, and even though in the end everything I wrote was bad, I still had no feeling for either what was ugly or degrading, sad or painful in this lonely state of mine, a loneliness, moreover, that is organic with me—as though I consisted only of bones. At the same time I was happy to think that I had detected the trace of an appetite in the region above my clogged intestines. The old lady, who had gone to fetch some milk for herself in a tin pot, returned, and before losing herself in her cards again asked me: "What are you writing? Notes? A diary?" And since she knew she would not understand my answer, she went right on with her questions: "Are you a student?" Without thinking of her deafness, I replied: "No, but I was one"; and while she was already laying out her cards again, I was left alone with my sentence, the weight of which compelled me to go on looking at her for a while.

We are two men sitting at a table with six or seven Swiss women. When my plate is half empty, or when I stare in boredom round me in the dining hall, I see plates rise up far off in the distance, rapidly draw near me in the hands of women (sometimes I call them Mrs., sometimes Miss), and slowly go back the way they came when I say, "No, thank you."

Le Siège de Paris par Francisque Sarcey: July 19, 1870, declaration of war. Those who were famous for a few days. —Changing character of the book as it describes the changing character of Paris.—Praise and blame for the same things. The calm of Paris after the surrender is sometimes French frivolity, sometimes French ability to resist.—September 4th, after Sedan, the Republic—workers and national guardsmen on ladders hammer the *N* off the public buildings—eight days after the Republic was proclaimed the enthusiasm still ran so high that they could get no one to work on the fortifications.—The Germans are advancing.

Parisian jokes: MacMahon was captured at Sedan, Bazaine surrendered Metz, the two armies have at last established contact.—The destruction of the suburbs ordered —no news for three months.—Paris never had such an appetite as at the beginning of the siege. Gambetta organized the rising of the provinces. Once, by good fortune, a letter from him arrived. But instead of giving the exact dates everyone was on fire to know, he wrote only *que la résistance de Paris faisait l'admiration de l'univers.*—Insane club meetings. A meeting of women in the Triat school. "How should the women defend their honor against the enemy?" With the *doigt de Dieu,* or rather *le doigt prussique. Il consiste en une sorte de dé en caoutchouc que les femmes se mettent au doigt. Au bout de ce dé est un petit tube contenant de l'acide prussique.* If a German soldier comes along, he is extended a hand, his skin is pricked and the acid is injected.—The Institute sends a scholar out by balloon to study the eclipse of the sun in Algeria.—They ate last year's chestnuts and the animals of the Jardin des Plantes.—There were a few restaurants where everything was to be had up to the last day.—Sergeant Hoff, who was so famous for murdering a Prussian to avenge his father, disappeared and was considered a spy.—State of the army: several of the outposts have a friendly drink with the Germans.—Louis Blanc compares the Germans to Mohicans who have studied technology.—On January 5th the bombardment begins. Doesn't amount to much. People were told to throw themselves on the ground when they heard the shelling. Street boys, grownups too, stood in the mud and from time to time shouted *gare l'obus.*—For a while General Chauzy was the hope of Paris, but met defeat like all the others; even at that time there was no reason for his renown, nevertheless, so great was the enthusiasm in Paris that Sarcey, even when writing his book, feels a vague, unfounded admiration for Chauzy.

A day in Paris at the time: Sunny and fine on the boulevards, people strolling placidly along; the scene changes near the Hotel de Ville where the Communards are in revolt, many dead, troops, excesses. Prussian shells whistle on the left bank. Quays and bridges are quiet. Back to the Théâtre Français. The audience is leaving after a performance of the *Mariage de Figaro.* The evening papers are just coming out, the playgoers collect in groups around the kiosks, children are playing in the Champs Elysées, Sunday strollers curiously watch a squadron of cavalry riding by with trumpets blowing.—From a German soldier's letter to his mother: *Tu n'imagines pas comme ce Paris est immense, mais les Parisiens sont de drôles de gens; ils trompettent toute la journée.*—For fourteen days there was no hot water in Paris.—At the end of January the four-and-a-half-month siege ended.

The comradely way old women behave to one another in a compartment. Stories about old women who were run over by automobiles; the rules they follow on a journey: never eat gravy, take out the meat, keep your eyes closed during the trip; but at the same time eat fruit down to the core, no tough veal, ask men to escort you across the street, cherries are the best fruit for roughage, the salvation of old women.

The young Italian couple on the train to Stresa joined another couple on the train to Paris. One of the husbands merely submitted to being kissed, and while he looked out of the window gave her only his shoulder to rest her cheek against. When he took off his coat because of the heat and closed his eyes, she seemed to look at him more intently. She wasn't pretty, there were only some thin curls around her face. The other woman wore a veil with blue dots one of which would frequently obscure her eye, her nose seemed to come too abruptly to an end, the wrinkles of her mouth were youthful ones, by which she could give expression to her youthful vivacity. When she bent her head her eyes moved back and forth in a way that I have observed at home only in people who wear eyeglasses.

The efforts made by all the Frenchmen one meets to improve one's bad French, at least temporarily.

Sitting inside our carriage, uncertain as we were of which hotel to choose, we seemed to be driving our carriage uncertainly too; once we turned into a side street, then brought it back on the right road; and this in the morning traffic of the Rue de Rivoli near the markets.

Stepped out on the balcony and looked around for the first time as though I had just awakened in this room, when in fact I was so tired from the night's journey that I didn't know whether I would be able to dash around in these streets the whole day, especially in view of the way they now looked to me from above, with me not yet on them.

Beginning of our Parisian misunderstandings. Max came up my hotel room and was upset that I wasn't ready. I was washing my face, whereas I had previously said that we should just wash up a little and leave at once. Since by "washing up a little" I had only meant to exclude washing one's whole body, and on the other hand it was precisely the washing of my face that I had meant by it, which I hadn't finished yet, I didn't understand his complaints and went right on washing, even if not with quite the same solicitude; while Max, with all the dirt of the night's journey on his clothes, sat down on my bed to wait. Whenever Max finds fault with someone he has the trick of knitting his mouth and even his whole face together in a sweet expression, he is doing it this very moment, as if on the one hand he intended by this to make his reproaches more understandable, and as if he wanted to indicate on the other hand that only the sweetness of his present expression keeps him from giving me a box on the ear. In the fact that I force him into a hypocrisy unnatural to him there is contained a further reproach which I feel him to be expressing when he falls silent and the lines of his face draw apart in a contrary direction—that is, away from his mouth—in order to recover from the sweetness they had expressed, which of course has a much stronger effect than did his first expression. I, on the other hand, out of weariness can retreat so deeply inside myself that these various expressions never reach to me (such was the case in Paris); which is why I can then behave in so lordly a fashion in my misery (out of a feeling of completest indifference and without a trace of guilt) as to apologize at once. This pacified him at the time in Paris, or so at least it seemed to, and he stepped out on the balcony with me and remarked on the view, chiefly on how Parisian it was. What I really saw was only how fresh

Max was; how assuredly he fitted into a Paris of some sort
that I couldn't even perceive; how, emerging from his dark
back room, he stepped out on a Paris balcony in the sunlight for the first time in a year and knew that he was deserving of it, while I, unfortunately, was noticeably more
tired than when I had first come out on the balcony shortly
before Max. And my tiredness in Paris cannot be got over
by sleep, but only by going away. Sometimes I even consider this one of the characteristics of Paris.

This was really written without ill will, but he was at my
heels at every word.

At first I was against the Café Biard because I thought
you could only get black coffee there. It turned out that
they have milk too, even if only with bad, spongy pastry.
Almost the only way to improve Paris that I can think of
is to provide better pastry in these cafés. Later, just before
breakfast, when Max had already sat down at the table, I
hit upon the idea of going about the side streets to look for
fruit. On the way to the café I kept eating a little of the
fruit, so that Max would not be too astonished. After a
successful attempt, in an excellent café near the Versailles
railroad station under the eyes of a waiter leaning over us in
the doorway, to eat apple strudel and almond cake bought
by us in a bakery, we do the same thing in the Café Biard,
and in this way discover that, apart from enjoying fine
pastry, you more decidedly enjoy the café's real advan-
tages; such as the complete lack of attention paid to you
in the relative emptiness of the place, the good service, and
your position near the people passing by the open door and
standing at the counter. You have only to put up with the
floor's being swept—something they do frequently because
the customers come in directly from the street and mill

back and forth at the counter—and their habitual disregard of their customers while they do it.

Looking at the tiny bars that line the route of the Versailles railroad, you would think it simple for a young couple to open one up and so lead a fine, interesting life involving no risk and no hard work except at certain hours of the day. Even on the boulevards you find cheap bars of this kind cropping up in the shadow at the corner of a wedge-shaped block of houses between two side streets.

The customers in whitewash-spotted shirts around little tables in the suburban inns.

The woman with a little barrow of books calling out her wares on the Boulevard Poissonière in the evening. Look through them, gentlemen, look through them, take your pick, they're all for sale. Without urging him to buy it, even without watching obtrusively, in the midst of her cries she at once quotes the price of the book that one of the bystanders picks up. She seems to ask only that the books be looked through with more speed, more speedily exchanged for others, all of which a person can understand when he watches the way here and there someone, myself, for instance, will slowly pick up a book, slowly leaf through it a little, slowly put it down and finally walk slowly away. The solemn way she quotes the prices of the books, which are full of such ludicrous indecencies that at first you can't imagine your ever deciding to buy a book under the eyes of all the people.

How much more decision is required to buy a book from a sidewalk stall than inside the store, for choosing a book in this way is really nothing but a free deliberation in the accidental presence of the books on display.

Sitting on two little chairs facing each other on the Champs Elysées. Children up much too late were still playing in the dusk and could no longer clearly see the lines they had drawn in the dirt.

A fat usherette at the Opéra Comique rather condescendingly accepted our tip. The reason for it, I thought, was our somewhat too hesitant approach one behind the other with the theater tickets in our hand, and I inwardly resolved the following evening to refuse a tip to the usherette at the Comédie to her face; stricken by shame in her presence and mine, however, I then gave her a large tip, though everyone else came in without giving one. I even said something at the Comédie to the effect that in my opinion tips were something "not indispensable," but nevertheless had to pay again when the usherette, this time a thin one, complained that she was not paid by the management and hung her head on her breast.

Boot-polishing scene at the beginning. How the children accompanying the watch walked down the stairs in step. The overture played perfunctorily to make it easy for the latecomers to take their seats. They used to do that only to operettas. A nice simplicity of scenery. Lethargic extras, as in every performance I have seen in Paris, whereas at home they can hardly contain their high spirits. The donkey for the first act of *Carmen* was waiting in the narrow street outside the entrance to the theater, surrounded by theater people and a small sidewalk audience, until the little entrance door was clear. On the steps out-

side I bought, almost purposely, one of those fake programs
which are sold in front of every theater. A ballerina sub-
stituted for Carmen in the dance in the smugglers' inn.
How her mute body labored during Carmen's song. Later
Carmen's dance, which seemed much prettier than it really
was because of the merits of her previous performance. It
was as if she had taken a few hasty lessons from the leading ballerina before the performance. The footlights whit-
ened her soles when she leaned against the table, listening
to someone, and crossed and uncrossed her feet below her
green skirt.

Man in the lobby talking to two ladies; had a somewhat
loosely hanging frock coat which, had it not been new,
had it fitted better and had he not been wearing it here,
could have come right out of the past. Monocle allowed
to fall and raised again. Tapped uncertainly with his stick
when the conversation halted. His arm continually trembled as if at any moment he intended to put it out and
escort the ladies through the center of the crowd. Worn,
bloodless skin of his face.

We were too tired to sit out the last act (I was too tired
even for the next to the last), went off and sat down in
a bar opposite the Opéra Comique; where Max out of
weariness sprayed soda over me and I out of weariness
couldn't keep from laughing and got grenadine in my nose.
Meanwhile the last act was probably beginning; we walked
home.

The German language's faculty of sounding beautiful in
the mouths of foreigners who haven't mastered it, and for
the most part don't intend to, either. So far as we have
observed, we never could see that Frenchmen took any
delight in the errors we committed in French, or even so

much as deigned to notice them, and even we, whose
French has little feeling for the language——

The very fortunate (from my point of view) cooks and
waiters: after the general meal they eat lettuce, beans and
potatoes mixed in large bowls, take only small portions
of each dish though a great deal is served them, and from
the distance look like the cooks and waiters at home.—The
waiter with the elegantly contracted mouth and little beard
who one day waited on me, I think, only because I was
tired, awkward, abstracted and disagreeable, and for this
reason was unable to serve myself, whereas he brought the
food to me almost without being aware of it.

At Duval's on the Boulevard Sébastopol at twilight.
Three customers scattered about the place. The waitresses
murmuring quietly to each other. The cashier's cage still
empty. I ordered a yogurt, then another. The waitress
silently brought it to me, the semidarkness of the place
added to the silence too, silently she took away the silver
that had been laid at my place in preparation for the evening meal and that might be in my way. It was very pleasant to have been able to sense a tolerance and understanding for my sufferings in this woman moving so silently
about me.

In the Louvre from one bench to the next. Pang if one
was skipped.—Crowd in the Salon Carré, the excitement
and the knots of people, as if the Mona Lisa had just been
stolen.—In front of the pictures the cross-bars that you
could conveniently lean upon, especially in the gallery
where the Primitives were hung.—This compulsion I have
to look with Max at his favorite pictures, though I am too

tired to look by myself.—Looking up admiringly.—The vigor of a tall young Englishwoman who walked up and down the length of the longest gallery with her escort.

Max's appearance as he was reading *Phèdre* under a street lamp in front of the Aristede, ruining his eyes on the small print. Why does he never listen to me?—But I profited from it, unfortunately, for on the way to the theater he told me everything he had read in his *Phèdre* on the street while I had been having supper. A short distance; Max's effort to tell me everything, everything; an effort on my part too. The military show in the lobby. The crowd had been pushed back several yards, and soldiers in military fashion were regulating the flow to the box office.

Apparently a claqueur in our row. Her applause seemed to follow the regular outbursts of the head claqueur busy in the last row above us. She clapped with her face absentmindedly bent so far forward that when the applause stopped she stared in astonished concern at the palms of her mesh gloves. But at once recommenced when it was called for. But in the end clapped on her own too, and so was no claqueur after all.

The feeling theatergoers must have of being on an equal footing with the play in order to arrive toward the end of the first act and make a whole row of people stand up.

A stage set that was never changed during the five acts made the performance more impressive, and was, even if only made of paper, more solid than one of wood and stone that is continually changed.

A group of pillars facing the sea and blue sky, overgrown by creepers. Direct influence of Veronese's *Banquet*, of Claude Lorrain too.

Oenone readily passed from one rigid pose into another; once, standing erect, her robe tightly wound about her legs, her arm raised and her fist steady, she delivered herself of a verse. Often veiled the expression of her face in her hands.

I was dissatisfied with the actress playing *Phèdre* when I remembered what satisfaction I had got from reading about Rachel in the period when she had been a member of the Comédie Française.

At a sight as surprising as the first scene offered, when Hippolyte, with his man-sized bow motionless at his side, was on the point of confiding in the Pedagogue, looking directly at the audience in quiet pride while he declaimed his verses as if they had been a holiday recitation, I had the impression—a slight one, though, as often in the past— that all this was taking place for the first time, and in my general admiration there was mingled admiration for something that had succeeded at its first attempt.

Sensibly conducted brothels. Clean shutters lowered everywhere over the large windows of the house. In the concierge's box, instead of a man, a decently dressed woman who would have been at home anywhere. In Prague already, I had often taken casual notice of the Amazonian character of brothels. Here it was even more pronounced. The female concierge who rang her electric bell, detained us in her box when she was notified that two visitors were just coming down the stairs; the two respectable-looking women upstairs (why two?) who received us; the light switched on in the adjoining room in the darkness or semidarkness of which were sitting the unengaged girls; the three-quarter circle (we made it a full circle) in which they stood around us, drawn up in postures calculated to reveal them to best advantage; the long stride with which the girl who had been chosen came forward; the grasp with which the madam urged me on, while I felt myself impelled toward the exit. I cannot imagine how I got to the street, it happened so quickly. It was difficult to see the girls clearly because there were too many of them, they blinked their eyes, but most of all because they crowded too closely around one. One would have had to keep one's eyes wide open, and that takes practice. I really only remember the one who stood directly in front of me. She had gaps in her teeth, stretched herself to her full height, her clenched fist held her dress together over her pudenda, and she rapidly opened and shut her large eyes and large mouth. Her blond hair was disheveled. She was thin. Anxious lest I should forget and take off my hat. Lonely, long, absurd walk home.

The assembled visitors waiting for the Louvre to open. Girls sat among the tall columns, read their Baedekers, wrote postcards.

Even when you walked round the Venus de Milo as slowly as possible, there was a rapid and surprising altera-tion in its appearance. Unfortunately made a forced re-mark (about the waist and drapery), but several true ones too. I should need a plastic reproduction to remember them, especially one about the way the bended left knee affected her appearance from every side, though sometimes only very slightly. My forced remark: One would ex-pect the body to grow slimmer above where the drapery leaves off, but at first it is even broader. The falling robe held up by the knee.

The front view of the Borghese Wrestler isn't the best one, for it makes the spectator recoil and presents a disjointed appearance. Seen from the rear, however, where for the first time you see his foot touching the ground, your eye is drawn in delight along the rigid leg and flies safely over the irresistible back to the arm and sword raised toward the front.

The subway seemed very empty to me then, especially in comparison with the time when, sick and alone, I had ridden out to the races. Even apart from the number of passengers, the fact that it was Sunday influenced the way the subway looked. The dark color of the steel sides of the cars predominated. The conductors did their work—opening and closing the car doors and swinging themselves in and out between times—in a Sunday afternoon manner. Everyone walked the long distances between branch connections in leisurely fashion. The unnatural indifference with which passengers submit to a ride in the subway was more noticeable. People seemed to face the door, or get off at unfamiliar stations far from the Opéra, as the impulse moved them. In spite of the electric lights you can definitely see the changing light of day in the stations; you notice it immediately after you've walked down, the afternoon light particularly, just before it gets dark. Arrival at the empty terminal of Porte Dauphine, a lot of tubes became visible, view into the loop where the trains make the curve they are permitted after their long trip in a straight line. Going through railroad tunnels is much worse; in the subway there isn't that feeling of oppression which a railroad passenger has under the weight—though held in check—of mountains. Then too, you aren't far off somewhere, away from people; it is rather an urban contrivance, like water pipes, for example. Tiny offices, most of them deserted, with telephones and bell systems, control the traffic. Max liked to look into them. The first time in my life I rode the subway, from Montmartre to the main boulevards, the noise was horrible. Otherwise it hasn't been bad, even intensifies the calm, pleasant sense of speed. Subway system does away with speech; you don't have to speak either when you pay or when you get in and out. Because it is so easy to understand, the subway is a frail and hopeful stranger's best chance to think that he has quickly and correctly, at the first attempt, penetrated the essence of Paris.

You recognize strangers by the fact that they no longer know their way the moment they reach the top step of the subway stairs; unlike the Parisians, they don't pass from the subway without transition into the bustle of the street. In addition, it takes a long time, after coming up, for reality and the map to correspond; we should never have been able, on foot or by carriage, to have reached the spot we stood on without the help of a map.

It is always pleasant to remember walks in parks: one's joy that the day was still so light, watching out that it didn't get dark suddenly—this and fatigue governed one's manner of walking and looking about. The automobiles pursuing their rigid course along the wide, smooth streets. In the little garden restaurant, the red-uniformed band, unheard amidst the noise of the automobiles, laboring at its instruments for the entertainment of those in its immediate vicinity only. Parisians never previously seen walking hand in hand. Men in shirt sleeves, with their families, in the semidarkness under the trees amid the flower beds, notwithstanding the "keep off" signs. There the absence of Jews was most noticeable. Looking back at the tiny train, which seemed to have rolled off a merry-go-round and puffed away. The path to the lake of the Bois de Boulogne. My most vivid recollection of the first sight of the lake is the bent back of a man stooping down to us under the canopy of our boat to give us tickets. Probably because of my anxiety about the tickets and my inability to make the man explain whether the boat went around the lake or across to the island, and whether it stopped off anywhere. And for this reason I was so taken by him that I often see him, with equal vividness, bent all by himself over the lake without there being any boat. A lot of people in summer clothes on the dock. Boats with unskilful rowers in them. The low bank of the lake, it had no railing. A slow trip, reminding me of walks I used to take alone every Sunday several years ago. Lifting our feet out of the water in the bottom of the boat. The other passengers' astonishment, when they heard our Czech, at finding themselves in the same boat with foreigners such as we were. A lot of people on the slopes of the western bank, canes planted in the ground, outspread newspapers, a man and his daughters flat in the grass, some laughter, the low eastern bank; the paths bounded by a low fence of curving sticks linked together, to keep the lap dogs off the lawns, something we did away with long ago back home; a stray dog was running across the meadow; rowers toiling solemnly at their oars, a girl in their heavy boat. I left Max over his grenadine, looking particularly lonely in the shadow at the edge of the half-empty garden café past which went a street that was intersected as if by chance by another street unknown to me. Automobiles and carriages drove out from the shadowy crossing into even more desolate-looking regions. Saw a large iron fence that was probably a part of the food tax bureau; it was open, however, and everyone could go through. Nearby you saw the glaring light of Luna Park, which only added to the twilight confusion. So much light and so empty. I stumbled perhaps five times on the way to Luna Park and back to Max.

Monday, September 11. Automobiles are easier to steer on asphalt pavement, but also harder to bring to a stop. Especially when the gentleman at the wheel, taking advantage of the wide streets, the beautiful day, his light automobile and his skill as a driver to make a little business trip, at the same time weaves his car in and out at crossings in the manner of pedestrians on the sidewalk. This is why such an automobile, on the point of turning off into a side street and while yet on the large square, runs into a tricycle; it comes gracefully to a halt, however, does little damage to the tricycle, has only stepped on its toe, as it were; but whereas a pedestrian having his toe stepped on in such fashion only hurries on all the faster, the tricycle remains where it is with a bent front wheel.

The baker's boy, who until this point had been riding along on his vehicle (the property of the N. Co.) without a thought, in that clumsy wobble peculiar to tricycles, climbs down, walks up to the motorist—who likewise climbs out—and upbraids him in a manner that is subdued by his respect for the owner of an automobile and inflamed by his fear of his boss. It is first a question of explaining how the accident happened. The automobile owner with raised palms simulates the approaching automobile; he sees the tricycle cutting across his path, detaches his right hand and gesticulates back and forth in warning to it, a worried expression on his face—what automobile could apply its brakes in time in so short a distance? Will the tricycle understand this and give the automobile the right of way? No, it is too late; his left hand ceases its warning motions, both hands join together for the collision, his knees bend to watch the last moment. It has happened, and the bent, motionless tricycle standing there can now assist in the description.

The baker's boy is hardly a match for the motorist. First of all, the motorist is a brisk, educated man; second, until now he has been sitting in the automobile at his ease, can go right back in and sit at his ease again; and third, he really had had a better view from the height of the automobile of what had happened. Some people have collected together in the meantime who don't stand in a circle round him but rather before him, as only befits the motorist's performance. The traffic meanwhile must manage without the space these people occupy, who in addition move back and forth with every new idea occurring to the motorist. Thus, for example, at one point they all march over to the tricycle to have a closer look at the damage that is so much under discussion. The motorist doesn't think it very serious (a number of people, all engaged in fairly loud discussion, agree with him), though he is not satisfied with just a glance but walks around it, peers into it from above and through it from below. One person, wanting to shout, sides with the tricycle, for the motorist is in no need of anyone's shouts; but is answered very well and loudly by an unknown man who has just come up, and who, if one were to believe him, had been with the motorist in the car. Every once in a while several spectators laugh aloud together, but then grow quiet at the thought of some new, weighty point.

Now there is really no great difference of opinion between the motorist and the baker's boy; the motorist sees around him a small, friendly crowd of people whom he has convinced, the baker's boy gradually stops monotonously stretching out his arms and uttering his protests, the motorist does not as a matter of fact deny that he has caused a little damage and by no means puts all the blame on the baker's boy, both are to blame, therefore none, such things just happen, etc. In short, the affair would finally have become embarrassing, the votes of the spectators, already conferring together over the costs of the repairs, would have had to be called for, if they hadn't remembered that they could call a policeman. The baker's boy, whose position in respect to the motorist is more and more a subordinate one, is simply sent off by him to fetch a policeman, his tricycle being entrusted to the motorist's protection. Without any dishonorable intention, for he has no need to build a faction for himself, the motorist goes on with his story even in his adversary's absence. Because you can tell a story better while you smoke, he rolls a cigarette for himself. He has a supply of tobacco in his pocket.

Uninformed newcomers, even if only errand boys, are systematically conducted first to the automobile, then to the tricycle, and only then instructed in all the details. If the motorist catches an objection from someone standing far back in the crowd, he answers him on tiptoe so as to look him in the face. It proves too much trouble to conduct the people back and forth between the automobile and the tricycle, so the automobile is driven nearer to the sidewalk of the side street. An undamaged tricycle stops and the rider has a look at things. As if to teach one a lesson in the difficulties of driving an automobile, a large motor bus has come to a halt in the middle of the square. The motor is being worked on up front. The passengers, alighting from the bus, are the first to bend down around it, with a real feeling of their more intimate relationship to it. Meanwhile the motorist has brought a little order into things and pushed the tricycle, too, closer to the sidewalk. The affair is losing its public interest. Newcomers now have to guess at what has happened. The motorist has withdrawn completely with several of the original onlookers, who are important witnesses, and is talking quietly to them.

But where in the meantime has the poor boy been wandering about? At last he is seen in the distance, starting to cut across the square with the policeman. No one had displayed any impatience, but interest is at once revived. Many new onlookers appear who will enjoy at no expense the extreme pleasure of seeing statements taken. The motorist leaves his group and walks over to the policeman, who has at once accepted the situation with a degree of calm that the parties involved were able to attain only after a half-hour's lapse. He begins taking statements without any lengthy preliminary investigation. With the speed of a carpenter, the policeman pulls an ancient, dirty but blank sheet of paper out of his notebook, notes down the name of the baking company, and to make certain of the latter walks around the tricycle as he writes. The unconscious, unreasonable hope of those present that the policeman will bring the whole matter to an immediate and objective conclusion is transformed into an enjoyment of the details of the statement-taking. The taking of the statements occasionally flags. Something has gone wrong with the policeman's notes, and for a while, in his effort to set it right, he hears and sees nothing further. He had, that is, begun to write on the sheet of paper at a point where for some reason or other he should not have begun. But now it is done in any case and his astonishment finds perpetual renewal. He has to keep turning the paper around over and over again to persuade himself of his having incorrectly begun the statements. He had, however, soon left off this incorrect beginning and begun to write in some other place; and so when he has finished a column he cannot tell—without much unfolding and careful scrutiny of the paper—where is the right place for him to go on. The calm the whole affair acquires in this way is not to be compared with that earlier calm which it had achieved solely through the parties involved.

TRIP TO WEIMAR AND JUNGBORN[82]
JUNE 28—JULY 29, 1912

Friday, June 28. Left from the Staatsbahnhof. Felt fine. Sokols [83] delayed the departure of the train. Took off my jacket, stretched out full length on the seat. Bank of the Elbe. The beautifully situated villages and villas, as on lake shores. Dresden. Clean, punctilious service. Calmly spoken words. Massive look of the buildings as a result of the use of concrete; though in America, for example, it hasn't this effect. The Elbe's placid waters marbled by eddies.

Leipzig, conversation with the porter. Opel's Hotel. The half-built new railroad station. Beautiful ruins of the old one. Room together. Buried alive from four o'clock on, for the noise made Max close the window. Great deal of noise, sounded like one wagon pulling another behind it. The horses on the asphalt like galloping saddle horses. The receding bell of the trolley by its pauses marking off the streets and squares.

Evening in Leipzig. Max's sense of direction, I was lost. But I discovered a beautiful oriel on the Fürstenhaus and was later confirmed by the guidebook. Night work on a construction job, probably on the site of Auerbach's Keller. A dissatisfaction with Leipzig that I couldn't throw off. The attractive Café Oriental. Dovecot, a beer parlor. The slow-moving, long-bearded proprietor. His wife drew the beer. Their two tall robust daughters served. Drawers in the tables. Lichtenhain beer in wooden jugs. Disgraceful smell when the lid was opened. An infirm habitué of the place, reddish, pinched cheeks, wrinkled nose; he sat with a large group of people, then stayed on alone; the girl joined him with her beer glass. The picture of the habitué, dead twelve years ago, who had been going there for fourteen years. He is lifting his glass, behind him a skeleton. Many heavily bandaged students in Leipzig. Many monocles.

Friday, June 29. Breakfast. The man who wouldn't sign the receipt for a money order on Saturday. Walk. Max to Rowohlt. Museum of the book trade. Couldn't contain myself in the presence of all the books. The ancient look of the streets of the publishing quarter, though there were straight streets too, and newer but less decorative houses. Public reading room. Lunch in the Manna. Bad. Wilhelm's winehouse; dimly lit tavern in a courtyard. Rowohlt: young, red-cheeked, beads of sweat between his nose and cheeks, moved only above the hips. Count Bassewitz, author of *Judas*, large, nervous, expressionless face. The movement in his waist, a strong physique carried well. Hasenclever, a lot of shadow and highlights in a small face, bluish colors too. All three flourished sticks and arms. Queer daily lunch in the winehouse. Large, broad wine cups with slices of lemon. In the Café Français, Pinthus, correspondent for the *Berliner Tageblatt*, a round, rather flat face, correcting the typescript of a review of *Johanna von Neapel* (première the previous evening). Café Français. Rowohlt was rather serious about wanting a book from me. Publishers' personal obligations and their effect on the average of the present-day German literature. In the publishing house.

Left for Weimar at five o'clock. The old maid in the compartment. Dark skin. Beautiful contours of her chin and cheeks. The twisted seams of her stockings; her face was concealed by the newspaper and we looked at her legs. Weimar. She got off there too, after putting on a large old hat. Later on I saw her again while looking at the Goethehaus from the market place.

Long way to the Hotel Chemnitius. Almost gave up. Search for a place to swim. Public beach on the Kirschberg. Schwanensee. Walked at night to the Goethehaus. Recognized it at once. All of it a yellowish-brown color. Felt the whole of our previous life share in the immediate impression. The dark windows of the uninhabited rooms. The light-colored bust of Juno. Touched the wall. White shades pulled part way down in all the rooms. Fourteen windows facing on the street. The chain on the door. No picture quite catches the whole of it. The uneven surface of the square, the fountain, the irregular alignment of the house along the rising slope of the square. The dark, rather tall windows in the midst of the brownish-yellow. Even without knowing it was the Goethehaus, the most impressive middle-class house in Weimar.

Sunday the 30th. Morning. Schillerhaus. The hunchbacked woman who came forward and in a few words, but mostly by the tone of her voice, seemed to be apologizing for the fact that these souvenirs still existed. On the steps, Clio, as diarist. Picture of the centennial birthday celebration, November 10, 1859; the decorated, enlarged house. Italian views, Bellagio, presents from Goethe. Locks of hair no longer human, yellow and dry as the beard on grain. Maria Pavlovna, slender neck, her face no broader, large eyes. Various Schiller heads. Well-arranged house for a writer. Waiting room, reception room, study, sleeping alcoves. Frau Junot, his daughter, resembled him. "Large-Scale Arboriculture Based on Small-Scale Experiments," his father's book.

Goethehaus. Reception rooms. Quick look into the study and bedroom. Sad, reminding one of dead grandfathers. The garden that had gone on growing since Goethe's death. The beech tree darkening his study.

While we were still sitting below on the landing, she ran past us with her little sister. The plaster greyhound on the landing is associated in my memory with this running. Then we saw her again in the Juno room, and again when we were looking out of the garden room. There were many other times I thought I heard her step and voice. Two carnations handed through the balcony railing. Went into the garden too late. I caught sight of her on a balcony. She came down only later on, with a young man. In passing I thanked her for having called our attention to the garden. But we did not leave yet. Her mother came up, a conversation sprang up in the garden. She stood next to a rosebush. Urged on by Max, I went over to her, learned of the excursion to Tiefurt. I'll go too. She's going with her parents. She mentioned an inn from where you can see the door of the Goethehaus. Gasthaus zum

Schwan. We were sitting among stands of ivy. She came out of the house. I ran over, introduced myself to everyone, received permission to accompany them and ran back again. Later the family arrived, without the father. I wanted to join them; no, they were going to have coffee first, I was supposed to follow with the father. She told me to go into the house at four. I called for the father after taking leave of Max.

Conversation with the coachman outside the gate. Walk with the father. Talked about Silesia, the Grand Duke, Goethe, the National Museum, photography and drawing, and our nervous age. Stopped in front of the house where they were drinking coffee. He ran up and called them all to the bay window; he was going to take a picture. Out of nervousness played ball with a little girl. Walked with the men, the two women in front of us, the three girls in front of them. A small dog scampered in and out among us. Castle in Tiefurt. Sightseeing with the three girls. She has a lot of those things in the Goethehaus too, and better. Explanations in front of the Werther pictures. Fräulein von Göchhausen's room. Walled-up door. Imitation poodle. Then left with her parents. Twice took pictures in the park; one on a bridge, it won't come out. At last, on the way home, a definite contact but without establishing any real relationship. Rain. Breslau carnival jokes told in the Archives. Took leave in front of the house. I stood around on Seifengasse. Max had meanwhile napped.

In the evening, incomprehensibly, ran into her three times. She with her girl friend. The first time we escorted them on their way. I can come to the garden any time after six in the evening. Now she had to go home. Then met her again on the Rundplatz, which had been got ready for a duel. They were talking to a young man in a manner more hostile than friendly. But then why hadn't they stayed home, since we had already escorted them to the Goetheplatz? They had had to go home as quickly as possible, hadn't they? Why were they now running out of Schillerstrasse down the small flight of steps into the out-of-the-way square, pursued by the young man or on their way to meet him, apparently without having been home at all? Why, after speaking a few words to the young man at a distance of ten paces and apparently refusing his escort, did they turn around again and run back alone? Had we, who had passed by with only a simple greeting, disturbed them? Later we walked slowly back; when we came to the Goetheplatz they once more came running out of another street almost into our arms, evidently very frightened. To spare them, we turned away. But they had already gone a roundabout way.

Monday, July 1. Gartenhaus am Stern. Sat in the grass in front of it and sketched. Memorized the verse on the Ruhesitz. Box bed. Slept. Parrot in the court calling Grete. Went without success to the Erfurter Allee, where she is learning to sew. Bathing.

Tuesday, July 2. Goethehaus. Garrets. Looked at the photographs in the custodian's quarters. Children standing around. Talked about photography. Continually on the alert for a chance to speak to her. She went off to her sewing with a friend. We stayed behind.

In the afternoon, Liszthaus. A virtuoso's place. Old Pauline. Liszt worked from five to eight, then church, then slept a second time, visitors from eleven on. Max took a bath, I went for the photographs, ran into her just before, walked up to the gate with her. Her father showed me the

pictures, but finally I had to go. She smiled at me mean-
inglessly, purposelessly, behind her father's back. Sad.
Thought of having the photographs enlarged. To the drug-
gist. Back to the Goethehaus again for the negatives. She
saw me from the window and opened the door.

Often ran into Grete. At the strawberry festival, in
front of Werther's Garden, where there was a concert.
The suppleness of her body in its loose dress. The tall officers who came out of the Russischen Hof. Every kind of
uniform. Strong slender fellow in dark clothes.

The brawl on the side street. "You're the biggest *Dreck-
orsch* there is!" The people at the windows. The departing
family, a drunk, an old woman with a rucksack, and two
boys tagging along.

I choke up at the thought of my having to leave soon.
Discovery of the Tivoli. The old snake charmer; her
husband who acts as the magician. The women German
teachers.

Wednesday, July 3. Goethehaus. Photographs were to
be taken in the garden. She was nowhere in sight so I
was sent to fetch her. She is always all atremble with movement, but stirs only if you speak to her. They snapped
the photographs. The two of us on the bench. Max showed
the man how to do it. She agreed to meet me the next
day. Öttingen was looking through the window and forbade Max and me, who happened to be standing alone at
the apparatus, to take photographs. But we weren't taking photographs at all! Her mother was still friendly then.

Not counting the schools and those who don't pay, there
are thirty thousand visitors every year.—Swim. The children boxing seriously and calmly.

Grand-ducal library in the afternoon. The praise of it

in the guidebook. The unmistakable Grand Duke. Massive chin and heavy lips. Hand inside his buttoned coat. Bust of Goethe by David, with hair bristling backward and a large, tense face. The transformation of a palace into a library, which Goethe undertook. Busts by Passow (pretty, curly-haired boy), Zach. Werner, narrow, searching, out-thrust face. Gluck. Cast from life. The holes in the mouth from the tubes through which he breathed. Goethe's study. You passed through a door straight into Frau von Stein's garden. The staircase that a convict fashioned from a giant oak without using a single nail.

Walk in the park with the carpenter's son, Fritz Wenski. His earnest speech. At the same time he kept striking at the shrubbery with a branch. He is going to be a carpenter too, and do his *Wanderjahre*. They no longer travel now in the way they did in his father's time, the railroad is spoiling people. To become a guide you would have to know languages, hence you must either learn them in school or buy the necessary books. Whatever he knew about the park he either learned in school or heard from the guides. Remarks plainly picked up from the guides which didn't fit in with the rest of his conversation; for instance, of the Roman house nothing but: This was the tradesmen's entrance.—Borkenhäuschen. Shakespeare monument.

Children around me on Karlsplatz. They discussed the navy. The children's earnestness. Ships going down. The children's air of superiority. Promise of a ball. Distribution of cookies. *Carmen* garden concert. Completely under its spell.

Thursday, July 4. Goethehaus. The promised appointment confirmed with a loud yes. She was looking out through the gate. I misinterpreted this, for she continued to

look out even when we were there. I asked once more:
"Even if it rains?" "Yes."

Max went to Jena, to Diederich's. I to the Fürsten-
gruft. With the officers. Above Goethe's coffin a golden
laurel wreath, donated by the German women of Prague
in 1882. Met everyone again in the cemetery. The Goethe
family vault. Walter von Goethe, b. Weimar, April 9,
1818, d. Leipzig, April 15, 1885: "With him the house of
Goethe ceased to be, whose name shall outlive the ages."
Inscription over the grave of Frau Karoline Falk: "Though
God took seven of her children, she was a mother to the
children of strangers. God shall dry all her tears." Charlotte
von Stein: 1742–1827.

Swim. Didn't sleep in the afternoon in order to keep an
eye on the uncertain weather. She didn't keep the appointment.

Found Max in bed with his clothes on. Both of us unhappy. If a person could only pour sorrow out the window.

In the evening Hiller, with his mother. I dashed away
from the table because I thought I saw her. Mistake. Then
all of us went to the Goethehaus. Said hello to her.

Friday, July 5. Walked to no avail to the Goethehaus.—
Goethe-Schiller Archives. Letters from Lenz. Letter from
the citizens of Frankfort to Goethe, August 28, 1830:

"A number of citizens of the old city on the Mayn, long
wont to greet the 28th of August with beakers in their
fist, would commend the favor of heaven could they welcome in person within the precincts of the Free City that
rare Frankfort man whom this day saw come into the
world.

"But as one year follows the next and they continue to hope and wait and wish, they must for the present be content to extend the gleaming bumper across woods and plains, frontiers and boundaries, to the lucky city on the Ilm, begging their honored fellow townsman the favor of clinking glasses with him and singing:

> *Willst Du Absolution*
> *Deinen Treuen geben,*
> *Wollen wir nach Deinem Wink*
> *Unablässig streben,*
> *Uns vom Halben zu entwöhnen*
> *Und im Ganzen Guten Schönen*
> *Resolut zu leben.*" [84]

1757 "Sublime Grossmama! . . ."
Jerusalem to Kestner: "Might I make so bold as humbly to ask to borrow Your Excellency's pistols for a journey I intend?"
Song of Mignon, without a single change.

Went for the photographs. Took them there. Waited around to no avail, delivered only three of the six photographs. And just the worst ones, in the hope that the custodian, to vindicate himself, would again take photographs. Not a chance.
Swim. Straight from there to Erfurter Strasse. Max for lunch. She came with two friends. I drew her aside. Yes, she had to leave ten minutes earlier yesterday, she just now learned from her friends that I had waited yesterday. She also had some difficulty with her dancing lessons. She certainly doesn't love me, but does respect me a little. I gave her the box of chocolates with the little heart and chain twined about it, and walked on with her a short distance.

A few words between us about a meeting. Tomorrow at eleven, in front of the Goethehaus. It can only be an excuse, she has to do the cooking, I'm sure, and then—in front of the Goethehaus! Nevertheless I agreed to it. Sad agreement. Went into the hotel, sat a little while with Max, who was lying in bed.

In the afternoon, an excursion to Belvedere. Hiller and his mother. Beautiful ride in the carriage along the single allee. The castle's surprising plan, which consists of a main section and four small buildings disposed along its sides, everything low and in muted colors. A low fountain in the middle. The front faces in the direction of Weimar. The Grand Duke hadn't been there for a number of years now. He hunts, and there is no hunting to be had here. Placid footman with clean-shaven, angular face who came to meet us. Sad, as perhaps are all people who move among masters. The sadness of domestic animals. Maria Pavlovna, daughter-in-law of the Grand Duke Karl August, daughter of Maria Fedorovna and of Czar Paul who was strangled. Many Russian things. Cloisonné, copper vessels with wires hammered on between which the enamel is poured. The bedrooms with their domed sky-painted ceilings. Photographs in the still habitable rooms were the only modern touch. How they too fell unnoticed into their proper places! Goethe's room, a corner room on the ground floor. Several ceiling paintings by Oeser, restored past all recognition. Many Chinese things. The "dark Kammerfrauenzimmer." Open-air theater with two rows of seats. The carriage with benches placed back to back, *dos à dos*, in which the ladies sat while their cavaliers rode in attendance beside them. The heavy carriage drawn by three teams of horses in which Maria Pavlovna and her husband drove from Petersburg to Weimar in twenty-six days on their wedding journey. Open-air theater and park were laid out by Goethe.

In the evening to Paul Ernst. (On the street asked two girls for the house of the writer, P. E. First they looked at us reflectively, then one nudged the other as if she wanted to remind her of a name she couldn't at the moment recall. Do you mean Wildenbruch? the other then asked us.) Mustache falling over his mouth and a pointed beard. Clasped his chair or his knees, and even when he had been angered (by his critics) wouldn't let go. Lives on the Horn. A villa, seemed to be entirely filled with his family. A dish of strong-smelling fish that they were about to carry upstairs was taken back into the kitchen when we appeared.—Father Expeditus Schmidt, whom I had already met once before on the steps of the hotel, came in. Is working in the Library on an edition of Otto Ludwig. Wanted to bring narghiles into the Archives. Reviled a newspaper as a "pious snake in the grass" because it attacked his *Heiligenlegenden*.

Saturday, July 6. To Johannes Schlaf's.[85] An elderly sister who looked like him received us. He wasn't in. We will return in the evening.

Walked for an hour with Grete. It would seem that she came with her mother's consent, whom she continued speaking to through the window even from the street. Pink dress, my little heart. Restless because of the big ball in the evening. Had nothing in common with her. Conversation broke off and kept resuming again. Our pace now very fast, now very slow. Straining at any cost to conceal the fact that there was not the slightest thread of a relation between us. What was it that drove us through the park together? Only my obstinacy?

Toward evening at Schlaf's. A visit to Grete before that. She was standing in front of the partly opened kitchen door in the ball dress whose praises she had already sung and which wasn't at all as beautiful as her usual dress. Eyes red from weeping, apparently because of her dancing partner, who had already caused her great distress. I said goodbye forever. She didn't know it, nor would it have mattered to her had she known. A woman bringing roses disturbed even this little farewell. Men and women from the dancing school everywhere on the streets.

Schlaf. Doesn't precisely live in a garret, as Ernst, who has fallen out with him, tried to persuade us. A man of great animation, his stout chest enclosed in a tightly buttoned jacket. His eyes only had a sick and nervous twitch. Talked mostly of astronomy and his geocentric system. Everything else, literature, criticism, painting, still clung to him only because he hadn't thrown it off. Besides, everything will be decided by Christmas. He hadn't the slightest doubt of his victory. Max said his position in relation to the astronomers was similar to Goethe's position in relation to the opticists. "Similar," he replied, continually taking hold of the table with his hand, "but much more favorable, for I have incontestable facts on my side." His small telescope for four hundred marks. He hadn't needed it to make his discovery, or mathematics either. He is entirely happy. The sphere of his activity is infinite, for his discovery, once recognized, will have great consequences in every field (religion, ethics, aesthetics, etc.) and he will naturally be the first to be called upon to reinterpret them. When we arrived he had just been pasting notices published on the occasion of his fiftieth birthday into a large book. "On such occasions they go easy on one."

Before that, a walk with Paul Ernst in the Webicht. His contempt for the present, for Hauptmann, Wassermann, Thomas Mann. In a little subordinate clause which you only caught long after it was said, with no regard for what our opinion might be, he called Hauptmann a scribbler. Otherwise vague utterances on the Jews, Zionism, races, etc., in all of which he showed himself remarkable only as being a man who had energetically used his time to good purpose.—Dry, automatic "yes, yes" at short intervals when someone else was speaking. Once he repeated it so often that I no longer believed my ears.

July 7. Twenty-seven, number of the porter in Halle.—Now at half-past six drop down on a long-sought bench near the Gleim Memorial. If I were a child, I should have to be carried, my legs ache so. No feeling of loneliness long after saying goodbye to you. And then fell into such an apathy again that it still wasn't loneliness.

Halle, a little Leipzig. These pairs of church towers here and in Halle which are connected by small wooden bridges in the sky. Even my feeling that you won't read these things right away, but only later, makes me so uncertain.— The cyclists' club meeting on the market place in Halle for an excursion. How difficult it is to go sight-seeing in a city, or even along a single street, by oneself.

A good vegetarian lunch. Unlike other innkeepers, it is just the vegetarian innkeepers with whom the vegetarian diet doesn't agree. Timid people who approach from the side.

Trip from Halle with four Jews from Prague: two pleasant, cheerful, robust elderly men, one resembling Dr. K., one my father, but much shorter; then a weak-looking young married man, exhausted by the heat, and his dreadful, stoutly built young wife whose face was somehow derived from the X family. She was reading a three-mark Ullstein novel by Ida Boy-Ed with a gem of a title that Ullstein had probably thought up: "One Moment in Paradise." Her husband asked her how she liked it. She had only begun it. "Can't say just yet." A nice German with dry skin and a whitish-blond beard beautifully parted over his cheeks and chin took a noticeably friendly interest in everything that went on among the four.

Railroad hotel [in Jungborn], room down on the street with a little garden in front. Went off into the city. A thoroughly ancient city. Timber framework seems to be the type of construction calculated to last the longest. The beams warp everywhere, the paneling sinks in or buckles out, but the whole keeps together; at most it shrinks a little with time and becomes even more solid. I have never seen people leaning so beautifully in windows. The center posts of most of the windows were immovable. People propped their shoulders against them, children swung from them. Sturdy girls were sitting on the bottom steps of the broad landing of a staircase, the skirts of their Sunday dresses spread out around them. Drachenweg Katzenplan. In the park on a bench with some little girls; we called it a girls' bench and defended it against some boys. Polish Jews. The children called them Itzig and didn't want to sit down on the bench right after them.

Jewish hotel N.N. with a Hebrew inscription. It is a neglected, castle-like building with a wide flight of stairs in front that stands out in the narrow streets. I walked behind a Jew who came out of the hotel and spoke to him. After nine. I wanted to know something about the community. Learned nothing. Looked too suspicious to him. He kept looking at my feet. But after all, I'm a Jew too. Then I can put up at N.N.—No, I already have a place to stay.—So.—Suddenly he moved close to me. Whether I wasn't in Schöppenstedt a week ago. We said goodbye in front of the gate of his house, he was happy to be rid of me; without my even asking about it, he told me how to get to the synagogue.

People in bathrobes on the doorsteps. Old, meaningless inscriptions. Pondered the possibilities offered me, on these streets, squares, garden benches and brooksides, of feeling thoroughly unhappy. Whoever can cry should come here on Sunday. In the evening, after walking around for five hours, on the terrace of my hotel in front of a little garden. At the table near by the landlord's family with a young, lively woman who looked like a widow. Unnecessarily thin cheeks. Hair parted and fluffed out.

July 8. My house is called "Ruth." Practically arranged. Four dormers, four windows, one door. Fairly quiet. Only in the distance they are playing football, the birds are loudly singing, several naked people are lying motionless in front of my door. All except me without swimming trunks. Wonderful freedom. In the park, reading room, etc. there are pretty, fat little feet to be seen.

July 9. Slept well in the cabin, which is open on three sides. I can lean against my door like a householder. Woke up at all hours of the night and kept hearing rats or birds gurgling or flitting in the grass around the hut. The man who was freckled like a leopard. Yesterday evening lecture on clothing. The feet of Chinese women are crippled in order to give them big buttocks.

The doctor, an ex-officer; affected, insane, tearful, jovial laughter. Buoyant walk. A follower of Mazdaznan. A face created to be serious. Clean-shaven, lips made to be compressed. He steps out of his examination room, you go past him to enter. "Please step in!" he laughs after you. Forbade me to eat fruit, with the proviso that I needn't obey him. I'm an educated man, I should listen to his lectures, they have even been published, should study the question, draw my own conclusions and then act accordingly.

From his lecture yesterday: "Though your toes may be completely crippled, if you tug at one of them and breathe deeply at the same time, after a while it will straighten out." A certain exercise will make the sexual organs grow. One of his health rules: "Atmospheric baths at night are highly recommended"—(whenever it suits me, I simply slip out of bed and go out into the meadow in front of my cabin)—"but you shouldn't expose yourself too much to the moonlight, it has an injurious effect." It is impossible to clean the kind of clothes we wear today!

This morning: washing, setting-up exercises, group gymnastics (I am called the man in the swimming trunks), some hymn singing, ball playing in a big circle. Two handsome Swedish boys with long legs. Concert by a military band from Goslar. Pitched hay in the afternoon. In the evening my stomach so upset that out of irritation I refused to walk a step. An old Swede was playing tag with several little girls and was so caught up in the game that once, while running, he shouted: "Wait, I'll block these Dardanelles for you." Meant the passage between two clumps of bushes. When an old, unattractive nursemaid went by: That's something you could really tap on (her back, in the black dress with white polka dots). Constant, senseless need to confide in someone. Looks at each person to see whether there is a possibility there, and whether an opportunity will present itself.

July 10. Sprained my ankle. Pain. Loaded new hay. In the afternoon walked to Ilsenburg with a very young Gymnasium professor from Nauheim; he may go to Wickersdorf [86] next year. Coeducation, nature cure, Cohen, Freud. Story about the group of boys and girls he took on an excursion. Storm, everyone soaked through, had to strip completely in a room in the nearest inn.

A fever during the night because of my swollen ankle. The noise the rabbits made running past. When I got up during the night three of these rabbits were sitting in the meadow in front of my door. I dreamt that I heard Goethe reciting, with infinite freedom and arbitrariness.

July 11. Talked to a Dr. Friedrich Sch., a municipal official of Breslau, had been in Paris for a long time to study municipal institutions. Lived in a hotel with a view into the court of the Palais Royal. Before that in a hotel near the Observatoire. One night there were two lovers in the next room. The girl shamelessly screamed with joy. Only when he spoke through the wall and offered to call a doctor did she grow quiet, and he was able to sleep.

My two friends disturb me; their path goes past my cabin and they always pause a moment at my door for a short chat or an invitation to take a walk. But I am also grateful to them for it.

In the *Evangelischen Missionzeitung*, July, 1912, about missions in Java: "Much as may justly be urged against the amateur medical activities extensively engaged in by missionaries, it is nevertheless the principal resource of their missionary work and cannot be dispensed with."

When I see these stark-naked people moving slowly past among the trees (though they are usually at a distance), I now and then get light, superficial attacks of nausea. Their running doesn't make things any better. A naked man, a complete stranger to me, just now stopped at my door and asked me in a deliberate and friendly way whether I lived here in my house, something there couldn't be much doubt of, after all. They come upon you so silently. Suddenly one of them is standing there, you don't know where he came from. Old men who leap naked over haystacks are no particular delight to me, either.

Walked to Stapelburg in the evening. With two people I introduced and recommended to one another. Ruins. Back at ten. Some nudists prowling about among the haystacks on the meadow in front of my cabin, disappeared into the distance. At night, when I walked across the meadow to the toilet, there were three of them sleeping in the grass.

July 12. Dr. Sch.'s stories. Traveled for one year. Then a long debate in the grass on Christianity. Old, blue-eyed Adolf Just who cures everything with clay and warns me against the doctor who had forbidden me fruit. The defense of God and the Bible by a member of the "Christian Community"; as the proof he needed at the moment, he read a Psalm. My Dr. Sch. made a fool of himself with his atheism. Foreign words—illusion, autosuggestion—didn't help him a bit. Someone we didn't know asked how it was that everything goes so well with the Americans, though they swear at every second word. With most of them it was impossible to discover what their real opinions were, though they all took a lively part in the discussion. The one who spoke so passionately of Flower Day and how it was just the Methodists who held back. The one from the "Christian Community" who lunches with his pretty little boy on cherries and dry bread wrapped in a small paper bag; otherwise he lies in the grass all day, three Bibles open before him, and takes notes. It has only been three years that he has been on the right path. Dr. Sch.'s oil sketches from Holland. Pont Neuf.

Two sisters, little girls. One with a narrow face, easy posture, nose coming delicately to a point, clear, not entirely candid eyes. Her face shone with so much intelligence that I found myself looking excitedly at her for several minutes. Something moved me when I looked at her. Her more womanly little sister intercepted my glances. —A newly arrived prim miss with a bluish look. The blonde with short, disheveled hair. Supple and lean as a leather strap. Coat, blouse and skirt, nothing else. Her stride!

With Dr. Sch. (forty-three years old) on the meadow in the evening. Going for a walk, stretching, rubbing, slapping and scratching. Stark naked. Shameless.—The fragrance when I stepped out of the writing room in the evening.

July 13. Picked cherries. Lutz read Kinkel's *Die Seele* to me. After eating I always read a chapter from the Bible, a copy of which is in every room. Evening, the children at play. Little Susanne von Puttkammer, nine years old, in pink drawers.

July 14. Picked cherries on the ladder with a little basket. Was high up in the tree. Religious services in the morning on Eckarplätzen. Ambrosian chant. In the afternoon sent the two friends to Ilsenburg.

I was lying in the grass when the man from the "Christian Community" (tall, handsome body, sunburned, pointed beard, happy appearance) walked from the place where he reads to the dressing cabin; I followed him unsuspectingly with my eyes, but instead of returning to his place he came in my direction, I closed my eyes, but he was already introducing himself: H., land surveyor, and gave me four pamphlets as reading matter for Sunday. When he left he was still speaking about "pearls" and "casting," by which he meant to indicate that I was not to show the pamphlets to Dr. Sch. They are: "The Prodigal Son," "Bought, or No Longer Mine (for Unbelieving Believers)," "Why Can't the Educated Man Believe in the Bible?" and "Three Cheers for Freedom: But What Is True Freedom?" I read a little in them and then went back to him and, hesitant because of the respect in which I held him, tried to make it clear why there was no prospect of grace for me at present. Exercising a beautiful mastery over every word, something that only sincerity makes possible, he discussed this with me for an hour and a half (toward the end an old, thin, white-haired, red-nosed man in linen joined in with several indistinct remarks). Unhappy Goethe, who made so many other people unhappy. A great many stories. How he, H., forbade his father to speak when he blasphemed God in his house. "Oh, Father, may you be stricken with horror by your own words and be too terrified to speak further, I wouldn't care one bit." How his father heard God's voice on his deathbed. He saw that I was close to grace. I interrupted all his arguments and referred him to the inner voice. Successfully.

July 15. Read Kühnemann's *Schiller.*—The man who always carries a card in his pocket to his wife in case of accident.—The Book of Ruth.—I read Schiller. Not far away a naked old man was lying in the grass, an umbrella open over his head.

Plato's *Republic.*—Posed for Dr. Sch.—The page in

Flaubert on prostitution.—The large part the naked body plays in the total impression an individual gives.

A dream: The sunbathers destroyed one another in a brawl. After the two groups into which they were divided had joked with one another, someone stepped out in front of one group and shouted to the others: "Lustron and Kastron!" The others: "What? Lustron and Kastron?" He: "Right." Beginning of the brawl.

July 16. Kühnemann.—Herr Guido von Gillshausen, captain, retired, writes poetry and music. A handsome man. Out of respect for his noble birth didn't dare look up at him; broke out in a sweat (we were naked) and spoke too softly. His seal ring.—The bowing of the Swedish boys.— Talked in the park with my clothes on to a man with his clothes on. Missed the group excursion to Harzburg.

Evening. Rifle meet in Stapelburg. With Dr. Sch. and a Berlin hairdresser. The wide plain rising gently to the Burgberg, bordered by ancient linden trees, incongruously traversed by a railroad embankment. The platform from which they shot. Old peasants made the entries in the scorebook. The three fife players with women's kerchiefs hanging down their backs. Old, inexplicable custom. Several of them in old, simple blue smocks, heirlooms made of the finest linen and costing fifteen marks. Almost everyone had his gun. Muzzle-loaders. You had the impression that they were all somehow bent from work in the fields, especially when they lined up in double file. Several former meetmasters in top hats with sabers buckled around them. Horses' tails and other old emblems were carried past; excitement; then the band played, greater excitement; then silence and drumming and fife playing, still greater excitement; finally, as the drums and fifes sounded for the last

time, three flags were brought out, climax of the excitement. Forward march and off they went. Old man in a
black suit, black cap, a somewhat pinched face and a not
too long, thick, silky, unsurpassable white beard encircling
his face. The former champion shot, also in a top hat and a
sash like a curtain around his body; the sash had little metal
shields sewn all over it on each of which was engraved the
name of the champion of a given year together with the
symbol of his trade. (The master baker had a loaf of bread,
etc.) Marching off in the dust to music under the changing
light of the thickly clouded sky. Doll-like appearance of a
soldier marching with them (a rifleman now in the army)
and his hopping step. People's armies and peasant wars. We
followed them through the streets. Sometimes they were
closer, sometimes farther away, since they stopped at the
houses of the various champion shots, played, and were
given some refreshments. The dust cleared toward the end
of the column. The last pair could be seen most distinctly.
From time to time we lost sight of them entirely. Tall
peasant with somewhat sunken chest, eternal face, top
boots, clothes that seemed made of leather; how ceremoni-
ously he detached himself from the gatepost. The three
women who were standing one behind the other in front
of him. The one in the center dark and beautiful. The two
women at the gate of the farmyard opposite. In each of the
two farmyards there was a giant tree that united with the
other above the wide road. The large targets on the houses
of the former champions.

The dance floor, in two parts, divided down the middle,
the band in a fenced-off section having two rows of seats.
Empty as yet, little girls slide across the smooth boards.
(Chess players, relaxing from their play and talking, disturb me as I write.) I offer them my soda, they drink, the

oldest first. Lack of a really common language. I ask
whether they have already eaten dinner [*genachtmahlt*],
complete lack of understanding; Dr. Sch. asks whether
they have already had supper [*Abendbrot*], they begin to
have a vague understanding (he doesn't speak clearly,
breathes too hard); they are able to give an answer only
when the hairdresser asks whether they have had their
grub [*gefuttert*]. They didn't want the second soda I ordered for them, but they wanted to ride on the merry-go-
round; I, with the six girls (from six to thirteen) around
me, flew to the merry-go-round. On the way the girl who
suggested the ride boasted that the merry-go-round belonged to her parents. We sat down and went around in a
coach. Her friends around me, one on my knees. Girls
crowding about who wanted to have some fun out of my
money too, but my girls pushed them away against my
will. The proprietor's daughter superintended the reckon-
ing so that I shouldn't have to pay for strangers. If they
wished, I was ready to go for another ride, but the proprietor's daughter herself said that it was enough; instead,
she wanted to go to the candy tent. In my stupidity and
curiosity I led the way to the wheel of fortune. As far as it
was possible, they were very sparing of my money. Then
off for the candy. The tent had a large stock, and was as
clean and neat as a store on the main street of a city. At the
same time the prices were low, just as they are at our fairs.
Then we went back to the dance floor. In all this I was
more sensible of the girls than of my own bounty. Now
they were ready for soda again, and thanked me prettily,
the oldest for all of them and each for herself. When the
dance began we had to leave, it was already a quarter to ten.

The hairdresser talking incessantly. Thirty years old,
with a square beard and pointed mustache. Ran after girls

but loved his wife, who was at home running the business and couldn't travel because she was fat and couldn't stand riding. Even when they once went to Rixdorf, she twice got out of the trolley to walk for a while and recover. She didn't need a vacation, she was satisfied just to sleep late once in a while. He was faithful to her, she provided him with everything he needed. The temptations to which a hairdresser is exposed. The young wife of a restaurateur. The Swedish woman who had to pay more for everything. He bought hair from a Bohemian Jew named Puderbeutel. When a delegation from the Social Democrats came to him and demanded that he take in the *Vorwärts* too, he said: "If that's what you're here for, then I didn't send for you." But finally gave in. When he was a "junior" (assistant) he was in Görlitz. He was an organized bowler. Was at the big bowlers' convention in Braunschweig a week ago. There are some 20,000 organized German bowlers. They bowled for three days until far into the night on four championship alleys. But you couldn't say that any one person was the best German bowler.

When I entered my cabin in the evening I couldn't find the matches, borrowed some in the next cabin and made a light under the table to see if they might have fallen down there. They hadn't, but the water tumbler was standing there. Gradually I discovered that my sandals were behind the wall mirror, the matches on a window sill, the hand mirror was hanging on a projecting corner. The chamber pot rested on top of the closet, my *Education sentimentale* was in the pillow, a clothes-hook under the sheet, my traveler's inkwell and a wet washcloth in the bed, etc. All this as a punishment for my not having gone to Harzburg.

July 19. Rainy day. You lie in bed and the loud thrumming of the rain on the cabin roof is as if it were beating against one's own breast. Drops appear at the edge of the eaves as mechanically as a row of lights lit along a street. Then they fall. An old man suddenly charges across the meadow like a wild animal, taking a rain bath. The drumming of the drops in the night. As though one were sitting in a violin case. Running in the morning, the soft earth underfoot.

July 20. Morning in the woods with Dr. Sch. The red earth and the light diffused from it. The upward soar of the trunks. The broad, overhanging, flat-leaved limbs of the beeches.

In the afternoon a group of maskers arrived from Stapelburg. The giant with the man dressed up as a dancing bear. The swing of his thighs and back. March through the garden behind the music. Spectators running over the turf, through the shrubbery. Little Hans Eppe when he saw them. Walter Eppe on the mailbox. The men dressed as women, with curtains as veils. An indecent sight when they danced with the kitchenmaids, who yielded seemingly without knowing that they were men in disguise.

In the morning read the first chapter of *Education sentimentale* to Dr. Sch. A walk with him in the afternoon. Stories about his lady friend. He is a friend of Morgenstern, Baluschek, Brandenburg, Poppenberg. His horrid complaining in the cabin in the evening, on the bed with his clothes on. Talked to Miss Pollinger for the first time, but she already knew all there was to know about me. Prague she knew from *Die Zwölf aus der Steiermark*. An ash-blonde, twenty-two years old, looks like a seventeen-year-old, always worrying about her deaf mother; engaged and a flirt.

At noon the departure of Frau von W., the Swedish widow who resembles a leather strap. Only a gray jacket over her usual clothes, a little gray hat with a bit of a veil. Her brown face looked very delicate in such a frame; only distance and concealment exercise an effect on regular features. Her luggage consisted of a small knapsack, there was not much more than a nightgown in it. This is the way she always travels, came from Egypt, is going to Munich.

Dance at Stapelburg in the evening. The celebration lasts four days, hardly any work is done. We saw the new champion shot, and on his back read the names of the champions from the beginning of the nineteenth century on. Both dance floors full. Couple stood behind couple around the hall. Each had only a short dance every fifteen minutes. Most of them were silent, not from embarrassment or any other reason, but simply silent. A drunken man was standing at the edge of the dance floor, knew all the girls, lunged for them or at least stretched out his arms to hug them. Their dancing partners didn't budge. There was a great deal of noise, from the music, and the shouting of the people at the tables down below and those standing at the bar. We walked vainly around for some time (I and Dr. Sch.). I was the one who accosted a girl. I had already noticed her outside when she and two friends were eating frankfurters with mustard. She was wearing a white blouse with flowers embroidered over her arms and shoulders. Her head was bent forward in a sweet and melancholy way, so that her breast was squeezed and her blouse puffed out. Her turned-up little nose, in such a posture, added to the melancholy. Patches of reddish brown here and there on her face. I accosted her just as she was descending the two steps from the dance floor. We stood face to face and she turned around. We danced. Her name was Auguste A., she was from Wolfenbüttel and had been employed on the farm of a certain Klaude in Appenroda for a year and a half. My peculiarity of not understanding names even after they have been repeated many times, and then not remembering them. She was an orphan and would enter a convent on October 1st. She hadn't told her friends about it yet. She had already intended to enter in April but her employers wouldn't let her go. She was entering the convent because of the bad experiences she had had. She couldn't tell me about them. We walked up and down in the moonlight in front of the dance hall, my little erstwhile friends pursued me and my "bride." Despite her melancholy she liked to dance very much, what was especially evident later on when I temporarily gave her over to Dr. Sch. She was a farm worker. She had to go home at ten o'clock.

July 22. Miss G., teacher, owl-like, vivacious young face with animated and alert features. Her body is more indolent. Mr. Eppe, private-school headmaster from Braunschweig. A man who gets the better of me. His speech is authoritative, impassioned if necessary, considered, musical —even hesitant, for form's sake. Soft face, a soft beard growing over his cheeks and chin. Mincing walk. I found myself diagonally across from him when he and I sat down together (it was his first time) at the common table. A silently chewing lot of people. He scattered words here and there. If the silence continued unbroken, there wasn't anything he could do. But if someone down the table said a word, he at once took it up, with no great to-do, however; rather to himself as though he had been the one addressed and was now being listened to, and at the same time looked down at the tomato he was peeling. Everyone paid attention except those who felt shamed and were defiant, like me. He laughed at no one, but when he spoke acknowledged all opinions. If no one stirred, then he continued humming softly while he cracked nuts or performed all those little preliminaries which are necessary when eating vegetables and fruit. (The table was covered with bowls and you mixed the foods as you pleased.) Finally he involved everyone in his own affairs on the pretext that he had to make a note of all the foods and send the list to his wife. After he had beguiled us with his wife for several days, he began all over again with some new stories about her. She suffers from melancholia, he said, has to go to a sanatorium in Goslar, will be accepted only if she pledges herself to stay for eight weeks, brings a nurse, etc.; the whole thing, as he had figured it up and as he once more figured it up for us at the table, will cost more than 1,800 marks. But no trace of an intention to excite sympathy. But still, anything as expensive as this needs to be thought over, everybody thinks things over. A few days later we heard that his wife was coming, perhaps this sanatorium will do for her. During the meal he received the news that his wife had just arrived with her two boys and was waiting for him. He was happy but ate calmly to the end, though there is no end to these meals, for they put all the courses on the table at the same time. His wife is young, fat, with a waist marked only by her clothes, clever blue eyes, high-combed blond hair, can cook, market, etc. very well. At breakfast— his family hadn't arrived at the table yet—while cracking nuts, he told Miss G. and me: His wife suffers from melancholia, weak kidneys, her digestion is bad, she suffers from agoraphobia, falls asleep only toward five o'clock in the morning; then if she is awakened at eight "she naturally frets herself into a temper" and becomes "furious." She has a very serious heart disorder, a severe asthma. Her father died in a madhouse.

NOTES · POSTSCRIPT · CHRONOLOGY
LIST OF AUTHORS, ARTISTS, PERIODICALS
AND WORKS

1 A play by Paul Claudel. Fantl, as well as Claudel, belonged to the so-called Hellerau circle. In Hellerau, a garden suburb of Dresden, Jacques-Dalcroze had his school for dancing and rhythmic gymnastics. There, in 1913, Jakob Hegner founded his publishing house, around which a circle of writers and intellectuals gathered.

2 A quotation from *Das Erlebnis und die Dichtung,* by Wilhelm Dilthey. Tellheim is the hero of Lessing's *Minna von Barnhelm.*

3 Kafka's eldest sister.

4 Czech writer and historian. Among other things he edited (in collaboration with Otto Pick) the Bohemian National Museum's manuscript letters of the correspondence between Casanova and J. F. Opiz.

5 This is the concluding entry of the seventh manuscript notebook of the *Diaries.* It began with the entry of May 2, 1913 (see *Diaries* 1910–1913, p. 284).

6 Robert Musil, who later won renown for his *Der Mann ohne Eigenschaften,* invited Kafka to collaborate in the publication of a literary magazine.

7 This and the two entries that follow were written almost two months before the war broke out. Soon thereafter, when the Russians conquered part of Austria, we witnessed scenes very like those Kafka describes here.

8 A preliminary sketch for *The Castle;* it was several years later that Kafka wrote the novel.

9 Kafka quotes P.'s remark ironically; P. in his innocence compared that rather important artist, Alfred Kubin, with an illustrator of pornographic books called "Marquis Bayros" who was in vogue at the time.

10 The name of a theater in a suburb of Prague.

11 Kafka, too, was buried in the same grave with his parents.

12 E., several times referred to later, was the sister of F.B.

13 Bl. was a friend of F.B.'s.

14 After the first breaking-off of his engagement, Kafka went on a short trip to Denmark with Ernst Weiss and the latter's friend.

15 Probably *Franziska*, a novel by Ernst Weiss.

16 Beginning with February 16, 1914, Kafka had been making his diary entries in two notebooks instead of one, alternating from one to the other. This first sentence of July 31 followed directly after the last sentence of July 29 (". . . I'll have the time") in the same notebook. The entries under July 30 were made in the other notebook.

17 Czech for "cheers."

18 The Czech diminutive for Adalbert.

19 Kafka had begun *The Trial*. Two years previously he had written "The Judgment" and parts of *Amerika*.

20 Part of the manuscript page has been torn off, leaving lacunae here and at the end of the entry of October 25.

21 A brother-in-law home from the front on furlough.

22 The two sentences in parenthesis were added as a kind of footnote.

23 Tabakskollegium, name of the place (in Königswuster-hausen, near Berlin) where Friedrich Wilhelm I of Prussia informally consorted with his ministers and advisers over beer and tobacco.

24 Published as a fragment in an appendix to the German edition of *The Trial*, under the title of "Fahrt zur Mutter."

25 Exegesis of "Before the Law"; "Before the Law" was originally published in the collection, *A Country Doctor*, and then incorporated into Chap. IX of *The Trial*. The "Legend" and its exegesis are published in *Parables* (No. 7, Schocken Library).

26 Later published as "The Giant Mole" in *The Great Wall of China*.

27 This story has not been preserved.

28 "The Man Who Disappeared," the title Kafka first gave to *Amerika*.

29 Miss F.R., a young woman from Lemberg whom Kafka met at a lecture course on world literature that I gave in a school for refugee Jewish children. Cf. also the entry of April 14, 1915, p. 119.

30 The Assicurazioni Generali, an Italian insurance company; Kafka's first job. The work cost him a great deal of effort.

31 Not the "Investigations of a Dog" in *The Great Wall of China.*

32 We Zionists took advantage of the presence of Eastern European Jewish war refugees to hold discussion evenings; it was our purpose to clarify the relations between the Jews of the East and the West. Needless to say, there were many misunderstandings at first; later, however, a fruitful collaboration ensued, and a mutual tempering of our views.

33 Kafka accompanied his elder sister Elli on a visit to her husband, a reserve officer, who had been moved up to the front.

34 An excursion spot near Prague.

35 A chance acquaintance we had made on our trip to Zurich in 1911 (see p. 244).

36 An unfinished novel of mine.

37 Georg Mordecai Langer, of Prague. For years, in Eastern Europe, he had sought to lead the life of a Hasid; later he wrote in Czech, German and Hebrew on Kabbalah and related subjects. Among other things he published two small volumes of Hebrew poems.

The wonder-rabbi mentioned here, a relative of the Zaddik of Belz, had fled with his disciples before the Russians from Grodek to Prague.

38 A suburb of Prague.

39 Rossmann and K. are the heroes of *Amerika* and *The Trial,* respectively.

40 Gerti was Kafka's niece, a child at the time. [The German word *Pferdefuss* means both the devil's cloven foot and, colloquially, clubfoot.—*Tr.*]

41 A model of a trench on exhibition near Prague.

42 A childhood friend of Kafka's; cf. Kafka's letters to him, in Vol. VI of the first German edition (Schocken Verlag) of his works.

43 Abraham Grünberg, a young and gifted refugee from Warsaw whom we saw a great deal of at the time. He died of tuberculosis during the war.

44 Kafka gave a humorous report of his visit to Mrs. M-T. Later he regretted his unintentional ridicule.

45 A talmudic scholar belonging to the pious Lieben family of Prague. Only two members of this extensive family were saved from the horrors of the Nazi occupation—the scholar mentioned here and a boy in a Palestinian kibbutz.

46 [Dream and weep, poor race of man, the way can't be found —you have lost it. With "Woe!" you greet the night, with "Woe!" the day.

I want nothing save to escape the hands that reach out for me from the depths to draw my powerless body down to them. I fall heavily into the waiting hands.

Words slowly spoken echoed in the distant mountains. We listened.

Horrors of hell, veiled grimaces, alas, they bore my body close-pressed to them.

The long procession bears the unborn along.]

47 Several entries in the octavo notebooks [see Postscript] fill, chronologically, the gap that occurs at this point in the *Diaries.* These entries, however, have a different, more "objective" character than the quarto notebooks of the *Diaries;* they are made up solely of short stories, the beginnings of stories, and meditations (aphorisms), but nothing that bears on the events of the day.

48 A Prague writer who (with Hugo Salus) had exercised a great influence on the generation that preceded ours. His poetic drama (adapted from the Spanish), *Don Gil von den grünen Hosen,* was famous.

49 This and a number of the succeeding entries are fragments of "In the Penal Colony."

50 The clause, "as if it bore witness to some truth," was struck out by Kafka in the manuscript.

51 Between this and the preceding entry the following occurred: the first medical confirmation was made of Kafka's tuberculosis; he again decided to break off his engagement to F., took a leave of absence from his job and went to live in the country, with his sister Ottla (in Zürau, Post Flöhau, about five kilometers east of Karlsbad). The trip to Ottla's house took place on September 12, 1917.

52 A nephew of Kafka's. He was murdered by the Nazis.

53 [The German word for atonement (*Versöhnung*) also means reconciliation.—*Tr.*]

54 Kafka's second fiancée, Miss J.W. The engagement lasted only six months or so.

55 A character in Knut Hamsun's *Growth of the Soil*, which Kafka was reading at the time. Kafka particularly loved and admired this writer.

56 The twelfth manuscript notebook of the *Diaries*, which ends at this point, consists only of a number of loose leaves between covers. Much of it was torn out by Kafka and destroyed.

57 Mrs. Milena Jesenská, whose acquaintance Kafka made at the beginning of 1920. She was a clever, able woman of liberal views; an excellent writer. A very intimate friendship developed between her and Kafka, one full of hope and happiness at first but which later turned into hopelessness. The friendship lasted a little more than two years. In 1939 Mrs. Jesenská was thrown into prison by the Nazis in Prague and murdered.

58 The magazine of the Czech scout movement. All problems of education interested Kafka.

59 "The Death of Ivan Ilyich," by Tolstoy. This and his *Folk Tales* ("The Three Old Men," particularly), were great favorites of Kafka's.

60 Addressed to Milena Jesenská.

61 This remark occurs in Kafka's first book, *Meditation*, in the piece entitled "Bachelor's Ill Luck." Cf. also *Diaries* 1910–1913, p. 151.

62 The last clause of this sentence is a reference to a line in Kafka's story, "A Country Doctor."

63 Joseph K., the hero of *The Trial;* the novel, written in 1914 and 1915, remained unpublished during Kafka's lifetime.

64 The seven ancient Jewish communities in Burgenland.

65 The beginning of a polemic against Hans Blüher's *Secessio Judaica.* Here Kafka throws up to Blüher the very faults Blüher maintains he finds in Jewish books.

66 The name of one of the exhibiting painters.

67 Makkabi was the name of a Zionist sports club. *Selbstwehr* was a Prague Zionist weekly. The Czech means: "I came to help you."

68 *Der grosse Maggid* (The Great Preacher), title of a book

by Martin Buber on the hasidic Rabbi Dow Baer of Mezritch, a disciple of the Baal Shem.

69 In southeastern Bohemia, where Kafka was recuperating at his sister Ottla's house.

70 Frydlant and Liberic, two old towns in northern Bohemia. The text retains Kafka's German spelling of the names.

71 Judging from the last entry in the diary of this trip (p. 243), it seems probable that Kafka visited these places on official business for the Workers' Accident Insurance Institute, by which he was employed.

This castle may perhaps have influenced Kafka's conception of the castle in his novel.

72 A recollection of the trip to Riva, Brescia, in 1909.

73 Kafka undertook this trip together with the Editor. We planned to write a novel together, called "Richard and Samuel," one chapter of which has been preserved under the title of "The First Long Train Journey." (See *Diaries* 1910–1913, *n* 14).

74 Alice R. is the woman who appears as Dora Lippert in "The First Long Train Journey." (See *Diaries* 1910–1913, *n* 21).

75 As shown in a drawing in the manuscript.

76 An allusion to the theory of the "Indistinct," with which the book *Anschauung und Begriff*, by Felix Weltsch and myself, begins. The "Indistinct" is represented there by the graphic symbol, $A + x$.

77 A Czech expression for the little envelopes that contain fortunes; a trained parrot would draw one out of a heap.

78 Writing entries in our diaries.

79 Paintings in the Louvre.

80 Paintings in the palace of Versailles.

81 From this point on the entries were made at the Erlenbach Sanatorium, Switzerland, whither Kafka had gone on alone while I returned home. His leave of absence was a little longer than mine. The entries, however, soon revert to the impressions of Paris that he had just absorbed.

82 Kafka and I went to Weimar together during our vacation, staying there until July 7. On July 8 Kafka left for the Jungborn nature therapy establishment in the Harz. Kafka was always interested in *Naturheilkunde* in all its various forms,

such as the raw food diet, vegetarianism, Mazdaznan, nudism, gymnastics, and anti-vaccinationism. The curious mixture of irony and respect in his attitude to these cults, and his efforts over the years to live in accordance with several of them, defy all analysis. The "Travel Diary" faithfully reflects Kafka's attitude.

83 Patriotic Czech gymnastic societies.

84 ["Confession," by Goethe. The following is a translation by Paul Dyrsen (1878):

> Absolution give to us!
>   And we shall forever
> To remember your command
>   Faithfully endeavor;
> Wholly love all worth and beauty
> And from doing half our duty
>   Resolutely sever.]

85 Johannes Schlaf, with Arno Holz one of the first men in German literature to write in the genre of modern realism, was one of the forerunners of Gerhart Hauptmann. In the years before our visit he had again made himself much talked about by advancing and vehemently defending an anti-Copernican theory according to which the sun moved around the earth.

86 Wickersdorf was a progressive country boarding school founded in Germany in 1906 in close conformity with the ideals of the German Youth Movement.

The text of the two volumes of the *Diaries* is as complete as it was possible to make it. A few passages, apparently meaningless because of their fragmentary nature, are omitted. In most instances no more than a few words are involved. In several (rare) cases I omitted things that were too intimate, as well as scathing criticism of various people that Kafka certainly never intended for the public. Living persons are usually identified by an initial or initials —that is, when they are not artists or political figures who because of their public activity must always anticipate criticism. Although I have used the blue pencil in the case of attacks on people still alive, I have not considered this sort of censorship necessary in the little that Kafka has to say against myself (partly in lighthearted playful mockery, and partly in earnest). The reader himself will know how to correct the false impression naturally arising out of this, that I was the only person against whom Kafka harbored anything. On this, as on many other points, I have followed the example of V. Chertkov in his editing of Tolstoy's diaries (cf. Chertkov's preface to that edition).

One must in general take into consideration the false impression that every diary unintentionally makes. When you keep a diary, you usually put down only what is oppressive or irritating. By being put down on paper painful impressions are got rid of. Pleasant impressions for the most part do not have to be counteracted in this way; you make note of them, as many people should know from experience, only in exceptional cases, or when (as in the case of a travel diary) it is your express purpose to do so. Ordinarily, however, diaries resemble a kind of defective barometric curve that registers only the "lows," the hours of greatest depression, but not the "highs."

This rule also holds true for the thirteen quarto notebooks that constitute Kafka's true diary. In the "Travel Diaries" of the same period a relatively brighter mood prevails. His good humor is seen with even more distinctness in his letters. A gloom begins to settle on the letters only as his illness grows worse, though then, to be sure, they are colored the deepest black of despair. For the most part, however, one can distinguish the following scale of brightness in Kafka's various forms of *personal* utterance (each of his *literary* works, of course, runs the gamut of the scale): the quarto notebooks show up as the darkest band of the spectrum; his travel notes are somewhat brighter; many of the letters (roughly, until the Zürau period, and even into it) are brighter still; in his conversations and daily intercourse there was often—even most often, during the early periods of his life—a gay ingenuousness one would scarcely credit to the author of the *Diaries*.

The bulk of the *Diaries* is contained in thirteen notebooks of quarto size.

The first, third, fourth and fifth notebooks Kafka numbered himself, in Roman numerals (the second notebook bears no number). Pages are numbered consecutively throughout, although a second pagination, also by Kafka, makes for some confusion. There was a further difficulty in arranging the material chronologically in the fact Kafka would occasionally, in the same notebook, write from the last page backward as well as from the first page forward, so that the entries met in the middle. Nevertheless, it was possible to establish the correct chronological order.

The first notebook begins with several undated entries. The first date noted is May 17-18, 1910. A few pages later there are entries for the period from February 19, 1911 to November 24, 1911. Notebook II, embracing the period from November 6, 1910 to May 1911, fills in the interval between May 1910 and February 1911, and also contains part of the first chapter of *Amerika*, "The Stoker." Notebook III goes from October 26, 1911 to November 24, 1911. Thus the first three notebooks dovetail—what is also the case with Notebooks VIII and IX. Notebook IV embraces the period from November 28, 1911 to the end of that year; Notebook V (in which several obviously erroneous dates had to be corrected) goes from January 4, 1912 to April 8, 1912; Notebook VI from May 6, 1912 to September 1912. Notebook VI contains "The Judgment" and the second part of "The Stoker." After an interval the diary is continued in Notebook VII from May 2, 1913 to February 14, 1914, and in Notebook VIII from February 16, 1914 to August 15, 1914. Notebook VIII, however, also contains (beginning on the last page and going backward) entries for the month of February 1913, and Notebook IX belongs to the period covered by the eighth notebook. Many pages have been torn out of the ninth and tenth notebooks. The latter notebook goes from August 21, 1914 (thus it follows directly after Notebook VIII) to May 27, 1915. Notebook XI contains entries for the period from September 13, 1915 to October 30, 1916, as well as a few from April to August 1917. Notebook XII, many of whose pages likewise were torn out by the author, begins in Zürau on September 15, 1917 and goes to November 10, 1917; after a lengthy interval it resumes with the entry of June 27, 1919, continuing on until January 10, 1920. The last—the thirteenth—notebook embraces the period between October 15, 1921 and November 1922, and also contains a few notes dated June 12, 1923. A part of the incomplete "Investigations of a Dog" (not the beginning, however) is sketched out in it in minuscule characters. In the earlier notebooks (the first eight) Kafka writes a large and swinging hand; later it gradually grows smaller and pointed.

These thirteen notebooks form a stylistic whole that I have tried to preserve. The writer notes down literary ideas, the beginnings of stories, or reflections passing through his head. The principles that guide him; the manner in which he looks to his literary efforts for a counterweight against the unfriendly world around him; the hated, arduous, indeed exhausting job—all this is repeatedly shown in detail in the entries themselves. In addition to the inspirations of his imagination, Kafka notes down occurrences in the workaday world, and also dreams—there are sketches where dreams predominate over relatively "realistic" entries; often they are the starting point for literary creation. In exceptionally happy cases the result, whether long or short, is a finished literary work in every respect. From these Kafka later chose a few for publication; they are to be found in Vol. I * of the *Gesammelte Schriften*. In the context of the *Diaries* an unexpected light is very often cast on the content of these pieces.

Thus, amidst daily notations which served the writer as a kind of springboard for literary creation, one sees many things that could have been published as independent fragments. One has the half-finished figure and the unworked marble before one at the same time.

* Published in translation under the title of *The Penal Colony*.

These thirteen quarto notebooks thus have a composition different from the "blue octavo notebooks," which are made up almost entirely of literary ideas, fragments and aphorisms (without reference to the everyday world). The octavo notebooks will be included in a future publication. Notations of a diary nature, dates, are found in them only as a rare exception. The three "Travel Diaries," on the other hand, have an entirely different character again: occurrences and experiences are noted in bare matter-of-fact fashion, in a way that would apparently provide no starting point for later work—just as a tourist would do. Of course, this tourist is Franz Kafka, and though his manner of observing things seems thoroughly natural, in a mysterious way it departs from everything customary.

Both—the bare factual and the partially wrought (which in happy cases became a finished work)—are uniquely mingled in the thirteen notebooks.

Tel Aviv, 1948.

MAX BROD

1883 Born July 3 in Prague

1901 Is graduated from the German Gymnasium *

1906 Doctorate in jurisprudence from the Karl-Ferdinand University in Prague

before 1907 Writes "Description of a Struggle" and "Hochzeitsvorbereitungen auf dem Lande"

1907–08 Temporary employment in the Assicurazioni Generali, an Italian insurance company

1908 Appointed to post with government-sponsored Arbeiter-Unfall-Versicherungs-Anstalt für das Königreich Böhmen in Prag

1909 Publication of "Conversation with the Supplicant" and "Conversation with the Drunken Man," two dialogues from "Description of a Struggle," in the literary periodical *Hyperion*
Publication of "The Aeroplanes at Brescia" in the Prague newspaper *Bohemia*

1910 Publication in *Bohemia* of several short pieces later included in *Meditation*

1911 Trip to Frydlant and Liberic
Trip to Switzerland, Italy, Paris and Erlenbach
Meets Yiddish theater troupe in Prague

1912 Publication in the literary periodical *Herderblätter* of "The First Long Train Journey," first chapter of "Richard and Samuel"
Trip to Weimar and Jungborn
Meets F.B.
Begins *Amerika*

* Incorrectly given in *Diaries 1910–1913* (Vol. I) as 1903.

Writes "The Judgment"

1913 Publication of *Meditation*

Publication of "The Judgment" in the literary yearbook *Arkadia*

Publication of "The Stoker," first chapter of *Amerika*

Trip to Riva

Writes "The Metamorphosis"

1914 Formal engagement to F.B.

Begins *The Trial*

Writes first draft of "In the Penal Colony"

Writes "The Giant Mole"

Trip to Denmark

1915 Publication of "The Metamorphosis"

Completes *The Trial*

Awarded the Fontane Prize for "The Stoker"

Moves from parental house into a rented room

1917 Tuberculosis

Sick leave from the Arbeiter-Unfall-Versicherungs-Anstalt

Final break with F.B.

1918 Writes "The Great Wall of China"

1919 Publication of the collection of stories, *A Country Doctor*

Short-lived second engagement, to J.W.

1920 Publication of "In the Penal Colony"

Stay in Meran, Austria

Resumes work at his office

Meets Milena Jesenská

1921 Stay in a sanatorium in the Tatra

Writes *The Castle*

Publication of "The Bucket Rider" in *Prager Presse*

1922 Publication of the story "A Hunger Artist" in *Neue Rundschau*

1923 Writes "Investigations of a Dog," "The Burrow," and "Josephine the Singer"

Meets Dora Dymant; goes with her to Berlin

1924 Publication of the collection of stories, *A Hunger Artist*

Dies June 3 in a sanatorium near Vienna

Buried June 11 in the Jewish cemetery in Prague-Strashnitz

It was not possible to identify all the authors and artists mentioned in the text. In such cases their names are not listed here.

Adler, Friederich (1857–1938), German Jewish poet and playwright from Prague: 172, *n* 48

Amerika, by Franz Kafka: 107, 188, *n* 19, *n* 28, *n* 39 (132)

Asmus Sempers Jugendland, by the German novelist Otto Ernst (1862–1926): 17

Az Est, Budapest newspaper: 120, 125

Baal Shem Tov, Israel B. Eliezer (*c.* 1700–1760), founder of Hasidism: 138–140, *n* 68 (229)

Bakunin, Mikhail (1814–1876), Russian anarchist: 118

Baluschek, Hans (1870–1936), German painter: 312

Bassewitz, Gerdt von (1878–): 288

"Bachelor's Ill Luck," by Franz Kafka: *n* 61 (207)

Baum, Oskar (1883–), Jewish author and music critic from Prague: 21, 103, 175

Belinski, Vissarion Grigorievich (1811–1848), Russian critic: 118

Bergmann, Hugo (1883–), Jewish philosopher from Prague, now professor at the Hebrew University: 121

Berliner Tageblatt, newspaper edited by Theodor Wolff, founded in 1872, later absorbed by Nazis: 255, 289

Bible: 130, 156, 158

Bizet, Georges (1838–1875), French composer: 274, 294

Black Flags, by Johan August Strindberg: 108, 111

Blanc, Louis (1811–1882), French revolutionary and historian: 268

"Blinde Gast, Der," story by Otto Pick: 95

Blüher, Hans (1888–), German writer, author of a number of anti-Semitic works: 225, 231, *n* 65

Böse Unschuld, Die, novel by Oskar Baum: 15

Bouvard et Pécuchet, by Gustave Flaubert: 115

Boy-Ed, Ida (1852–1928), German popular novelist: 301

Brandenburg, Hans (1885–), German poet and critic: 312

Briefe, die neueste Literatur betreffend (1759), a series of

337

* Listed only when mentioned in the text as an author.